# Transactions
# of the
# Royal
# Historical
# Society

SIXTH SERIES

# XXX

CAMBRIDGE
UNIVERSITY PRESS

Published by the Press Syndicate of the University of Cambridge
University Printing House, Shaftesbury Road, Cambridge CB2 8BS,
United Kingdom
One Liberty Plaza, Floor 20, New York, NY 10006, USA
477 Williamstown Road, Port Melbourne, VIC 3207, Australia
C/Orense, 4, Planta 13, 28020 Madrid, Spain
Lower Ground Floor, Nautica Building, The Water Club,
Beach Road, Granger Bay, 8005 Cape Town, South Africa

First published 2020

*A catalogue record for this book is available from the British Library*

ISBN 9781108833189 hardback

SUBSCRIPTIONS. The serial publications of the Royal Historical Society, *Royal Historical Society Transactions* (ISSN 0080-4401) and Camden Fifth Series (ISSN 0960-1163) volumes, may be purchased together on annual subscription. The 2020 subscription price, which includes print and electronic access (but not VAT), is £216 (US $360 in the USA, Canada, and Mexico) and includes Camden Fifth Series, volumes 59, 60 and Transactions Sixth Series, volume 30 (published in December). The electronic-only price available to institutional subscribers is £181 (US $301 in the USA, Canada, and Mexico). Japanese prices are available from Kinokuniya Company Ltd, PO Box 55, Chitose, Tokyo 156, Japan. EU subscribers (outside the UK) who are not registered for VAT should add VAT at their country's rate. VAT registered subscribers should provide their VAT registration number. Prices include delivery by air.

Subscription orders, which must be accompanied by payment, may be sent to a bookseller, subscription agent, or direct to the publisher: Cambridge University Press, University Printing House, Shaftesbury Road, Cambridge CB2 8BS, UK; or in the USA, Canada, and Mexico: Cambridge University Press, Journals Fulfillment Department, One Liberty Plaza, Floor 20, New York, NY 10006, USA.

SINGLE VOLUMES AND BACK VOLUMES. A list of Royal Historical Society volumes available from Cambridge University Press may be obtained from the Humanities Marketing Department at the address above.

*Printed in the UK by Bell & Bain Ltd, Glasgow*

# CONTENTS

*Transactions of the RHS* 30 (2020), pp. 1–28 © The Author(s), 2020. Published by Cambridge University Press on behalf of the Royal Historical Society
doi:10.1017/S0080440120000018

TRANSACTIONS OF THE
# ROYAL HISTORICAL SOCIETY
## PRESIDENTIAL ADDRESS

## By Margot C. Finn

## MATERIAL TURNS IN BRITISH HISTORY: III. COLLECTING: COLONIAL BOMBAY, BASRA, BAGHDAD AND THE ENLIGHTENMENT MUSEUM*

READ 6 DECEMBER 2019

ABSTRACT. This lecture explores the history of Enlightenment-era collecting of antiquities to probe the claims to universality of Western museums. Focusing on the British Museum's Enlightenment Gallery, it underscores the imperial and familial contexts of British collecting cultures. Questioning received narratives of collecting which highlight the role played by individual elite British men, it suggests that women, servants and non-European elites played instrumental parts in knowledge production and the acquisition of antiquities. The private correspondence of the East India Company civil servant Claudius Rich – the East India Company's Resident or diplomatic representative at Baghdad 1801–1821 – and his wife Mary (née Mackintosh) Rich illuminates social histories of knowledge and material culture that challenge interpretations of the British Museum's Enlightenment Gallery which privilege trade and discovery over empire.

What is Enlightenment? In 1784, the German philosopher Immanuel Kant famously asked and answered this question, declaring that 'Enlightenment is mankind's exit from its self-incurred immaturity.' 'Public' enlightenment, Kant urged, was 'nearly inevitable', if only the public were 'allowed freedom'. For Enlightenment, 'nothing more is required than *freedom* ... namely the freedom to make a public use of one's reason in all matters', he proclaimed.[1] Ostensibly universalist and cosmopolitan, Kant's vision of Enlightenment was predicated on a belief that the autonomous exercise of reason was a fundamental characteristic of humanity. As twenty-first-century philosophers and intellectual

---

*For assistance and suggestions during the research and writing of this article, I am most grateful to Elizabeth Eger, Onni Gust, Jon Parry, Grace Redhead and John Styles. All errors remain my own.

[1] Immanuel Kant, 'An Answer to the Question: What is Enlightenment?', trans. James Schmidt, in *What Is Enlightenment?: Eighteenth-Century Answers and Twentieth-Century Questions*, ed. James Schmidt (Berkeley, 1996), 58–9. Emphasis in original.

historians have, however, abundantly demonstrated, Kant's universalism was both imbricated with and undercut by his repeated theorisations and exemplifications of human difference. 'In the critical philosophy Kant writes as if all humans, regardless of race or gender, have reason,' Theodore Vial observes. 'Yet in [his] writings about non-Europeans and women, many people seem to be deficient in reason.'[2] Kant's 1775 essay 'Of the Different Human Races', his 1785 essay on 'Determination of the Concept of Human Race' and his 1788 essay 'On the Use of Teleological Principles in Philosophy', indeed, played such foundational roles in theorising 'natural' human differences that some scholars credit him 'with "inventing" the concept of race'.[3] Feminist critics have likewise underlined the exclusionary implications of Kant's dim view of women's ability to reason. Any laboured learning 'or painful pondering' the female of the species undertook, Kant suggested, worked against the natural grain of her limited understanding; a scholarly woman, he observed, 'might as well even have a beard'.[4]

Over the past two decades, historians have done much to illuminate the central tension in Enlightenment treatises between universalism, on the one hand, and perceptions of gender- and race-based difference, on the other.[5] In this lecture I build on those foundations, by interrogating the imperial and material pathways by which universalism, gender and race came to be instantiated in – and erased from – the Enlightenment museum. Eighteenth-century European museums were physical, material and organisational structures calculated to elicit the autonomous, public exercise of reason.[6] They thus lie at the heart of the Enlightenment project, and share its conflicted, questionable claims to universalism. To surface these issues, I explore the colonial collecting practices that brought material objects from the Middle East into Europe's Enlightenment museums. Beginning my lecture in Bloomsbury, in the present-day Enlightenment Gallery of the British Museum, I travel to Enlightenment-era Bombay, Basra and Baghdad, with brief excursions to the ruins of ancient Babylon and to Kurdistan, before returning

---

[2] Theodore Vial, *Modern Religion, Modern Race* (Oxford, 2016), 24.

[3] *Ibid.*, 22–3, 54 n. 6 (citation from chapter abstract of online edition).

[4] Citations from Mari Mikkola, 'Kant on Moral Agency and Women's Nature', *Kantian Review*, 16 (2011), 89–111, 89. Mikkola however argues against the most severe feminist critiques of Kant.

[5] See for example *Women, Gender, and Enlightenment*, ed. Sarah Knott and Barbara Taylor (New York, 2005); Silvia Sebastiani, *The Scottish Enlightenment: Race, Gender, and the Limits of Progress* (New York, 2013); *A New Imperial History: Culture, Identity, and Modernity in Britain and the Empire, 1660–1840*, ed. Kathleen Wilson (Cambridge, 2004).

[6] *Enlightening the British: Knowledge, Discovery and the Museum in the Eighteenth Century*, ed. R. G. W. Anderson, M. L. Caygill, A. MacGregor and L. Syson (2003); *Enlightenment: Discovering the World in the Eighteenth Century*, ed. Kim Sloan with Andrew Burnett (2003).

to contemporary London. This vantage point affords an opportunity to integrate an analysis of late Enlightenment colonial collecting cultures with some preliminary reflections on potential next steps for the twenty-first-century agenda of decolonising the museum.[7]

My lecture is underpinned by three basic research questions. It begins by asking, 'How "universal" is the universal museum?' The Altes Museum in Berlin, the British Museum in Bloomsbury, Paris's Louvre and New York's Met are all commonly described as universal museums. This usage has recently become a central plank in museums' defensive platforms, in the face of increasingly clamorous claims for the restoration of heritage objects.[8] Assertions of the European museum's universalism, of course, have an extended geneal-ogy, one that is rooted in the museum's Enlightenment function as a built environment designed to foster the public's exercise of reason through scientific scrutiny of global material cultures.[9] Here, instead, I underscore the contribution of Enlightenment imperialism to the making of these museum collections. My second research question, then, is 'How colonial or imperial was the Enlightenment universal museum?' This is hardly a novel material turn on my part.[10] My book-shelves bulge with studies of Enlightenment collectors such as Sir Joseph Banks and Sir Hans Sloane, contextualised within a colonial frame, and excellent new studies are now extending this line of analysis to less familiar eighteenth- and nineteenth-century museum donors.[11] My third research question is more novel. It adds another gender to this male

---

[7] For an introduction to the museum decolonisation literature, see John Giblin, Imma Ramos and Nikki Grout, 'Thoughts on Representing Empire and Decolonising Museums and Public Spaces in Practice: An Introduction', *Third Text*, 33 (2019), 471–86; *Museums and Communities: Curators, Collections, Collaboration*, ed. Viv Golding and Wayne Modest (2013); Claire Wintle, 'Decolonising the Museum: The Case of the Imperial and Commonwealth Institutes', *Museum and Society*, 11 (2013), 185–201.

[8] A foundational text in this debate is the 'Declaration on the Importance and Value of Universal Museums' signed by eighteen museum directors in 2002: http://archives.icom. museum/pdf/E_news2004/p4_2004-1.pdf. See also James Cuno, *Who Owns Antiquity? Museums and the Battle over Our Ancient Heritage* (Princeton, 2008). For the opposing view, see for example Rafia Zakaria, 'Opinion: Looted Art and the "Universal Museum": Can 21st-Century Collections Ever Escape Colonialism's Violent Legacy?', *Frieze* (28 November 2018): https://frieze.com/article/looted-art-and-universal-museum-can-21st-century-collections-ever-escape-colonialisms.

[9] See esp. *Enlightenment*, ed. Sloan.

[10] *Art and the British Empire*, ed. T. J. Barringer, Geoff Quilley and Douglas Fordham (Manchester, 2007); *Curating Empire: Museums and the British Imperial Experience*, ed. Sarah Longair and John McAleer (Manchester, 2012).

[11] Neil Chambers, *Endeavouring Banks: Exploring the Collections from the* Endeavour *Voyage 1768–1771* (2016); James Delbourgo, *Collecting the World: The Life and Curiosity of Hans Sloane* (2017); Kate Donington, *The Bonds of Family: Slavery, Commerce and Culture in the British Atlantic World* (Manchester, 2019), esp. ch. 7.

mix by asking: what happens to our understanding of the universal museum and its entanglement with Enlightenment colonial collecting practices if we not only posit that there were women in the Enlightenment, but also acknowledge that imperialising women contributed to the making of the Enlightenment museum? By inserting women back into the Enlightenment Gallery of the British Museum, I hope to accomplish two main goals. The first is to reveal more fully the broad spectrum of social, material and political practices that undergirded East India Company collecting cultures in the Enlightenment era. My second purpose is to use the archival traces left by European women to recover contributions made to colonial collecting by male and female South Asian and Middle Eastern labourers, servants, go-betweens and governing elites. For, if we are to contextualise – much less to decolonise – the museum, these historical agents and their vital engagement with the Enlightenment's conflicted universal histories will also demand to be acknowledged.

# I

To visit the British Museum's Enlightenment Gallery today is to stand in the centre of a universal museum. Or, is it? The celebration of the Museum's 250th anniversary in 2003 saw this gallery reopen after a major refurbishment engineered to explore 'the way people of the time looked at the "natural and artificial curiosities" being collected from all over the world by scholars and collectors, who then sought to make sense of their past and their present'. For Neil MacGregor, then the Museum's director, Enlightenment universalism was the taproot that had fed the Museum's evolving practices of collecting and display from its foundation in 1753 through the late Enlightenment of the 1820s. MacGregor argued that Enlightenment universalism, recast for 'an age of global citizenship', also provided the justification for the Museum's continued existence in the twenty-first century. 'The universal scope of the Museum's collections', he suggested, made the British Museum 'a unique repository of the achievements of human endeavour' and thus 'truly the memory of mankind'.[12] Part I of the exhibition catalogue published to accompany the gallery's relaunch was, appropriately, entitled 'The Universal Museum', and the title of the volume itself celebrated the European Enlightenment's 'discovery' of the world.[13]

From the vantage point of 2019, the 'discovery' paradigm now appears inherently flawed, suggesting that Europe is the centre of the universe, and that Europeans were precocious or are exceptional in the exercise

[12] Neil MacGregor, 'Preface', in *Enlightenment*, ed. Sloan, 6.
[13] *Enlightenment*, ed. Sloan, esp. part I.

of their reason.[14] Three significant absences, moreover, mark the Enlightenment Gallery's celebration of an enduring universalism born in the age of reason. The first is empire, and is closely implicated with the second – which is slavery. Both of these defining features of the Enlightenment universe are at once conspicuously on display in the gallery's material culture and curiously invisible in the textual interpretations that elaborate on exhibited objects' identity and meanings. An informed visitor is, for example, struck by the embodiment of imperialism and slavery manifest in the gallery's many busts. Sir Hans Sloane, the Irish physician whose collecting began in earnest in 1687 when he resided in the British slave colony of Jamaica and whose West Indian specimens were among the British Museum's founding collections, and Sir Joseph Banks, the botanist who accompanied Captain Cook on his first Pacific voyages and later advised the British government to colonise Australia, are both prominently on display.[15] Textual references to empire and slavery – much less to indigenous or enslaved peoples – are, however, exceptionally thin on the ground.[16] The Enlightenment Gallery's explanatory leaflet observes that the room that houses its objects was completed in 1828 and 'now contains an exhibition about the Age of Enlightenment, a time when people – including the collectors who created the British Museum – used reason and first-hand observation of the world around them to understand it in new ways'.[17] The leaflet, like the gallery itself, proceeds to organise the Enlightenment within seven broad themes. Concealed within the seventh theme, 'trade and discovery', empire and slavery lie submerged under a rubric that depicts the violently acquisitive practices of 'Merchants, diplomats, explorers and collectors' as a modernising, scientific impulse 'in which objects were classified by culture rather than as exotic curiosities'.[18]

Complementing this amnesia with respect to empire and slavery is the third salient absence from the Enlightenment Gallery: the roughly half of adult humankind who are women. To be sure, there are female forms in

---

[14] For a powerful critique of the 'discovery' paradigm of British and European history, see Sujit Sivasundaram, *Waves across the South: A New History of Revolution and Empire* (New York, 2020).

[15] Banks, indeed, is the only historical figure in the Enlightenment Gallery to merit two busts. The visual analysis of the gallery in this lecture is based on visits made to the British Museum in August–November 2019.

[16] Significantly, slavery is 'dealt with' in passing by referencing abolitionism: Kim Sloan, '"Aimed at universality and belonging to the nation": The Enlightenment and the British Museum', in *Enlightenment*, ed. Sloan, 23–5. For the representation and repression of Jamaican slavery in Sir Hans Sloane's eighteenth-century publications, see Kay Dian Kriz, *Slavery, Sugar and the Culture of Refinement: Picturing the British West Indies, 1700–1840* (New Haven, 2008), ch. 1.

[17] 'Enlightenment: Room 1: Discovering the World in the 18th Century' (London, n.d.), n.p.

[18] Ibid.

this room: no fewer than four goddesses and seven female mythic figures grace the Enlightenment Gallery. A lion-headed Egyptian goddess and a Roman statue of Demeter are thus visibly displayed.[19] We can, perhaps, also deduce the presence (offstage) of yet another mythical woman from the fact that the Roman cupid on display is depicted stringing his bow. Historical women are, however, entirely absent. Only by exiting the gallery and turning left into the corner of an adjacent room do we encounter an Enlightenment woman who is also a human. Here Sarah Sophia Banks is mentioned as an Enlightenment collector – albeit one who was 'Less well-travelled' than her eminent brother, Sir Joseph Banks, and whose collection, 'put together at home', featured 'popular prints … and general ephemera', rather than the universalising global goods encased next door in the Enlightenment Gallery.[20] The texts that elaborate on the Enlightenment Gallery's material objects likewise ignore women, or relegate them to an historical side-room. The gallery leaflet depicts Sir Hans Sloane's bust prominently on its cover and cites two named men in its synopsis, but it otherwise effaces gender from its analytical repertoire, employing instead putatively generic collective nouns such as 'people', 'Europeans', 'scholars', 'collectors' and 'Britain'.[21] 'Women too' were part of the Enlightenment, the exhibition catalogue does acknowledge.[22] But a visitor to the gallery is hard-pressed to find them in the figures that embellish the exhibition itself.

In the decade and a half since the relaunch of the Enlightenment Gallery, a burgeoning scholarship on Enlightenment women has made this absence much more obvious than it can possibly have been in 2003.[23] In what follows, two types of archaeology serve to reveal

---

[19] The Enlightenment Gallery can be explored virtually via Google Arts & Culture: https://www.britishmuseum.org/collection/galleries/enlightenment.

[20] For Sarah Sophia Banks, see John Gascoigne, 'Banks, Sarah Sophia (1744–1818)', *Oxford Dictionary of National Biography* (Oxford, 2004), which begins by describing her as a 'collector of antiquarian items'. See also Valerie Schutte, 'Cutting, Arranging, and Pasting: Sarah Sophia Banks as Collector', *Early Modern Women*, 9 (2014), 127–40, and Catherine Eagleton, 'Collecting African Money in Georgian London: Sarah Sophia Banks and Her Collection of Coins', *Museum History Journal*, 6 (2013), 23–38. Citations are from the British Museum descriptions on display in Room 2. The material culture and texts depicting Sarah Sophia Banks are telling: small reproductions of original images of her, rather than the originals, are on display, under a rubric entitled 'The Age of Curiosity'.

[21] The named individuals are Robert Smirke (the Enlightenment architect who designed the room) and George III. The full list of human categories is: 'people', 'collectors', 'European collectors', 'man-made', 'antiquaries', 'specialist historians and archaeologists', 'the British Museum's founders', 'Europeans', 'scholars', 'Britain', 'Merchants, diplomats, explorers and collectors'.

[22] Sloan, '"Aimed at universality"', 20.

[23] See for example JoEllen DeLucia, *A Feminine Enlightenment: British Women Writers and the Philosophy of Progress, 1759–1820* (Edinburgh, 2015); *Bluestockings Displayed: Portraiture, Performance and Patronage, 1730–1830*, ed. Elizabeth Eger (Cambridge, 2013); Patricia Fara,

women whose histories are both materially present and entirely hidden from the public in the Enlightenment Gallery's display cabinets. By deploying forms of reason that include the well-tested methodologies of feminist historical recovery – that is, digging into both new and old archives and reading manuscripts and the printed record against the grain – and by looking for actual women who participated in Enlightenment archaeological digs, this lecture both expands upon and challenges the universalising claims of Enlightenment museum collections.[24] Case 15 of the Enlightenment Gallery, labelled 'The Search for Modern Babylon', provides my point of departure.

## II

Focusing on early nineteenth-century excavations in what was then a marginal outpost of the Ottoman Empire and is now Iraq, Case 15 is subdivided into six sections. Three upper compartments contain a combination of small objects and textual exegeses, while the three compartments below display larger archaeological finds from ancient Nineveh and Babylon. The descriptive texts that interpret these objects recite a familiar late Enlightenment narrative, inflected by English nationalism.[25] 'In the seventeenth century', they assert, these ancient cities 'were still undiscovered'. With the coming of Enlightenment, however, and the arrival of 'A young Englishman, Claudius James Rich', Babylon and Nineveh were 'discovered' by European collectors. Scientific practices – exemplified by Claudius Rich's geographical mapping of these sites and his removal from them of material artefacts destined for the British Museum – gave birth to a new, modern form of alchemy. Through archaeological investigation, 'rubble' was distilled by reason into scholarly knowledge of the ancient world.[26]

Who was Claudius Rich, and how did his collections come to embody English Enlightenment in the British Museum? We can only answer

---

*Pandora's Breeches: Women, Science and Power in the Enlightenment* (2004); and *Women, Gender, and Enlightenment*, ed. Knott and Taylor.

[24] For feminist methodology in the British colonial context, see esp. Antoinette Burton, 'Archive Stories: Gender in the Making of Imperial and Colonial Histories', in *Gender and Empire*, ed. Philippa Levine (Oxford, 2004), 281–93. For the early history of women in archaeology (and their erasure from the discipline), see Amara Thornton, *Archaeologists in Print: Publishing for the People* (2018), esp. ch. 3.

[25] For the heroic narrative of masculine archaeology in this region, see Eleanor Robson, 'Old Habits Die Hard: Writing the Excavation and Dispersal History of Nimrud', *Museum History Journal*, 10 (2017), 217–32, esp. 218–21.

[26] The case description reads: 'In the seventeenth century … the sites of the destroyed cities of Nineveh and Babylon were still undiscovered. During the Enlightenment, new attempts were made to find the ruins of these cities, famous from descriptions in the Bible … A young Englishman, Claudius James Rich, discovered the site of Babylon, mapped ancient Nineveh and gathered artefacts and inscriptions. This "rubble" … inspired … a century of … scholars.'

these questions if we subvert the logic of the Enlightenment Gallery by interrogating his Englishness and situating Rich in the context of empire. To unpack Case 15 fully, we need as well both to follow the money and to *cherchez la femme*. Rich features in Case 15 as 'A young Englishman', but he was born in France, the bastard son of a military officer of Scottish and Irish heritage who had been cashiered from the British army for his leading part in a notoriously brutal wartime scandal in Europe's West Indian slave colonies.[27] Rich's illegitimacy is reflected in the uncertainty that continues to surround the precise date and place of his birth. It is also registered in his surname: Rich was the maiden name of his Irish paternal grandmother; his father was Colonel (later Sir) James Cockburn.[28] Raised and educated in Bristol, Rich as we shall see insisted that he was Irish.[29] Lacking a family fortune but displaying a precocious ability to master foreign languages, he was an obvious candidate for employment in the East India Company. Appointed in London to the Bombay civil service in 1804, Rich was first dispatched to Aleppo, Alexandria and Cairo, honing his Oriental languages. He fetched up (dressed as a turbaned Mamlūk) in colonial Bombay in September 1807.[30]

Bombay in 1807 had a population of a few hundred East India Company men. The city was also home to at least ninety-nine adult British women, accompanied by their many daughters. Enumerated among these women in a census of 1806 was Lady Mackintosh, the second wife of the Recorder of Bombay's main court.[31] It was to the Mackintosh residence that Claudius Rich repaired upon his arrival, swiftly gaining the approval and patronage of the Whig historian, politician and judge Sir James Mackintosh, and also winning the heart of Sir James's eldest daughter, Mary. Seventeen years old when she met Claudius Rich and just eighteen when they wed a few months later, Mary Mackintosh had been educated by a combination of boarding school, a governess and her father. She spoke French, Italian and

[27] His reputed father was Sir James Cockburn, 5th Bt: Alastair W. Massie, 'Cockburn, Sir James, fifth baronet (1723–1809)', *Oxford Dictionary of National Biography* (Oxford, 2004). Edmund Burke denounced the British plundering of St Eustatius in parliamentary speeches of 14 May 1781 and 4 December 1781. See *The Writings and Speeches of Edmund Burke*, vol. 4: *Party, Parliament, and the Dividing of the Whigs: 1780–1794*, ed. P. J. Marshall, Donald C. Bryant and William B. Todd (Oxford, 2015), 66–94, 104–14.

[28] Constance M. Alexander, *Baghdad in Bygone Days: From the Journals and Correspondence of Claudius Rich, Traveller, Artist, Linguist, Antiquary, and British Resident at Baghdad, 1808–1821* (1928), 1–3.

[29] *Ibid.*, 4.

[30] *Ibid.*, 9–10, 13–17.

[31] *The Bombay Calendar and Register, for the Year 1806; With an Almanac* (Bombay, [1806]), 181–3. The Calendar enumerated 176 'Ladies' of Bombay Presidency and 99 for Bombay itself, but did not include any of Lady Mackintosh's three teenage stepdaughters, including the eldest, Mary.

German and was a voracious reader of both history and novels.[32] Like her husband – with whom she was deeply in love – she lacked a fortune: her father's improvidence had forced the sale of his Highland estate in 1801, precipitating his exile to the Bombay judiciary, where Mackintosh's spendthrift habits continued unabated.[33] His patronage, however, secured Claudius Rich's appointment as the East India Company's Resident or diplomatic representative at Baghdad. Within a few weeks of the couple's marriage in January 1808, they were sailing from Bombay for Basra.[34]

Both a major Persian Gulf port and a caravan city, Basra lay at the interface between the Indian Ocean world and the Ottoman Empire. Its roadways carried commerce to Persia, Syria, Kurdistan, Armenia and Asia Minor; its waterways carried goods and people, via the Tigris and Euphrates, 300 miles north-west to Baghdad, and thence toward Constantinople.[35] The city's population was dominated by Sunni Arabs but was also home to Shia tribesmen, Armenians, Jews, Syrian Christians, Indians and Europeans.[36] English merchants had been trading at Basra since 1635, and the East India Company had established its first factory (or warehouse) there in 1723.[37] The Company's agent at Basra when the Riches' ship docked in March 1808 was Samuel Manesty. The eighth son of a successful Liverpool slave trader, Manesty had been in the Company's employ since 1778, acting as Resident at Basra from the early 1780s and developing a lucrative

[32] Alexander, *Baghdad in Bygone Days*, 19–22, 24. They sailed on the *Princess Augusta* East Indiaman. Mary's half-brother recalled the presence of a German governess and that Mackintosh educated the children on the voyage by reading them Milton's works and Addison's *Spectator* articles. Sir James recorded in a letter of 16 July 1806 that 'I read through the whole of Gibbon, with such omissions and explanations as children require', as well as Robertson's *Charles V* and *America* 'with the very delightful interludes of Walter Scott and Miss Baillie'. *Memoirs of the Life of the Right Honourable Sir James Mackintosh*, ed. Robert James Mackintosh (2 vols., 1835), I: 203–4, 254, 291, 438 (citation from 291). He read both Burke and Hume to them as part of 'a regular course of the political history of England' (291).

[33] Christopher J. Finlay, 'Mackintosh, Sir James of Kyllachy (1765–1832)', *Oxford Dictionary of National Biography* (Oxford, 2004). For the sale of Mackintosh's estate, and his improvident lifestyle thereafter, see *Memoirs*, ed. Mackintosh, I: 169, 188. As his son notes, prior to his Bombay appointment, Mackintosh had been offered a position as a judge at Trinidad (*ibid.*, 187), a reminder of the extent to which the empires of Britain's Atlantic and Indian Ocean worlds were connected through their governing elites.

[34] Alexander, *Baghdad in Bygone Days*, 22–4. Mary may have been the only 'lady' sailing with the fleet. She reported reading the theologian William Paley on board. Mary Rich (henceforth MR) to Lady Mackintosh, 18 February–31 March 1808, British Library (henceforth BL), BL, Add MS 80751, fol. 7v.

[35] Thabit A. J. Abdullah, *Merchants, Mamluks, and Murder: The Political Economy of Trade in Eighteenth-Century Basra* (Albany, 2001), 3, 11–13.

[36] *Ibid.*, 13, 17, 25–7.

[37] *Ibid.*, 28.

private trade both as the owner of substantial shipping and as the husband of an Armenian Christian whose family owned extensive date plantations.[38] Claudius Rich took an instant dislike to Manesty and refused to allow his wife to disembark at Basra, determined that Mary should not be tainted by contact with Manesty's spouse, who Rich insisted was merely a concubine and whom he described in a letter to Sir James Mackintosh as both a 'Trull' and 'a dirty Armenian drab'.[39] The first salvo in an extended battle between Rich and Manesty, this comment – which Rich's in-laws in Bombay found deeply offensive – conveys the fragility of his class, race and gender identities as the unacknowledged illegitimate son of a disgraced British military officer.[40]

From Basra the Riches sailed by schooner to Baghdad, arriving in May at this provincial seat of government. By 1808, Baghdad had been under the turbulent dynastic rule of Mamlūk pashas for decades. The Mamlūks were Georgian warriors, enslaved and imported as boys by the Ottomans, converted to Islam and set to govern the empire's unruly Iraqi borderlands.[41] By the later eighteenth century the Baghdad province or *pashalik* had attained an unstable quasi-independence.[42] Claudius and

---

[38] For Manesty, see Robin P. Walsh, 'Manesty, Samuel (1758–1812)', *Oxford Dictionary of National Biography* (Oxford, 2010), and M. E. Yapp, 'The Establishment of the East India Company Residency at Baghdad, 1798–1806', *Bulletin of the School of Oriental and African Studies*, 30 (1967), 323–36, esp. 323–5.

[39] Claudius Rich (henceforth CR) to William Erskine, from Basra, 31 March 1808, BL, Add MS 80751, fol. 17; Alexander, *Baghdad in Bygone Days*, 25–7. Walsh, 'Manesty', cites Lachlan Macquarie's April 1807 description of Mrs Manesty as being 'an Armenian by Birth of a respectable Family, and has brought her Husband no less than 13 Children … Mrs Manesty is still a beautiful Woman, and very pleasing in her manners.' See also X. W. Bond, 'Claudius Rich and Samuel Manesty', Untold Lives Blog (4 March 2016), https://blogs.bl.uk/untoldlives/2016/03/claudius-rich-and-samuel-manesty.html, who ascribes Rich's comment instead to 'Orientalist' concerns. Mary recorded the incident on 23 March 1808 to her stepmother, Lady Mackintosh. Manesty's letter to Claudius was very pleasant, she observed, but he wished her to meet '<u>Mrs Manesty</u> at the Factory … We must if possible contrive some excuse as it is totally out of the question. No I am not quite so <u>dawdling</u> as all that comes to visit <u>a dirty Armenian</u> drab as Claudius calls her.' BL, Add MS 80751, fol. 12. The couple were convinced that Manesty was not married, and that the invitation was intended to dupe them into thinking that 'Mrs Manesty was indeed a wife'. *Ibid.*, 13v–14.

[40] Mary wrote to Maitland on 30 August 1808 expressing sorrow on learning that their father and stepmother disapproved of the couple's response to Manesty and his wife, repeating the rumour that Mrs Manesty was an '<u>Armenian Trull</u>' and saying that she had written to her stepmother for advice on the propriety of their actions. BL, Add MS 80751, fol. 37. On the next folio (38), in contrast, she reported a pleasant visit with the Armenian wife of her husband's servant Coja Mokeill: her perceptions of both Armenian and 'native' Iraqi women varied both over time and by context.

[41] Charles Tripp, *A History of Iraq* (Cambridge, 2014), 8–10.

[42] Abdullah, *Merchants, Mamluks*, 11–12; Tom Nieuwenhuis, *Politics and Society in Early Modern Iraq: Mamlūk Pashas, Tribal Shayks and Local Rule between 1802 and 1831* (The Hague, 1982), vii, 9–13, 76, 80.

Mary Rich's residence in the city from 1808 to 1821 coincided with a period of instability that saw successive sons and sons-in-law of the Mamlūk pasha Sulaymān the Great vie for power.[43] Defeat in these dynastic contests was violent and decisive, resulting in the death and beheading of successive vanquished pashas. Women in Baghdad – as Mary Rich was to find to her discomfort – lived enclosed lives physically confined to their own and each other's female quarters within the home. But it would be mistaken to assume that the wives, sisters and mothers of Mamlūk men lacked power or political agency. To the contrary, their role as dynastic marriage partners, their personal immunity from beheading during episodes of regime change and their ability to accumulate substantial fortunes ensured that 'Many Mamlūk pashas owed the continuation of their power to the use of status and wealth brought to them through their wives.'[44] In this context, Mary – who, unlike her husband, could socialise freely with the ladies of Baghdad in their homes, and who learned Turkish to do so – proved a valuable asset to Claudius as a diplomat.[45]

Baghdad mattered to the British in these years chiefly because they feared that Napoleon's troops would use Mesopotamia as a route to reach and conquer the Indian subcontinent.[46] Claudius Rich's duties as the Company's Resident combined official diplomatic relations with management of an extensive spy-ring that transferred clandestine information about the French and their allies between Britain and India via Basra and Constantinople.[47] In defiance of the Company's orders, he

[43] Nieuwenhuis, *Politics and Society*, 15–16.

[44] *Ibid.*, 16–17, 23–4 (citation from 24). See more broadly *Ottoman Women in Public Space*, ed. Ebru Boyar and Kate Fleet (Leiden, 2016).

[45] She mentioned in a letter to Maitland that she was learning Turkish when she reported her first visit with Baghdad women ('two Armenian ladies') three days after arriving in Baghdad (7 May 1808, BL, Add MS 80751, fol. 19). On 12 June 1808 she wrote to Lady Mackintosh: 'I have been so busily occupied in copying dispatches for Claudius that I have hardly a few moments left me to write a few words to you.' *Ibid.*, fol. 23. Recognition of the roles played by diplomatic wives has emerged as a key component of the 'new diplomatic history'. See Jennifer Mori, 'How Women Made Diplomacy: The British Embassy in Paris, 1815–1841', *Journal of Women's History*, 27: 4 (2015), 137–59; *Women, Diplomacy and International Politics since 1500*, ed. Glenda Sluga and Carolyn James (2015).

[46] For fears of military invasion as a motive for engagement with Baghdad in the Napoleonic era, see for example John Macdonald Kinneir, *Journey through Asia Minor, Armenia, and Koordistan, in the Years 1813 and 1814; With Remarks on the Marches of Alexander, and the Retreat of the Ten Thousand* (1818), esp. viii and 512–39. Twenty-first-century historians dispute the economic and political motives for British diplomacy in Baghdad. See Jonathan Parry, 'Steam Power and British Influence in Baghdad, 1820–1860', *Historical Journal*, 56 (2013), 145–73, 147, esp. fn. 6.

[47] England obtained commercial concessions from the Ottoman sultan in 1809 through the Treaty of Dardanelles. See Iftikhar Ahmad Khan, 'Indian Shipping at Basra: The Incident of 1820', *Proceedings of the Indian History Congress*, 54 (1993), 724. For Rich's engagement in espionage, see Nieuwenhuis, *Politics and Society*, 85.

also intervened in Mamlūk succession disputes. Over 100 letters to family in Bombay written by Mary and Claudius Rich survive from these years. In this correspondence, Mary's letters veer between thinly veiled expressions of terror during the violent coups that marked Mamlūk succession disputes, and prolonged recitals of the couple's great boredom and lassitude during the interminable summer months.[48] They document her own and her husband's political views, their diplomatic endeavours and their labile, racialised perceptions of the Ottoman population. Her correspondence also positively pullulates with material objects. It is animated with thick descriptions of the couple's strategic circulation of luxury goods, obtained in the modern consumer markets of Europe, India, the Persian Gulf and the Ottoman Empire; it also registers Claudius's efforts to extract ancient artefacts and medieval manuscripts from Mesopotamian, Kurdish and Indian collectors.

The Riches rapidly established a twofold pattern of material and epistolary communication with Mary's kith and kin in Britain and India.[49] By sail, letters and goods travelled to and fro between London, Bombay, Basra and Baghdad; at the same time – on horseback and in caravans – boxes, parcels and correspondence journeyed via the overland route between continental Europe, Constantinople and Kurdistan to Baghdad, from whence the Riches dispatched selected items onward to Bombay via Basra.[50] In both the overland and the maritime iterations of this communication network, material goods flowed alongside – and enabled – a constant exchange of gossip, tactical information, political news, patronage, scholarly expertise, emotion, labour and human beings.

---

[48] Writing to Maitland on 10 July 1808, she wished one of her sisters would come and stay with her, 'but I am afraid you young gay ladies would find it rather a bore being shut up in a Haram all day'. On 13 July 1808, again writing to Maitland, she reported that Wahhabi tribesmen had appeared 'in swarms' outside the gates of Baghdad and that the pasha and his troops, having marched out against them, decided it 'more prudent to retreat'. A few years previously, the Wahhabi had, she reported, murdered 8,000 men, women and children of Baghdad, 'shewing not the least quarter or mercy and it is even said drank in exaltation the blood of their victims. They remind me of the Musselmen in the time of Mahomet and the first Calihs.' She knew the latter from Gibbon. BL, Add MS 80751, 31–31v, 32–32v. Many of her letters, in contrast, are marked by the generic ennui of white experiences of imperialism, as detailed by Jeffrey Auerbach, *Imperial Boredom: Monotony and the British Empire* (Oxford, 2018).

[49] The first goods recorded as being dispatches to Bombay were the bottles of red wine from Shiraz that Claudius purchased at Bushire, en route to Basra, for Sir James Mackintosh. MR to Maitland Mackintosh, 16 March 1808, BL, Add MS 80751, fol. 7v.

[50] For the communication networks upon which they relied, see Joshi Chitra, 'Dak Roads, Dak Runners, and Reordering of Communication Networks', *International Review of Social History*, 57 (2012), 169–89 and Edward Ingram, 'Directing the Mail from Baghdad', in Edward Ingram, *Empire-building and Empire-builders: Twelve Studies* (1995), 30–46.

Most of the couple's surviving letters from Baghdad were written by Mary Rich to her sister Maitland in Bombay. Named by her father to honour the trustee of his debt-ridden Highland estate, Maitland Mackintosh at age seventeen married a Bombay civil servant several years her senior.[51] Her husband, William Erskine, had been her father's private secretary before obtaining his judicial appointment, and became a distinguished scholar of Indian languages and history.[52] In Bombay, Claudius Rich had lived with Erskine before his marriage to Mary. The brothers-in-law shared a passion for Oriental manuscripts and material culture, an ambition to compensate for their lack of inherited wealth by accumulating cultural capital, and a sense of humour about their own personal idiosyncrasies. Although Mary wrote the great bulk of their surviving letters, these manuscripts also include letters and insertions authored by Claudius, which allow us to see the couple's sexual division of marital labour and the extent to which his diplomacy, mental health, scholarship and collecting activities rested on his wife's intellectual, social and acquisitive investment in global material cultures.

In keeping with established gender norms, Mary assumed responsibility for provisioning the household at the Baghdad Residency and for ensuring that her own and her husband's material comfort appropriately registered their identities, dignity and status. Her requests for snuff, shoes, textiles, books and musical instruments were at once a means of retaining links to distant family, and assertions that even in distant Baghdad the Riches upheld elite, contemporary, Enlightenment values of propriety and elegance. Mary was an exacting commissioner of goods, determined to combine economy, taste and signification through her vicarious purchasing.[53] Having discovered that only slippers could be obtained in Baghdad, she requested many pairs of shoes from her sister in Bombay, but instructed her to send footwear made in Bengal or China, instead of 'vulgar ill made Bombay shoes'.[54] Not just nail brushes but 'Smyths Nail Brushes' must be dispatched to her; the flute for Claudius 'must be a Patent Flute of the newest kind with all the

---

[51] For Maitland's naming, see Finlay, 'Mackintosh'. James Maitland was the eighth Earl of Lauderdale. Her naming reflects Mackintosh's early commitment to including his daughters fully in his patronage networks.

[52] For Erskine, Katherine Prior, 'Erskine, William (1773–1852)', *Oxford Dictionary of National Biography* (Oxford, 2004).

[53] Notwithstanding Mary's location in Baghdad, her provisioning activities mirror in many ways those described for propertied provincial Englishwomen in Amanda Vickery, *The Gentleman's Daughter: Women's Lives in Georgian England* (New Haven, 1998).

[54] MR to Maitland, 15 September 1808, 1 October 1809 and 29 April 1811, BL. Add MS 80751, fols. 40v, 113 and 270 (citation from fol. 270).

additional keys'.[55] In return, she sent Persian Gulf and Ottoman luxuries that included attar of roses, pearls, embroidered Turkish handkerchiefs, velvet and silk, as well as mobilising the overland European route via Constantinople to obtain yard upon yard of fine but inexpensive French lace.[56]

These commissioned goods served political ends, allowing the Riches to express specific national identities and to mobilise selected forms of Britishness when engaging in Mamlūk diplomacy. The couple's seemingly obsessive demands for Irish linen for Claudius's trousers illustrate the ways in which material culture bolstered their unstable personal claims of belonging. His contemporaries associated Claudius with Bristol, but both he and Mary laboured to underline his essential Irishness, and thus his association with his reputed father's Cockburn family line.[57] Assertions that Claudius was Irish had a habit of surfacing when husband and wife perceived his status to be under threat. Suspected lapses in their acquaintances' sexual propriety and references to their own economic precarity both triggered their invocation of Rich's Irish identity. It is thus unsurprising that Claudius couched his objection to Mary meeting with Samuel Manesty's Armenian wife in Basra in terms of his own Irish nationality, or that Mary ascribed their lack of a Scottish country seat to having 'married an Irishman' rather than to her Scottish father's notorious improvidence.[58] This leitmotif of Irish identity took material form in Mary's persistent efforts to clothe Claudius's nether regions in Irish linen. In 1809 she wrote to remind Maitland that she had commissioned two dozen pairs of Irish linen

---

[55] MR to Maitland, 29 April 1811 and 22 January 1810, BL, Add MS 80751, fols. 274 and 133. On 4 November 1810, she wrote to Maitland: 'I do not much like the music you sent me', observing that Claudius had described it as 'd—d dull' (*ibid.*, fol. 206).

[56] For the Ottoman trade in luxury textiles, see *Threads of Global Desire: Silk in the Pre-modern World*, ed. Dagmar Schäfer, Giorgio Riello and Luca Molà (Woodbridge, 2018), introduction and chs. 4–5. Examples of French lace, which Mary was very keen for Maitland to provide comparative Bombay prices for, include MR to Maitland, 20 February 1811 and 24 October 1812, BL, Add MS 80751, fols. 243, 274; 24 October 1812, BL, Add MS 80752, fol. 35v.

[57] For example, Rich's patron, Richard Hall, writing to Sir James Mackintosh on 30 December 1803, stated that 'He is of Bristol, where I had the pleasure lately of seeing him.' Hall continued, 'He is a young man of good family', without elaborating on Rich's parentage. *Memoirs*, ed. Mackintosh, I: 201.

[58] 'Do you know the Fellow had actually the impudence to imagine that I would suffer Mrs Rich to keep company with his Trull. Oh how my Irish blood boiled.' CR to Erskine, 31 March 1808, BL, Add MS 80751, fol. 17. Mary did not visit Scotland until her return to Britain in the 1820s, but wrote of Inverness, the nearest town to her father's erstwhile Highland estate: 'I always claim [it] as my Town and will certainly persuade Mr Rich though no Seat to visit your & Major Campbell's in the Highlands from which I am forever exiled having married an Irishman.' MR to Mrs Campbell, 30 September 1809, BL, Add MS 80751, fol. 108v.

trousers for Claudius, which had yet to arrive.[59] Repeated reminders that Claudius would soon have nothing decent to wear gave way, when the commissioned trousers finally arrived, to complaints that the cloth was 'so horribly coarse' that Claudius had 'declared he will not wear anything you have sent'.[60] Worse yet, on inspection the 'Irish linen' trousers Maitland had sent proved instead to be merely 'Indian long cloth, and so tight & rotten that hardly any of them now remain'.[61]

Mary's rejection of Indian textiles was selective, focusing primarily on Claudius's person and his personal dignity as the British representative in Baghdad.[62] The Dardanelles Treaty of Peace, Commerce and Secret Alliance signed in 1809 ended the Anglo-Turkish War, pledging the British to protect Ottoman interests and restoring British access to Turkish markets.[63] In this context, Mary not only commissioned Maitland to supply fine Indian textiles for her own Baghdad wardrobe, but also ordered items from the subcontinent to serve as diplomatic gifts at the Mamlūk pashas' court. As in India, the Company's Residents were, soon after their arrival at Baghdad, invested with robes of honour to mark their incorporation into the ruler's ambit, and were expected to offer fine gifts in return as signs of fealty. As pasha succeeded beheaded pasha, Claudius repeatedly processed to the palace to be invested with a pelisse made from cloth of gold and lined with sable.[64] In return, he

---

[59] MR to Maitland, 1 October 1809, BL, Add MS 80751, fol. 114. Interestingly, she now asked as well for multicoloured Turkish-style nankeen pantaloons, tied at the ankles, but it was to the Irish linen trousers that her letters repeatedly returned, for example in a letter to Maitland of 4 November 1810 (fol. 205v). Trousers entered genteel British men's wardrobes in response to colonial and imperial trade and warfare in the eighteenth century, as discussed by Beverly Lemire, 'A Question of Trousers: Seafarers, Masculinity and Empire in the Shaping of British Male Dress, c. 1600–1800', *Cultural and Social History*, 13 (2016), 1–22, esp. 13–18.

[60] MR to Maitland, 29 April 1811, BL, Add MS 80751, fol. 270. Claudius added a note, telling Maitland that he was using some of the goods for his annual clothing allowance for his guard, and made a point of noting 'as for my wearing them that is all a joke'. John Styles (personal communication) notes that Irish flaxen linen imported into Bombay, although a cool textile well-suited to the tropics, would likely have been intended for plebeian nautical use and very coarse.

[61] MR to Maitland, 27 July 1812, BL, Add MS 80752, fol. 23. E. M. Collingham, *Imperial Bodies: The Physical Experience of the Raj, c. 1800–1947* (Cambridge, 2001), ch. 2, esp. 62–3, 65–6, discusses the gendered regimes that governed East India Company clothing and fashions.

[62] Mary herself – although exceptionally punctilious with respect to the weight, composition, colour, pattern and ornamentation of material for her gowns – accepted that Indian textiles were well suited for her own wardrobe. See for example her letter to Maitland, 21 September 1810, BL, Add MS80751, fol. 189.

[63] Allan Cunningham, 'Robert Adair and the Treaty of the Dardanelles', in *Anglo-Ottoman Encounters in the Age of Revolution: Collected Essays*, ed. Allan Cunningham (1993), 103–43.

[64] See for example MR to Erskine, 27 March 1809, BL, Add MS 80751, fol. 71v. The horse was caparisoned 'in the Turkish manner'. See similarly MR to Maitland, 29 October 1810, BL, Add MS 80751, fol. 221. The analogous investiture ceremonies for East India Company

offered expensive gifts of luxuries, the cost of which Mary sought to reduce by commissioning Indian textiles from her sister in Bombay.[65]

In time, moreover, Mary emerged as a diplomat in her own right. The norms of Sunni propriety in Baghdad prohibited her from meeting with Muslim men other than her household servants.[66] Mary's circle of even female acquaintances was, moreover, initially very narrow: there was only one other Englishwoman in Baghdad when she arrived, and the Anglo-Turkish war prevented the ladies of the pasha's family from visiting. Armenian women did come to the Residency, and were duly entertained with coffee and sweetmeats, but Mary initially reported that they were 'disgustingly ugly and indecent and I am obliged to keep them at a great distance'.[67] In sharp contrast, when the cessation of war allowed her to visit the Muslim ladies of the pasha's court, their elite status trumped their race and religion, and Mary fulsomely praised their pleasing politeness.[68] Her sometimes esteem for elite Ottoman men derived from their solicitude for these women, which protected them from physical violence when successive pashas were overthrown. As Mary observed to Maitland in the midst of the bloody coup of 1810, 'The respect and tenderness of Turks towards women is astonishing, and in a different manner equals any of the most civilized nations in Europe.'[69]

Once welcomed into the women's quarters of Baghdad's courtly elite, Mary Rich reported to her sister that she had become the frequent recipient of 'very handsome presents, [and] of course I am obliged to do the same, but find Jewellery so very expensive that I wish much to procure some Indian goods which they will esteem more, as they are not to be procured here'.[70] Deploying domestic sociability, limited

---

Residents on the subcontinent are discussed in Margot Finn, 'Material Turns in British History: II. Corruption: Imperial Power, Princely Politics and Gifts Gone Rogue', *Transactions of the Royal Historical Society*, 29 (2019), 1–25.

[65] She complained to Maitland on 29 May 1811 that the failure of the 'Poonah Chintzes' to arrive was especially irksome 'as Mr Rich is now preparing to <u>make the present</u> to the Pasha and … the Chintzes would have been very acceptable & saved me great expence as now I shall be obliged to set them down in my own account whereas otherwise they would have been purchased for the Company & been much admired by the Turks.' BL, Add MS, 80751, fol. 277–277v.

[66] MR to Kitty Mackintosh, 23 December 1810: 'A Turk would not allow even his dearest friend even to mention the name of his wife and two men would be intimate for 30 years without either presuming to speak concerning their Haram.' BL, Add MS, 80751, fol. 226v.

[67] MR to Maitland, 10 July 1808, BL, Add MS 80751, fol. 27.

[68] MR to Maitland, 1 October 1809, BL, Add MS 80751, fol. 111.

[69] MR to Maitland, 5 October 1810, BL, Add MA 80751, fols. 196v–197. The complexities and internal contradictions of Enlightenment 'Orientalist' interpretations of Ottoman gender norms are explored by Joanna de Groot, 'Oriental Feminotopias? Montagu's and Montesquieu's "Seraglios" Revisited', *Gender and History*, 18 (2006), 66–86.

[70] MR to Maitland, 19 March 1810, BL, Add MS 80751, fol. 149. She went on to specify Madras gold muslin, Pune muslin embroidered with gold and silver, and kincob from

verbal communication and the exchange of luxury goods, Mary Rich cultivated unprecedented European relations with Baghdad's govern-ing-class women.[71] We can see the impact of her friendships in Claudius Rich's repeated interventions to save the male kin of deposed pashas from execution in the aftermath of violent succession disputes: it was the women whom Mary entertained at the Residency and whose houses she visited who pleaded for Claudius Rich to appeal to the newly installed pashas who had supplanted their sons and husbands. Already in 1812, trust between Mary and these women was sufficiently robust to allow the late pasha's widow to defy etiquette and travel to the British Residency, where she appealed directly to Claudius to inter-vene on behalf of her son.[72] This behaviour reflects a new style of European material diplomacy exercised by the Riches as a couple, rather than – as the extant secondary literature suggests – providing yet another example of Claudius Rich's personal charisma and his excep-tional command of the 'Oriental mind'.[73]

### III

What of collecting, archaeological excavation and Enlightenment science? Here too we can only understand Claudius Rich's contributions if we recognise his reliance on and partnership with his wife. Neither Mary nor her sister read Oriental languages, a major impedi-ment to participating actively in the accumulation of Arabic, Persian and Syriac texts – to which their husbands devoted much time, effort and money.[74] Their correspondence, however, demonstrates that the

Gujarat: 'mind however in choosing them not to consider your own taste, but to let them be as gaudy as possible'.

[71] She told Maitland that she could now follow their conversations in Turkish, but not yet participate in them. 22 December 1810, BL, Add MS 80751, fol. 226. Mary Rich's status as a wife and a Christian was important in this context. Both Claudius's predecessor as Baghdad Resident and Samuel Manesty at Basra had been entangled in diplomatic rows involving European men's alleged or actual relations with Muslim women in the *pashalik*. For Sir Harford Jones, who was expelled from Baghdad in 1804 as a result of such allegations, see Yapp, 'Establishment', 331–2. For Manesty, Mirza Abu Taleb Khan, *The Travels of Mirza Abu Taleb Khan, in Asia, Africa, and Europe, during the Years 1799, 1800, 1801, 1802, and 1803. Written by Himself, in the Persian Language*, trans. Charles Stewart (2 vols., 1810), 371–6.

[72] MR to Maitland, 19 May 1812, BL, Add MS 80752, fols. 11–11v. See also MR to Erskine, 12 March 1817, BL, Add MS 80752, fols. 230–230v.

[73] Alexander, *Baghdad in Bygone Days*, exemplifies this characteristic interpretation of Claudius Rich: 'He ... had the gift given to few Europeans, that of thoroughly understand-ing the Oriental mind and outlook ... He understood the Oriental phlegm and patience, and could become as Oriental as themselves.' (32–3).

[74] Rich had begun to seek out manuscripts for his brother-in-law within a few days of his arrival in Baghdad: 'I have instituted a search for such MSS as I think you should like', he wrote four days after their schooner docked. CR to Erskine, 8 May 1808, BL, Add MS 89751, 21v.

two men expected their wives both to facilitate and to take an active interest in their acquisitions. Claudius thus wrote to Maitland, rather than to William Erskine, to report that he had purchased 'a very famous work' of Arabic 'natural magic' for her husband, which although the price was 'rather extravagant' was 'just the thing he wants'.[75] Mary's letters to her sister routinely interlarded information about consumer goods with information about the acquisition of manuscripts and antiquities; her correspondence brought together in the same sentences and paragraphs news that she was sending 'excellent velvet' from Constantinople, complaints that she was yet again disappointed by her sister's dispatch of ersatz Irish linen, and notification that she was sending books of Oriental scholarship which Claudius had ordered from Constantinople, Vienna and Paris.[76]

Both ancient history and archaeology, moreover, allowed Mary Rich to participate directly in Claudius's scholarship and collecting. In preparation for the couple's archaeological excursions, Mary read ancient history avidly. Shortly after arriving in Baghdad, she took up the multi-volume *Universal History* produced by eighteenth-century London booksellers to bolster her understanding of the history of Islam.[77] A year later, Mary was supplementing the *Universal History* with the works of Enlightenment historians such as Edward Gibbon and developing a preference for Islamic military culture. 'I have lately been reading again with fresh instruction and delight the Chapters in Gibbon respecting these Countries, and his most elegant account of Mahomet, and the first Arabian Heroes for surely they deserved that appellation in contradistinction to the cowardly & effeminate Greeks,' she observed in a letter to Maitland.[78]

---

[75] CR to Maitland, 14 December 1810, BL, Add MS 80751, fols. 223–223v. Lindsay Allen offers an excellent analysis of the wider context of East India Company families and the collection of antiquities in '"Come Then Ye Classic Thieves of Each Degree": The Social Context of the Persepolis Diaspora in the Early Nineteenth Century', *Iran*, 51 (2013), 207–34.

[76] MR to Maitland, 27 February 1812, BL Add MS 80752, fols. 20–3.

[77] Claudius, for example, recommended that she read the multi-volume eighteenth-century *Universal History*, in the edition with a preface by Mr Sale, and at his recommendation Mary read Robertson's *Charles V* aloud to him. MR to Maitland, 10 July 1808 and 15 September 1808, BL, Add MS 80751, fols. 27v–28 and fol. 43. MR to Maitland, 12 June 1808: 'I am now reading the first Vols of the second part of the Universal history containing the History of Life of Mahomedt which I believe [is] reckoned the best part of the whole book. Though rather dry I read it with great pleasure & interest & after I intend going through carefully Monsieur Sale's prefatory treatise on the Arabs. Claudius has recommended [it] to me as the best book I could possibly read on that subject.' *Ibid.*, fols. 28–28v. For the *Universal History*, see Guido Abbattista, 'The Business of Paternoster Row: Towards a Publishing History of the Universal History, 1736–65', *Publishing History*, 17 (1985), 5–50.

[78] MR to Maitland, 1 October 1809, BL, Add MS 80751, fol. 112.

Historical understanding was a collaborative, not an individualistic, enterprise in the Rich household. The couple replicated the sociable practices of domestic reading Sir James Mackintosh had instituted in Bombay to instruct his family in history. In the long, hot afternoons at the Baghdad Residency, Mary read aloud from historians such as Gibbon, allowing Claudius simultaneously to refresh his historical knowledge of the ancient world and to hone his skills of drawing and draughtsmanship as he listened to her.[79] These artistic and technical skills came into active use as the couple began to venture beyond Baghdad to explore the ruins of ancient Babylon, 60 miles to the southwest. The precise location of this famous biblical city was hotly disputed by East India Company men of science.[80] Cartography was an Enlightenment and an imperial science par excellence, and Claudius Rich's initial visit to the reputed site of Babylon in 1811 figures in twenty-first-century historiography as a case study in Enlightenment reason put to the service of empire.[81] Wielding astronomical, mathematical and surveying instruments,[82] Claudius Rich exercised his reason in the rubble of Babylon to dispute his predecessors' assumptions – which had been based on armchair cartography – about the ancient city's location relative to the banks of the Euphrates.[83] More than merely measuring, Claudius set his companions to dig in the ruins. These excavations amid what Claudius in his journals repeatedly described as the 'rubble' of Babylon, revealed the inscribed cuneiform bricks, clay tablets, coins and cylinder seals that now populate Case 15 of the British Museum's Enlightenment Gallery.

[79] MR to Maitland, 26 September 1808, BL, Add MS 80751, fol. 43.

[80] Rich's first excursion was framed by a desire to test the assertions of the Company's official surveyor, James Rennell, with actual fieldwork. Rennell's arguments are found in James *Herodotus Rennell, Geographical System of Herodotus Examined and Explained by a Comparison with Those of Other Ancient Authors, and with Modern Geography. In the Course of the Work are Introduced, Dissertations on the Itinerary State of the Greeks, the Expedition of Darius* (1800). See Rich's *Memoir on the Ruins of Babylon. With Three Plates* (1815), esp. 51–2.

[81] For this argument with respect to the East India Company in particular, see Matthew H. Edney, *Mapping and Empire: The Geographical Construction of British India, 1765–1843* (Chicago, 1990). Edney, however, does not mention Rich. For Rich in this context, see Robert J. Mayhew, *Enlightenment Geography: The Political Languages of British Geography, 1650–1850* (Basingstoke, 2000), ch. 10, esp. 205. For an argument that the nexus between empire and geography was more heterogeneous and less relentlessly instrumental, see Felix Driver, *Geography Militant: Cultures of Exploration and Empire* (Oxford, 2001).

[82] Or so the advertisement for the probate sale of these goods claimed they were: *Bombay Gazette*, 17 April 1822.

[83] Rennell disputed Rich's interpretation in 'Remarks on the Topography of Ancient Babylon', *Archaeologia* (1816). Mayhew, *Enlightenment Geography*, 205, notes that it was Rich, not Rennell, who undertook observational fieldwork.

Absent from modern accounts of Rich's excavations at Babylon are both Mary Rich and her errant younger sister, Kitty Mackintosh.[84] Both were indisputably present, as their letters to their sister Maitland in Bombay attest. Kitty Mackintosh had been dispatched at the age of fifteen by her father to Baghdad to keep Mary company. Described by her elder sister as a 'madcap' and only lightly chaperoned, on shipboard she had attracted the attention of a twenty-seven-year-old naval lieutenant, whose proposal of marriage Kitty rashly accepted.[85] She was rescued before the marriage could take place by the Riches, who – as Mary reported to Maitland – set sail hastily from Baghdad to the port of Bushire 'to restore our giddy sister I hope to her senses'.[86] Sequestered with the Riches for several months at the Baghdad Residency, Kitty remained resolute in her marital intentions, and it was immediately prior to her marriage, aged sixteen, that the Riches travelled *en famille* to the site of Babylon.[87] Now a safe distance from the strictly policed gender regime of Sunni Baghdad, Kitty ranged freely over the ruins with Mary, and observed that she was 'very pleased' with the ancient site. She also reported to Maitland that 'Mary has told me that she has sealed her letter to you with a seal dug up at Babylon & therefor begs you will observe it particularly.'[88]

When in 1813 Claudius Rich began to bring his analysis of the 'heaps of rubbish' he had excavated at Babylon into the public domain, he erased Mary and Kitty entirely from the record of his scientific investigations.[89] His popular *Memoir on the Ruins of Babylon* thanked 'a gentleman who accompanied me (Mr. Lockett), who superintended' the surveying operations, referred to both Arabic and European male scholars and

---

[84] For example, Michael Seymour offers a perceptive account of Rich's 1811 investigations at Babylon, but mentions Mary only in the context of her subsequent sale of his collection to the British Museum. Michael Seymour, *Babylon: Legend, History and the Ancient City* (2016), 133–8, esp. 137.

[85] For the description of Kitty (born 1795) as a 'madcap', see MR to Maitland, 29 May 1811, BL, Add MS 80751, fol. 275.

[86] MR to Maitland, 9 April 1811, BL, Add MS 80751, fol. 261.

[87] The marriage took place in Baghdad on 8 January 1812, and may have been performed by Rich as Resident. The Riches and Kitty left Baghdad for Babylon on 9 December 1811. MR to Maitland, 18 December 1811, BL, Add MS 80751, fol. 311.

[88] Kitty (Catherine) Mackintosh to Maitland, from Babylon, 18 December 1811, fols. 313–313v.

[89] The first edition of the *Memoir* was published in Vienna in 1813 in the journal *Mines de l'Orient*. It was republished without corrections in London 1815, a second edition appeared in 1816 and a third in 1818. A *Second Memoir on the Ruins* also appeared in 1818. Mary Rich additionally published his 'Narrative of a Journey to the Site of Babylon in 1811' in an edited compilation of his and her journals and writing published in London in 1836: Claudius James Rich, *Narrative of a Residence in Koordistan, and on the Site of Ancient Nineveh; With Journal of a Voyage down the Tigris to Bagdad and an Account of a Visit to Shirauz and Persepolis* [ed. Mary Rich] (2 vols., 1836).

mentioned in passing his use of Turkish men as 'native' informants.[90] Rich expressly wrote both this text and his 1818 *Second Memoir of the Ruins of Babylon* in the style of a reasoned scholarly conversation among men, principally conducted with Major James Rennell, the East India Company's renowned surveyor general of Bengal. In these publications, Rich made relentless use of personal pronouns and possessives – 'I', 'me', 'myself' and 'my' – to describe his research methodology: these four words appear no fewer than thirty-seven times in the first four pages of the *Second Memoir*.[91] His usage prefigures the stylistic convention that was to be adopted in the 1830s by Mary's half-brother, Robert James Mackintosh. When Robert composed a memoir of their father, Sir James Mackintosh, he too was to write Mary and her sisters out of the annals of Enlightenment science. In Robert's memoir, Claudius James Rich and his relations with Sir James Mackintosh merited many pages of attention. Mary's first mention in this work – without the dignity of a name – occurred only when she married Claudius. Like her sister Maitland, with whom she thus became indistinguishable in the text, Robert signified her presence in the historical record only by the letter 'M', followed by a dash.[92]

If we allow these persistent forms of erasure to stand uncontested, we lose sight of multiple layers of Enlightenment universalism. For effacing the records left by European women such as Mary Rich and her sisters also erases from the record South Asian and Middle Eastern women and men who participated in Enlightenment knowledge-making. Mary's descriptions of domestic life in Baghdad and the couple's travels in the wider Ottoman territories highlight this point. Servants, go-betweens and political elites from the Indian subcontinent and a cosmopolitan mélange of Armenians, Arabs, Baghdadis, Jews, Kurds, Mamlūks, Syrians and Turks enabled the Riches to read, write, eat, travel, dig and collect during Claudius's tenure as Resident.[93] His texts are unusual in acknowledging the existence and role of many of these

---

[90] Claudius James Rich, *Memoir of the Ruins of Babylon: With Three Plates* (3rd edn, 1818). Lockett is mentioned on 3; the Kurdish historian and geographer Abu 'l-Fida (1273–1331), for example, on 8; and the Turkish man on 29.

[91] Claudius Rich, *Second Memoir on Babylon: Containing an Inquiry into the Correspondence between the Ancient Descriptions of Babylon and the Remains Still Visible on the Site: Suggested by the "Remarks" of Major Rennell in the* Archæologia (1818), 1–4.

[92] *Memoirs*, ed. Mackintosh, I: 366, 432, 435, 438.

[93] For the role of 'native' men as brokers of Enlightenment knowledge, see esp. Kapil Raj, *Relocating Modern Science: Circulation and the Construction of Scientific Knowledge in South Asia and Europe, Seventeenth to Nineteenth Centuries* (Basingstoke, 2007), and *The Brokered World: Go-Betweens and Global Intelligence, 1770–1820*, ed. Simon Schaffer, Lisa Roberts, Kapil Raj and James Delbourgo (Sagamore Beach, 2009).

collaborators,[94] but by consulting Mary's unpublished personal correspondence as well as the careful annotations and footnotes of her editions of his posthumous works, we can add both substantial volume and human detail to her husband's records. Indeed, it is precisely Mary's female gender identity, her responsibility as a married woman for management of her husband's household, which predisposes her writings to the task of recovering the lost names and voices of their servants in particular.

The 'servant problem' is a cliché in middle- and upper-class British household history. Locating, training, tolerating, disciplining, paying and perhaps most of all retaining servants was a perennial source of anxiety for British and imperial women alike.[95] Mary Rich was no exception. Claudius brought thirty Indian sepoys with him to Baghdad to act as a personal bodyguard and also employed a small troop of European hussars; he had a Company surgeon, who served as his assistant, at least one manservant, a Slavic household steward, grooms and several interpreters and clerks.[96] Mary's letters underscore the relative paucity of her available human resources in Baghdad. Unlike the ladies of the pashas' families with whom she socialised, who could rely on bevies of slave girls imported from the Caucuses to boost their status and perform their menial tasks, she had brought only one Indian maidservant with her in 1808. By autumn, this woman insisted on leaving for Bombay with Claudius's Indian manservant, Abdullah – 'indecent conduct' that her mistress decried as 'abominable'.[97] Mary then reluctantly made do with a young female relation of Claudius's Armenian chief interpreter.[98] In 1810 she added an Indian tailor from Madras to her minuscule establishment of servants.[99] Several months later, the arrival of a so-called

---

[94] Seymour, *Babylon*, 135–6, notes that 'A final merit of Rich's account, no doubt enhanced by the author's long residence in Iraq and linguistic ability, is its incidental coverage of local and non-European tradition relating to the site [of Babylon], a subject that is only now reappearing in archaeological discourse generally.'

[95] For British instances, see for example R. C. Richardson, 'The "Servant Problem", Social Class and Literary Representation in Eighteenth-Century England', in *Literature as History: Essays in Honour of Peter Widdowson*, ed. Simon Barker and Jo Gill (2010), 106–17; Carolyn Steedman, 'Servants and Their Relationship to the Unconscious', *Journal of British Studies*, 42 (2003), 316–50. Colonial examples include Charlotte Macdonald, 'Why Was There No Answer to the "Servant Problem"? Paid Domestic Work and the Making of a White New Zealand, 1840s–1950s', *New Zealand Journal of History*, 51 (2017), 7–35.

[96] Alexander, *Baghdad in Bygone Days*, 60. She estimates that there were fifteen hussars; the steward, who stayed with Rich until his death, was known as Pietro.

[97] MR to Maitland, 18 November 1808, BL, Add MS 80751, fol. 59v.

[98] Alexander, *Baghdad in Bygone Days*, 60, states that an Armenian maid was her only servant, but the information in the letters and journals that record her travels speak of 'attendants', and name the mother of Claudius's dragoman (chief interpreter) among them.

[99] MR to Maitland, [November 1810], BL, Add MS 80751, fols. 211–212v. She was to pay him 30 rupees per month, half to the tailor himself and half to his family in Madras, an arrangement that proved very difficult to effect.

'Portuguese' – a term denoting a mixed-race Indian Christian – swiftly confirmed Mary's existing race prejudices about the colonial lower orders. To her 'no small annoyance in such a place as Bagdad [*sic*] where they are remarkably particular in everything respecting a [harem]', Kitty's maid 'proved a useless idle creature' and was soon discovered to be with child. Mary promptly sacked her, and wrote to Maitland to 'beg you will immediately stop her wages & to never let me see the face of a Portuguese woman again'.[100]

It is nonetheless through Mary's anxious correspondence with Maitland about servants that we first catch fleeting glimpses of non-European agency, personal preferences, prejudice and reason. The initial reactions of Claudius's Indian manservant, Abdullah, to the Muslim women of Baghdad were captured by Mary in a letter to Maitland a few days after their arrival at the Residency, in which she described a visit from the wife and mother-in-law of one of Claudius's officers. 'You never saw such witch-like figures in your life as they all appear coming into a room with a thick black gauze veil over their face and a blue-check shawl covering their body,' she reported. 'Abdulla very genteelly calls them so many <u>Devils</u>.'[101] A few months later, despite Mary's offers of presents and additional payments, her Indian maidservant emphatically articulated her dislike for Baghdad and desire to travel with Abdullah home to Bombay, and voted with her feet. The Portuguese maidservant who arrived in 1811 – already pregnant when she set sail from Bombay – may instead have seen the Baghdad Residency as a conveniently distant Company home in which to bear an illegitimate child.[102] The instrumental uses to which empire could be put were not enjoyed equally by the Riches and their servants, but neither were the latter entirely powerless within the imperial master–servant relationship.[103]

In Baghdad, Claudius's physical and mental health declined sharply from 1812 onward. Mary's letters record an alarming escalation of symptoms such as fits, fevers and fainting, and she and Claudius both wrote openly about his mounting 'melancholy' and inability to shake off the

[100] MR to Maitland, 28 October 1811, BL, Add MS 80751, fols. 307–307v.
[101] MR to Maitland, 7 May 1808, BL, Add MS 80751, fol. 19v.
[102] The ability of 'subaltern' Indian women to negotiate East India Company power hierarchies in this period is discussed by Durba Ghosh, 'Making and Un-making Loyal Subjects: Pensioning Widows and Educating Orphans in Early Colonial India', *Journal of Imperial and Commonwealth History*, 31 (2003), 1–28.
[103] Mary's letters are punctuated with requests that the Erskines would forward the correspondence of the Riches' Indian tailor to his family in Madras, to prevent him from leaving their household in Baghdad. See for example MR to Maitland, 5 August 1812, BL, Add MS 80752, fol. 26.

'blue devils' of depression.[104] Seeking relief from the social isolation, political upheaval and intolerable heat of Baghdad, they made extended journeys to the Kurdish provinces to the north, using their travels to explore ancient ruins and collect both antiquities and manuscripts. These activities necessitated large-scale mobilisations of colonial labour.[105] Their Kurdish expedition of 1820, for example, was undertaken with perhaps sixty tent-pitchers, muleteers and other skilled labourers – Arabs, Christians, Indians, Jews, Persians and Turks, commanded by Claudius's Armenian steward, Aga Minas.[106] Combing Mary Rich's writings yields many more records of the personnel who enabled their travels and excavations than does reading her husband's journals alone. For Mary's records also allow us to enumerate and name specific women among their servants, go-betweens and interlocutors.

Both Claudius and Mary kept journals of their 1820 Kurdish expedition, and Mary chose to print her text as well as Claudius's when she published a posthumous edition of his works in 1839. Before the couple departed Baghdad, they were feted, at gender-segregated events, by the men and women of Baghdad's governing elite, many of whom they had now known for over a decade. Claudius's account of these festivities mentions that Mary's exclusively female gathering included 'her friend Salkha Khatoon, one of the widows of old Suleiman Pasha'. Mary's account also mentions this powerful woman, but describes her as 'my Koordish friend Salkha Khanum', and endows her with both a birthplace and opinions, by suggesting that her friend 'seemed not a little to envy me my excursion to her native mountains'. Additionally, Mary named 'my constant and intimate friend Hanifa Khatoon, who was very angry at our fancy, as she called it, of flying off to such a solitary savage place as Koordistan, and leaving all the comforts and amusements of Baghdad'. A third named female friend in Mary's account was Zabit Khatoon, who in stormy weather, had mounted her horse and arrived at the women's gathering late at night, to bid Mary farewell.[107]

---

[104] See for example MR to Maitland 24 June 1812, 19 November 1812, 7 May 1813 and 21 May 1813, and CR to Erskine, 26 April 1813, BL, Add MS 80752, fols. 14–14v, 47, 90–90v, 94 and 68.

[105] For this aspect of East India Company knowledge-making, see esp. Onni Gust, 'Mobility, Gender and Empire in Maria Graham's *Journal of a Residence in India* (1812)', *Gender & History*, 29 (2017), 273–91.

[106] Rich, *Narrative of a Residence*, I: 5. Aga Minas 'had all the patience and good humour which such a post required – was unwearied in his endeavours to make everyone comfortable, and most zealous in the discharge of his duty'. Significantly, this detailed description comes not from Rich's text but from Mary's editorial footnote.

[107] *Ibid.*, I: 3 (CR), 331–2 (MR).

Just as Mary Rich's letters to Maitland registered – however schematically – the volition and views of her domestic servants in Baghdad more fully than Claudius's writings, so too her Kurdish travel narrative attended more carefully to servants' identities, lives and labour than did his. Claudius for example mentioned that he was accompanied by a bodyguard of twenty-five Indian sepoys and that Mary initially travelled in a covered mule-litter or takhtrawan and was 'attended by women servants, and all the state of a haram'.[108] Mary's parallel description identifies her two attendants: one was her maidservant 'Taqui' and the other was the mother of Claudius's interpreter, Aga Minas. She accorded them an ethnicity and a social identity. And unlike Claudius, whose comments spoke only of the great dignity with which he and his wife travelled, Mary's account elaborated on the discomfort her female attendants must have endured. She travelled in a recumbent position in her takhtrawan, but her attendants instead journeyed sitting up in 'mohoffas, or a kind of cages, two of which are swung on one mule, and balance each other', she reported. 'It is by no means a comfortable conveyance, owing to the constrained posture the person is obliged to sit in.'[109]

In Kurdistan, as in Baghdad, Mary continued to visit the harems of the governing elite, meeting the mothers, sisters and wives of Kurdish pashas and, if they spoke Turkish, conversing with them. The couple stayed for several months in Sulaimani, a northern provincial capital and Kurdish seat of learning where Claudius avidly sought Oriental manuscripts and Mary too engaged in the work of Enlightenment. In June 1820, accompanied by her female attendants, she was greeted at the pasha's harem by 'a crowd of slave-girls' and introduced to the 'ladies of the family'. The pasha's wife was a woman of Mary's own age, Adela Khanum. Mary noted in her journal that she was the pasha's only wife, and that 'they ... have been endeared to one another by their common sorrow for the death of many children by the smallpox'. Adela Khanum had learned Turkish as a child in Baghdad, and Mary – by birth, marriage and personal inclination a daughter of Enlightenment science – mustered her own Turkish language skills to convince her new friend of the wisdom of vaccinating her surviving son. 'Perhaps too when they hear their Pasha has consented to try the vaccine on his only child, the common people may be induced to allow us to vaccinate their children,' she mused, in keeping with a Kantian conviction in the power of public reason.

[108] *Ibid.*, I: 2.
[109] *Ibid.*, I: 2 (CR), 333 (MR). She notes that as 'Minas's mother is very stout, and Taqui very slender, it was a difficult and nice operation to make the balance equal by throwing in a quantity of stones on Taqui's side.'

'Our journey to Koordistan will then indeed not have been in vain.'[110] Conducted in good faith, this experiment ended fatally. The vaccine ordered at Mary's behest by express delivery from Baghdad duly arrived in the autumn, but both Adela Khanum's young son and her infant nephew died of the disease itself, an outcome Claudius blamed on the inept administration of the vaccine by a Turkish inoculator.[111]

## IV

What do the imperial and material lives of Mary and Claudius Rich tell us about the claims to universalism of 'Western' museums today? How can we best acknowledge the myriad, cross-cultural forms of Enlightenment knowledge production – powerfully marked by empire, slavery and patterns of prejudice – which extended from Bombay to Basra, Baghdad and Babylon? Should we bin the Enlightenment as a concept, or perhaps boycott the Enlightenment Gallery of the British Museum?

I think not. Instead, in concluding this lecture, I make three modest proposals. The first is that, beginning with Case 15, the British Museum should take a first step toward 'universalising' its history by acknowledging the existence of Enlightenment women and their contribution to public forms of reasoning. Mary Rich was with Claudius Rich for every day and night of his tenure at the Baghdad Residency. She kept him in Europeanised clothing, read Gibbon's history aloud to him, wrote letters for Claudius, copied his diplomatic correspondence, tended him through a succession of physical and mental illnesses, negotiated on his behalf with the East India Company when he fell out of their favour and accompanied him on archaeological digs and manuscript purchasing expeditions.[112] When he died of cholera in 1821, it was Mary who settled his estate, preserved his collections, shipped them to England

---

[110] 'Fragment of a Journal from Bagdad [sic] to Sulimana by Mrs. Rich', in *ibid.*, I: 373–5 (citations from 374). For Enlightenment British women and vaccination, see esp. Michael Bennett, 'Jenner's Ladies: Women and Vaccination against Smallpox in Early Nineteenth-Century Britain', *History*, 93 (2008), 497–513, and Daniel Grey, '"To bring this useful invention into fashion in England": Mary Wortley Montagu as Medical Expert', in *British Women and the Intellectual World in the Long Eighteenth Century*, ed. Teresa Barnard (Farnham, 2015), 15–32.

[111] Rich, *Narrative of a Residence*, I: 303, 268. For the mixed record of such vaccination campaigns, see also Susan Heydon, 'Death of the King: The Introduction of Vaccination into Nepal in 1816', *Medical History*, 63 (2019), 24–43; Katherine Foxhall, 'The Colonial Travels and Travails of Smallpox Vaccine, c.1820–1840', in *Migration, Health and Ethnicity in the Modern World*, ed. Catherine Cox and Hilary Marland (New York, 2013), 83–103.

[112] Her trip to London (while Claudius remained behind in Paris) to negotiate with the East India Company on his behalf is detailed in CR to Erskine, 24 October 1815, BL, Add MS 80752, fol. 189.

and (with her father's assistance) sold them to the British Museum.[113] In the 1830s, as the race to decipher cuneiform began to accelerate in Europe, it was she who carefully annotated and produced scholarly editions of Claudius's published and unpublished works.[114] Surely she too deserves some mention.

My second modest proposal is that we acknowledge that Claudius Rich worked collaboratively not only in tandem with his European wife but also with a wide, cross-cultural universe of servants, agents and go-betweens that included princely elites in Baghdad and Kurdistan who shared his collecting habits as well as the grooms, muleteers and river navigators whose skills ensured that his wife and his collections journeyed safely via Baghdad, Basra and Bombay to Britain. Mary Rich's writings, as I have argued here, enhance our ability to recognise – and in some instances, even to name – specific non-European persons who – sometimes wittingly, and not always willingly – sustained Claudius's colonial collecting. Just as her letters chronicle domestic scenes that allow us briefly to glimpse moments of opportunism or resistance among the servants of the Rich household, so too the fakes from the Rich collection that are displayed in Case 15 remind us that the empire does strike back.[115] We know from her writings that Mary Rich had opinions – about politics, about history and about the myriad Mesopotamian peoples with whom the Riches lived for over a decade. Although many of her views are unpalatable today, by writing Mary Rich back into the historical and material record of the European Enlightenment we can nonetheless take steps toward 'universalising' the Museum by recognising the existence, labour and agency of these men and women. They too merit explicit reference in Case 15 of the Enlightenment Gallery.

Third and finally, we need to name empire and colonialism – rather than merely referencing 'trade and discovery' – in the Enlightenment Gallery, and more broadly in the universal museum. Acknowledging histories of both race and slavery is vitally important in that context. But

---

[113] Claudius Rich died intestate; Mary was awarded administration of his estate in Bombay in February 1822. The decision to send his 'variety of valuable oriental Manuscripts and natural curiosities' to England for sale reflected the assessment that they could not be sold at Bombay 'except at a ruinous sacrifice'. Account of the estate of Claudius Rich, 5 April 1823, BL, IOR/L/AG/34/27/391, 1–7 (citation from 1).

[114] Rich, *Narrative of a Residence*. In addition to including an excerpt from her own journals in this volume, Mary Rich used the footnotes to register her own presence in her husband's life and career.

[115] Forgeries of antiquities attest to the agency of 'native' men and women caught up in East India Company collecting cultures. Case 15 notes the presence of nineteenth-century forgeries of ancient figurines in the Claudius Rich collection, which it purchased from Mary Rich in 1825. See for example the fired clay figurine, British Museum number 91893 (Registration number R. 97).

recovering the full range of gender at play in colonial collecting is also integral to the task of decolonising the museum. In defending Britain's 'universal' museums from restitution claims, Tristram Hunt has recently argued that 'There remains something essentially valuable about the ability of museums to position objects beyond particular cultural or ethnic identities, curate them within a broader intellectual or aesthetic lineage, and situate them within a wider, richer framework of relationships.'[116] Gender is entirely absent from this ostensibly universalising gaze. The history of Mary and Claudius Rich reminds us, however, that it is precisely such sweeping claims to universalism that have, historically, allowed us to write the roughly half of humankind who are non-men out of museum histories, and in so doing to entrench the effacement of non-Europeans from 'universal' museum collections. Today, at so many levels, Immanuel Kant's argument of 1784 – that 'Public' enlightenment is 'inevitable', if only the public is 'allowed freedom' – may ring hollow. Perhaps, by replacing the 'bearded' learned ladies of Kant's imagination with analyses of actual historical women who engaged with Enlightenment reason, we can begin to improve upon this partial and unsatisfactory interpretative tradition by replacing the 'universal' with the 'human'.

---

[116] Tristram Hunt, 'Should Museums Return Their Colonial Artefacts?', *The Guardian* (29 June 2019). The alternative case is made by Felwine Sarr and Bénédicte Savoy, *The Restitution of African Cultural Heritage: Toward a New Relational Ethics*, trans. Drew S. Burk (November 2018): http://restitutionreport2018.com/sarr_savoy_en.pdf.

*Transactions of the RHS* 30 (2020), pp. 29–54 © The Author(s), 2020. Published by Cambridge University Press on behalf of the Royal Historical Society
doi:10.1017/S008044012000002X

# THE EDICT OF PÎTRES, CAROLINGIAN DEFENCE AGAINST THE VIKINGS, AND THE ORIGINS OF THE MEDIEVAL CASTLE

By Simon MacLean ⓘ

READ 8 FEBRUARY 2019

ABSTRACT. The castle was one of the most characteristic features of the western European landscape in the Middle Ages, dominating social and political order from the eleventh century onwards. The origins of the castle are generally assigned to the ninth and tenth centuries, and the standard story begins with the defensive fortifications established against the Vikings during the reign of the West Frankish king Charles the Bald (843–77). In this article I argue that there are serious problems with this origin story, by re-evaluating some of the key sources on which it rests – particularly the Edict of Pîtres (864). I seek to demonstrate that my analysis of this source has important implications for how we think about the relationship between fortifications and the state in the Carolingian Empire; and by extension the evolution of the castle in north-western Europe between the ninth and twelfth centuries.

## I Introduction

The Edict of Pîtres of 25 July 864 is one of the most celebrated of the 350 or so capitularies promulgated by the kings and emperors of the Carolingian dynasty. The Carolingians ruled the Frankish kingdoms which dominated western Europe during the eighth and ninth centuries, and the capitularies were their characteristic form of legislation – a heterogeneous genre, but broadly speaking recognisable as records of royal proclamations divided into chapters, often expressed in a legislative or exhortatory voice.[1] The Edict was issued by one of the most enthusiastic Carolingian legislators: Charles the Bald, who ruled the West Frankish kingdom (approximately equivalent to modern France) between 843 and 877. One reason for its fame is the notable range and detail of its thirty-seven clauses, which dealt at length with the standard of the coinage and other matters related to the regulation of royal dues (land,

---

[1] The website of the Capitularies project at the University of Cologne is the best starting point for anyone interested in these texts: http://capitularia.uni-koeln.de/en/.

labour and military service) (Table 1).[2] Another is the unusually grand
rhetoric used to articulate the Edict's demands. Many of the clauses
echoed or quoted laws from the Roman imperial past, with the aim
being to present Charles as a new version of the famous legislating
emperor Theodosius II (402–50).[3] For these reasons, the Edict has
justly been called 'the largest single legislative act by a north European
king before Edward I'; and 'the most remarkable piece of legislation
between Justinian's Novels and the twelfth century'.[4]

The ambitious presentation of Charles as heir to a long tradition of
imperial legislation tells us something about the moment at which it was
issued. In 864 the king was at the peak of his power, having prevailed
over a series of serious rebellions. In 858 he was effectively deposed
after an invasion by his brother Louis, king of East Francia, and only
just held onto his throne thanks to the loyalty of his bishops, marshalled
by the Edict's primary author Archbishop Hincmar of Rheims. In 862
the king's son, also Louis, rebelled alongside some of the most powerful
aristocrats in northern and western Francia. Another persistent opponent,
Charles's nephew Pippin II (would-be king of Aquitaine), was finally captured in 864.[5] Having seen off these threats, in summer 864 Charles was
triumphantly riding the crest of a comeback wave. This was made very
clear to those present at the Pîtres assembly itself, where Pippin II was publicly condemned.[6] But Charles's victory over his relatives was not the end
of the story, because the foregoing dynastic conflicts had drawn large
groups of Vikings into the lower Seine region in the late 850s and early
860s. Pîtres (dép. Eure, about 12 miles south-east of Rouen) was at the epi-
centre of their activity, and one contemporary text even refers to it as 'the
seat of the Northmen'.[7] The Edict's neo-imperial propaganda was therefore not a static piece of posturing by a ruler proclaiming his status at a
moment of extraordinary power, but the vehicle for a targeted attempt

[2]  *Edictum Pistense*, ed. A. Boretius and V. Krause, MGH Capitularia Regum Francorum
II (Hanover, 1897), no. 273, 310–28.
[3]  J. L. Nelson, 'Translating Images of Authority: The Christian Roman Emperors in the
Carolingian World', in J. L. Nelson, *The Frankish World* (1996), 89–98; S. Corcoran,
'Hincmar and his Roman Legal Sources', in *Hincmar of Rheims: Life and Work*,
ed. R. Stone and C. West (Manchester, 2015), 129–55.
[4]  P. Wormald, *The Making of English Law: King Alfred to the Twelfth Century* (Oxford, 1999),
51; Nelson, 'Translating Images', 93.
[5]  Hincmar as primary author: Nelson, 'Translating Images', 96–7. Rebellions:
J. L. Nelson, *Charles the Bald* (1992), 181–209.
[6]  *Annales Bertiniani*, ed. F. Grat *et al.* (Paris, 1964), s.a. 864, p. 113. The Edict's Roman
legal echoes may have had specific contemporary resonance to the Aquitanians:
S. Esders, 'Montesquieu, the Spirit of Early Medieval Law, and "the Modern Origins of
the Early Middle Ages"' (forthcoming).
[7]  *Capitula Pistensia*, ed. A. Boretius and V. Krause, MGH Capitularia Regum Francorum
II (Hanover, 1897), no. 272, 302–10, at 303.

Table 1.    *Summary of constituent chapters of the Edict of Pîtres*

| | |
|---|---|
| Preamble 1–3: Welcome, exhortations to keep the peace as agreed two years earlier in the same place | |
| 1–4 | Protection of church, orphans, widows; respect for king's vassals |
| 5 | Safeguarding of royal lands |
| 6–7 | Lawless behaviour and disruption of justice caused by Vikings |
| 8–24 | Regulation of the coinage |
| 25 | Prohibition on selling arms and armour outside the kingdom |
| 26–7 | Regulation of military service |
| 28–30 | Regulation of rents and services due to the king |
| 31 | Attempt to limit population mobility caused by Vikings |
| 32–5 | Regulation of counts' courts and swearing of oaths; debtors |
| 36 | Exhortation to disseminate and heed the capitularies |
| 37 | Nobody to stay in the lodge built by the king at the Seine crossing, which had been destroyed by passers-by and had to be rebuilt |
| Additional clauses 1–3: Exhortation to loyalty; destruction of unauthorised fortifications; obligation to attend court; reminder to keep the agreed peace | |

to deal with the disturbance caused by Scandinavian war-bands to the normal operation of society in north-west Francia.

The present article is concerned more with the Edict's practical than its ideological features, and specifically with its material on fortifications and military matters. Although these clauses form a relatively small proportion of the text's whole, they have cast a long historiographical shadow. In chapters 26 and 27 Charles expanded the criteria for service in the army, which was now effectively required of anyone who could get his hands on a horse; and added a new obligation that those lacking the necessary resources to fight should instead contribute work on 'fortifications, bridges and swamp crossings'.[8] The most significant of those crossings was a fortified bridge across the Seine where it met the Eure and the Andelle at Pont-de-l'Arche near Pîtres. The substantial twin towers of this bridge, situated on opposite banks, were intended to guard this important confluence and prevent the Vikings from passing further upriver.[9] Chapter 37 railed against people who had delayed

[8]  G. Halsall, *Warfare and Society in the Barbarian West* (London and New York, 2003), 99–100; S. Coupland, 'The Carolingian Army and the Struggle against the Vikings', *Viator*, 35 (2004), 49–70.

[9]  S. Coupland, 'The Fortified Bridges of Charles the Bald', *Journal of Medieval History*, 17 (1991), 1–12; J. Le Maho, 'Un grand ouvrage royal du IXe siècle: le pont fortifié dit "de

this project by misusing and damaging the buildings on the construction site.

Best known of all is a further clause in the postscript to the Edict which required that any other fortifications built without the king's permission should be destroyed by their proprietors or, failing that, the king's counts. If the latter were unwilling to carry out the destruction before the first day of August, five weeks hence, they would be dismissed. This chapter has played a vital role in shaping modern ideas about the origins of the medieval castle: it is the key witness to the hypothesis that the Carolingian kings enjoyed a formal monopoly on the construction of fortifications, and that their ability to enforce this right was now crumbling. The collapse of this supposedly age-old monopoly in the later ninth century is traditionally seen as heralding the emergence of a fully medieval landscape of 'private' power dominated by the lordly castle, which would soon eclipse the essentially 'public' political landscape of the Carolingians. The core purpose of this article is to draw attention to some serious problems in the structure of this grand narrative. Via a re-examination of the relevant sections of the Edict, I aim to show that some basic features of the text have been misunderstood; and that what it tells us about the history of the castle in the ninth century and beyond needs to be reassessed. My argument has three main parts. First, I will highlight the significance of the Edict to the ways that historians have for over a century discussed the origins of the medieval castle. Second, I will offer a new analysis of the relevant clauses of the Edict. Finally, I will discuss the implications of my analysis for the way we think about the origins of the medieval castle and the nature of public authority in the Carolingian Empire.

## II Modern historiography on the rise of the castle

The widely accepted story of the medieval castle begins with the death throes of the Carolingian Empire in the later ninth century, with Viking attack and crumbling royal authority leading to the 'privatisation' of the political landscape. This story is based on clear patterns in the written sources. Put simply, ninth-century narratives rarely mention fortifications of any kind, much less castles; while tenth-century authors saw them everywhere. Readers of the so-called *Annals of St-Bertin* written at Rheims between 861 and 882 by Charles the Bald's close adviser Archbishop Hincmar will find events playing out across a classically Carolingian landscape articulated around assemblies, episcopal synods, and royal visits to palaces and hunting grounds. By contrast, in the

Pîtres" à Pont-de-l'Arche (Eure)', in *Des châteaux et des sources: archéologie et histoire dans la Normandie médiévale*, ed. E. Lalou *et al.* (Mont-Saint-Aignan, 2008), 143–58.

pages of the *Annals* by Flodoard of Rheims, written in exactly the same place between 919 and 966, the same landscape looks very different: Flodoard shows us a world of sieges, truces and armed competition for territory prosecuted by kings and aristocrats based in places called things like *castrum*, *castellum* and *arx*.[10] The main catalyst for this shift is held to have been the Scandinavians, since all manner of sources make clear that cities, monasteries and palaces were fortified in response to intensifying Viking raids in the later ninth century. To symbolise changing Carolingian attitudes to fortification, another example from Rheims is often used: around 820, one archbishop removed stones from the city walls to repair his church; but around 885, his successor reinforced the walls using material from a damaged church.[11]

Although fortified churches and cities are not castles, it is in this context that the age of the castle is presumed to have begun – with rudimentary fortifications built against Viking attacks in the later ninth century. In the world of Flodoard, which emerged in the decades after the empire's end in 888, these initial castles are thought to have evolved into centres of incipient lordship. By the middle of the eleventh century, the castle was undoubtedly one of the defining features of the medieval European landscape, and by the twelfth it was a basic unit of political power recognisable to the point of cliché. 'He dragged a castle at his horse's tail', went a contemporary bon mot about the power and status of Duke Frederick of Swabia; while the English chronicler William of Newburgh called castles 'the bones of the kingdom'.[12] Nobody in the ninth century had spoken in such terms.

Crucial validation for this narrative comes from the clause in the 864 Edict which forbade unauthorised fortifications and mandated the destruction of any already built. What else could these forbidden structures be, but early aristocratic castles?[13] The Edict is valued not only for giving us a first glimpse of such 'proto-castles', but also an explanation for their appearance. Charles's demand that unauthorised fortifications be dismantled implies that Carolingian kings enjoyed a monopoly on the right to fortify – that the legitimacy of any fortification, in other words, depended on rarely granted royal authorisation. It also seems to imply that this monopoly was starting to crumble under Viking pressure.

---

[10] *Annales Bertiniani*, ed. Grat *et al.*; Flodoard, *Annales*, ed. P. Lauer (Paris, 1906).

[11] Flodoard, *Historia Remensis Ecclesiae*, ed. M. Stratmann, MGH Scriptores 36 (Hanover, 1998), 1.12, 2.19, 4.8, pp. 114, 179, 399.

[12] Otto of Freising, *Gesta Friderici I*, ed. G. Waitz and B. Simson, MGH SRG 46 (Hanover and Leipzig, 1912), I.12, p. 28; M. Strickland, 'The Bones of the Kingdom and the Treason of Count John', in *Culture politique des Plantagenêt, 1154–1224*, ed. M. Aurell (Poitiers, 2004), 143–72.

[13] M. W. Thompson, *The Rise of the Castle* (Cambridge, 1991), 33; A. Debord, *Aristocratie et pouvoir. Le rôle du château dans la France médiévale* (Paris, 2000), 28, 36–8.

The existence and then disintegration of royal control over fortifications therefore appears to explain both the absence of castles from Carolingian written sources, and their ubiquity in the post-Carolingian material. Further ballast for this argument comes from comparison with southern England, where, despite an equivalent experience of Viking raids, no castles are mentioned as such in written sources until the reign of Edward the Confessor on the eve of the Norman Conquest (at which point they were explicitly referred to as a novelty). The Anglo-Saxon state, then, has been used as a control example to show that early medieval states were capable of reserving fortifications to the public authority.[14] The unauthorised proto-castles of Pîtres are something like the evil twins of the fortified Alfredian *burhs*, symbolising weak Frankish rule and privatisation in contrast to sound English government and organised central power.

The paradigm of the Carolingian royal monopoly received its most comprehensive modern working-out in a 1909 book by Erich Schrader, since when it has been canonised by inclusion in the authoritative German encyclopedias of historical/legal concepts which codify the analytical categories of modern scholarship.[15] The concept appears regularly in histories of the Carolingian era, albeit with a sceptical eyebrow usually raised about the extent to which the monopoly was really effective.[16] Stronger versions of the thesis can be found in work dealing specifically with the history of castles. In this branch of the historiography, the monopoly appears as one of the archetypal regalian rights or public powers (alongside the right to mint coins and the right to appoint counts) whose gradual privatisation explains the transformation of the Carolingian Empire into the more fragmented (traditionally 'feudal') landscape of the tenth and eleventh centuries.[17] But despite the

---

[14] R. Higham and P. Barker, *Timber Castles* (Exeter, 2004), 39.

[15] E. Schrader, *Das Befestigungsrecht in Deutschland von den Anfängen bis zum Beginn des 14. Jahrhunderts* (Göttingen, 1909); A. Coulin, *Befestigungshoheit und Befestigungsrecht* (Leipzig, 1911); K. H. Allmendigen, 'Befestigungsrecht', in *Handwörterbuch zur deutschen Rechtsgeschichte*, ed. A. Erler and E. Kaufmann (Berlin, 1971–7), s.v.; F. Schwind *et al.*, 'Burg', in *Lexikon des Mittelalters*, ed. L. Lutz *et al.* (Munich and Zurich, 1977–99), s.v.; D. Kerber, 'Die Burg im mittelalterlichen Territorium. Das Burgenbauregal', in *Burgen in Mitteleuropa. Ein Handbuch*, ed. H. W. Böhme *et al.* (Stuttgart, 1999), 66–8.

[16] Nelson, *Charles the Bald*, 207; C. Wickham, *The Inheritance of Rome: A History of Europe from 400 to 1000* (2009), 517; O. Creighton, *Early European Castles* (2012), 47.

[17] C. Coulson, 'Fortresses and Social Responsibility in Late Carolingian France', *Zeitschrift für Archäologie des Mittelalters*, 4 (1976), 29–36; Higham and Barker, *Timber Castles*, 95; J. Henning, 'Wandel eines Kontinents oder Wende der Geschichte? Das 10. Jahrhundert im Spiegel der Frühmittelalterarchäologie', in *Europa im 10. Jahrhundert. Archäologie einer Aufbruchszeit*, ed. J. Henning (Mainz, 2002), 15; P. Ettel, 'Der Befestigungsbau im 10. Jahrhundert in Süddeutschland und die Rolle Ottos des Großen am Beispiel der Burg von Roßtal', in *Europa*, ed. Henning, 370; C. Coulson, *Castles in Medieval Society: Fortresses*

occasional volley of drive-by scepticism, the existence of this royal power over fortifications has almost never been seriously questioned.[18] Indeed, its influence on the study of the origins of the castle is so great that in many scholarly traditions it still governs the interpretation of archaeological evidence: fortified sites datable before the tenth century are *ipso facto* characterised as something other than castles – they are assumed to belong somehow to the 'public' rather than the 'private'. The paradigm appears to be corroborated by the archaeology mainly because it has been used as the interpretive framework *for* the archaeology.[19]

The idea of the Carolingian fortification monopoly is so deeply embedded that it has helped shape modern interpretations about forms of authority in western Europe right down to the twelfth century. The charters of tenth- and eleventh-century France have been scoured for evidence of royal or ducal involvement in castle-building which might be interpreted as lingering traces of the Pîtres 'public' monopoly – Count Fulk's prodigious encastellation programme in Anjou around the millennium has been interpreted as a prime example.[20] Rights to control fortification have long been considered part of the Carolingian legacy inherited by ducal Normandy, reflected especially in a clause in the *Consuetudines et iusticie* (1091/6) which implies that the dukes had the right to garrison their subjects' castles.[21] The baton then passes from Normandy to England, where castles spread rapidly in the wake of the conquest in 1066. The so-called *Laws of Henry I* (*c.*1115) contains two clauses forbidding '*castellatio* without licence'.[22] '*Castellatio*' is

in England, France and Ireland in the Central Middle Ages (Oxford, 2003), 20–2. For the connotations of 'feudal' in this context, see R. Abels, 'The Historiography of a Construct: "Feudalism" and the Medieval Historian', *History Compass*, 7 (2009), 1008–39.

[18] Scepticism: K. U. Jäschke, *Burgenbau und Landesverteidigung um 900. Überlegungen zu Beispielen aus Deutschland, Frankreich und England* (Sigmaringen, 1975), 44, 76–8; T. Kohl, 'Befestigungen in der Karolingerzeit und ihr Umfeld: Eine historische Perspektive', in *Bronzezeitliche Burgen zwischen Taunus und Karpaten*, ed. S. Hansen and R. Krause (Bonn, 2018), 196.

[19] As pointed out by L. Bourgeois, 'Les résidences des élites et les fortifications du haut moyen âge en France et en Belgique dans leur cadre européen: aperçu historiographique (1955–2005)', *Cahiers de civilisation médiévale*, 49 (2006), 114–15.

[20] R. Aubenas, 'Les châteaux forts des Xe et XIe siècles. Contribution à l'étude des origines de la féodalité', *Revue historique de droit français et étranger*, ser. 4, 16 (1938), 548–86; B. Bachrach and D. Bachrach, *Warfare in Medieval Europe, c.400–1453* (London and New York, 2017), 125–6.

[21] *Consuetudines et iusticie*, in C. H. Haskins, *Norman Institutions* (Cambridge, MA, 1918), 278–84; J. Yver, 'Les premières institutions du duché de Normandie', in *I Normanni e la loro espansione in Europa, Settimane di Studio del Centro Italiano sull'Alto Medioevo 16* (Spoleto, 1969), 303–4; D. Bates, *Normandy before 1066* (1982), 163; C. Coulson, 'Fortress Policy in Capetian Tradition and Angevin Practice: Aspects of the Conquest of Normandy by Philip II', in *Anglo-Norman Castles*, ed. R. Liddiard (Woodbridge, 2003), 332–3; M. Hagger, *Norman Rule in Normandy, 911–1144* (Woodbridge, 2017), 442–3.

[22] *Leges Henrici Primi*, ed. L. J. Downer (Oxford, 1972), cc. 10.1, 13.1, pp. 108–9, 116–17.

glossed somewhat mysteriously as 'fortifications of three walls', and may therefore refer not to the erection of castles per se, but to their activation for war by the addition of extra ramparts or ditches. This text has none-theless been interpreted as an expression of 'Carolingian nostalgia' – as has Henry II's attempted destruction in 1154 of the so-called 'adulterine' (unauthorised) castles built during the war-torn reign of his predecessor Stephen.[23] And although the history of the medieval castle is often ima-gined to be a predominantly Anglo-French debate, it has from the very beginning also interested historians of Germany and the Low Countries searching for the origins of the high medieval aristocratic residence, the so-called 'Adelsburg'. In Germany, clear evidence for fortification licences first appears, as in England and France, around the end of the twelfth century.[24] For Schrader and his successors, this was nothing other than the consummation of a process that began with the Edict of Pîtres – the definitive re-establishment, at last, of the Carolingian public monopoly.[25] Only the historiography of Italy, whose *incastellamento* paradigm developed independently of the northern Frankish model, has seemed immune to the Edict's influence.[26]

These attempts to join the dots between the public powers of the Carolingians and the increasingly sophisticated governments of the period around 1200 are so deeply internalised in the modern historiog-raphy because they perfectly reflect one of the central impulses of twen-tieth-century medievalism: the attempt to rescue the Middle Ages from its Enlightenment dismissal as a millennium of 'feudal chaos'.[27] The coherence of these arguments can, however, mask the fact that the lines traced between the sources depend on a considerable amount of scholarly ingenuity. In truth, none of the normative sources before the end of the twelfth century speaks unambiguously of a royal right to authorise fortification – with the notable exception of the 864 edict itself. Implicitly or explicitly, Pîtres is a core element in all the stories out-lined above. It is the Rosetta Stone which seemingly brings together the

---

[23] C. Coulson, 'The Castles of the Anarchy', in *The Anarchy of King Stephen's Reign*, ed. E. King (Oxford, 1994), 75; Coulson, 'Fortress Policy', 339. For a very helpful historio-graphical discussion see R. Eales, 'Royal Power and Castles in Anglo-Norman England', in *Anglo-Norman Castles*, ed. Liddiard, 41–67.

[24] *The Saxon Mirror: A Sachsenspiegel of the Fourteenth Century*, trans. M. Dobozy (Philadelphia, 1999), III.65–8, pp. 133–4.

[25] In addition to the works cited in n. 15, see G. Fehring, *The Archaeology of Medieval Germany* (London and New York, 1991), 118–20; W. Hechberger, *Adel im fränkisch-deutschen Mittelalter* (Ostfildern, 2005), 331–46; T. Zotz, 'Burg und Amt – zur Legitimation des Burgenbaus im frühen und hohen Mittelalter', in *Burgen im Breisgau. Aspekte von Burg und Herrschaft im überregionalen Vergleich*, ed. E. Beck *et al.* (Ostfildern, 2012), 141–52.

[26] On Italy see C. Wickham, *Medieval Rome: Stability and Crisis of a City, 900–1150* (Oxford, 2015), 42–52.

[27] Coulson, 'Castles of the Anarchy', 77.

other fragments from the tenth to twelfth centuries into a coherent picture. The story normally told about the origins of the European castle and its changing relationship to public authority not only begins with the Edict of Pîtres, but also depends on it. What, then, does the relevant section of the Edict actually say?

## III The 'additional chapters'

The key clause, in the first of the Edict's three 'additional chapters', runs as follows:

> We remind you of your loyalty, so that you will steadfastly observe this, and will always be prepared as chosen men, faithful to ourself and to God, so that if problems arise for us against the pagans or anyone else, as soon as the news reaches any one of you and you hear of our need, you will be ready to fight without delay, and will be able to travel in the service of God and ourself for the common good, and to join us swiftly. And it is our wish and express command that if anyone has built castles, fortifications or hedges [*castella, firmitates, haias*] at this time without our permission, such fortifications shall be demolished by the beginning of August, since those who live nearby and round about are suffering many difficulties and robberies as a result. And if anyone is unwilling to demolish them, then the counts in whose districts they have been built shall destroy them. And if anyone tries to stop them, they shall be sure to let us know at once. And if they neglect to implement this our command, they should know that, as it is written in these chapters and in the capitularies of our predecessors, we shall look for counts who are willing and able to obey our orders, and appoint them in their districts.[28]

This passage prompts some obvious questions: who was building these structures, and why were the locals suffering? As already noted, the most common interpretation is that they were 'proto-feudal' castles build by lords exercising arbitrary power over the less powerful in the area; flies in the ointment of Carolingian public authority, as if beamed in from eleventh-century Anjou. This is certainly one possible interpretation, but not the only one. The text does not specify that the locals were suffering through the actions of the castles' inhabitants, but from the very fact that the castles had been built. The assembly at Pîtres had been called to urge completion of the king's bridge project at Pont-de-l'Arche to fortify the Seine against the Vikings who were established in the region. Perhaps the complaint was that labour had been diverted from the bridge works into the private projects of powerful aristocrats while the king's back was turned? That would echo clauses in the main body of the Edict referring to delays on the bridge project and the misappropriation of labour. Such anxieties are also reflected elsewhere in the capitulary record, such as a prohibition from *c.*820 on the

---

[28] *Edictum Pistense*, ed. Boretius and Krause, postscript c. 1, 328. All translations taken from the text by S. Coupland at www.academia.edu/6680741/The_Edict_of_P%C3%AEtres_-_translation.

forcing of freemen into working on royal game parks.[29] Another (albeit less likely) possibility is that the 'difficulties and robberies' were inflicted not by castle-dwelling lords, but by the Vikings themselves. If aristocrats in this area were building fortifications as residences or refuges for their own benefit, the 'locals and those living round about' may have been left unprotected as a result.

Still, whatever the exact problem presented by these troublesome buildings, the clause does imply that they should have been subject to royal authorisation. Charles complains that the castles, private or not, had been built 'without our permission [or: command]' – and this clearly suggests that others *had* been built with his licence. The king undoubtedly believed himself able to give or withhold such permission. There are, however, two good reasons to doubt that the basis for this entitlement was an abstract public right. The first is the very fact that Charles's demands were not explicitly phrased as the exercise of an assumed prerogative, but justified in a quite different manner: with reference to the suffering of the locals. Might the principle at stake here not simply have been the king's duty to protect his people from predation?[30] A further problem is hinted at by chapter 27 in the main body of the Edict, which deals with military service. Here, the drafters explicitly quoted a ruling of Charles's father Louis the Pious which instructed royal agents to find out how many freemen lived in their counties and thereby establish how many fighters they could afford to equip between them.[31] According to the Edict, this was to be done 'so that those who are unable to join the army can work on new fortifications, bridges and swamp crossings, following ancient practice and the custom of other nations, and can do guard duty in the fortifications and in the border area'.[32] Significantly, this additional phrase was a novelty not found in the source text, showing that the Edict's drafters could not refer to any clear precedent in Carolingian tradition for obliged fortification duty. It was, though, a duty expected of freemen in contemporary southern England.[33] Charles's justification of this

---

[29] *Capitula de functionibus publicis*, ed. A. Boretius, MGH Capitularia Regum Francorum I (Hanover, 1883), no. 143, c. 4, 295.

[30] This point was made by Jäschke, *Burgenbau*, 78; Zotz, 'Burg und Amt'.

[31] *Capitula ab episcopis in placito tractanda*, ed. A. Boretius and V. Krause, MGH Capitularia II, no. 186, c. 7, 7. The provenance of this text is more complex than realised by Boretius and Krause – a more accurate edition by S. Patzold *et al.* is forthcoming.

[32] *Edictum Pistense*, ed. Boretius and Krause, c. 27, 321–2.

[33] Jäschke, *Burgenbau*, 32, 111. Anglo-Saxon obligations: N. P. Brooks, 'The Development of Military Obligations in Eighth and Ninth Century England', in *England before the Conquest. Studies in Primary Sources Presented to Dorothy Whitelock*, ed. P. Clemoes and K. Hughes (Cambridge, 1971), 69–84. This was not the first time that Hincmar compared Frankish and English military organisation: J. L. Nelson, 'The Church's Military Service in the

demand by appealing to 'the custom of other nations' appears to be a reference to these Anglo-Saxon requirements; while 'ancient practice', as elsewhere in the Edict, is more likely a general appeal to the (Theodosian?) past than to Frankish practice. This was special pleading, showing Charles, Hincmar and their drafters grasping at any rhetorical straw in order to get their bridge built. The fact that there was any pleading at all implies that they did not expect the king to be able to demand fortification work as a matter of course – far less monopolise it.

The second reason for doubt is even more important: the clause forbidding 'castles, fortifications or hedges' is not actually *in* the Edict of Pîtres. That the nineteenth-century editors of the MGH text included it as part of a group of 'additional chapters' need not alarm us unduly, for Carolingian capitularies only survive in recipient copies. These could be transmitted in a variety of forms and did not always retain their structural integrity – we cannot always be sure exactly what the original versions looked like. In the case of Pîtres, though, we have extra information in the shape of the *Annals of St-Bertin*, written by Archbishop Hincmar of Rheims:

> On 1 June at a place called Pîtres, Charles held a general assembly, at which he received not only the annual gifts but also the tribute from Brittany ... Then Charles ordered fortifications to be constructed there on the Seine to prevent the Northmen from coming up the river. With the advice of his faithful men and following the custom of his predecessors and forefathers he drew up *capitula* to the number of 37, and he gave orders for them to be observed as laws throughout his whole realm.[34]

Hincmar's testimony that the legislative core had thirty-seven clauses needs to be taken seriously because he was almost certainly the Edict's primary author.[35]

How, then, should we interpret the additional six clauses (three as preamble, three as postscript) included in the modern edition? On closer inspection it becomes clear that the preamble and the epilogue are presented not as part of the legislation itself, intended to be distributed through the realm, but as the king's direct speech made to those present at the Pîtres assembly in 864. That is more or less explicit in the titles given to these sections: 'The announcement of Lord Charles at Pîtres' (preamble); 'And after all these things were read' (epilogue). The opening of the preamble speech indicates what was on Charles's mind:

Ninth Century: A Contemporary Comparative View', in J. L. Nelson, *Politics and Ritual in Early Medieval Europe* (1986), 117–32.

[34] *Annales Bertiniani*, ed. Grat *et al.*, s.a. 864, p. 113; *The Annals of St-Bertin*, trans. J. L. Nelson (Manchester, 1991), 118.

[35] Above, n. 5.

We give you many thanks for the faithfulness and goodwill which you continually display to us through all your help and obedience, just as your ancestors did to our ancestors, and for largely keeping the peace which we affirmed and had recognised here together two years ago. Since then the agreement has been upheld in many places, and most of you have observed it, though not all of you, as we had hoped. We also thank you for coming to this our assembly in such numbers and in peace.[36]

The rest of the preamble continues in a similar vein. In the second chapter Charles again stresses the peace made two years earlier and reminds his audience to 'labour manfully, unfailingly and unremittingly on the defensive works which we have begun here against the Northmen'; and in the third he introduces the main body of the Edict and requires that it be copied and distributed for reading out and keeping in every county. The epilogue also harks back to the earlier agreement: 'we remind you of your loyalty', it begins.

The 'peace' agreement referred to repeatedly in the king's speech was made at an assembly at Pîtres in 862 at which some of the 864 Edict's core themes had first been aired. In particular, it was then that the king had first urged his men to work together on the construction of his new bridge at Pont-de-l'Arche.[37] In the capitulary recording the 862 assembly, Charles laments the presence of the Vikings and fumes at the absence of coordination among the Franks. Too many people, said the king, were taking advantage of the disruption and therefore making the situation worse rather than better. He threatened 'malefactors' with public penance and reiterated the public duties of counts and other royal agents. Charles also pointedly condemned 'coniurationes et conspirationes et seditiones', terms often used in ninth-century capitularies to describe 'gatherings and sworn associations that could promote self-help'.[38] Such associations had always been viewed with suspicion by the Carolingians, but in Viking-beset northern Francia around 860 the ruling class seems to have harboured almost pathological hostility towards autonomous local action. The most shocking manifestation of this had taken place in 859, when members of a local militia set up to resist the Scandinavians were afterwards slaughtered by 'the more powerful men' of the Franks for this act of supposed insubordination.[39]

The preamble and prologue to the Edict of Pîtres must be read against this background. When Charles spoke at length in 864 about 'the agreed peace' that he expected his audience to observe, he was not talking in general terms – he was referring explicitly to the sworn agreement made in June 862 by what he claimed was the same audience. The

---

[36] *Edictum Pistense*, ed. Boretius and Krause, preface c. 1, 311.

[37] *Annales Bertiniani*, ed. Grat *et al.*, s.a. 862, p. 91.

[38] *Capitula Pistensia*, ed. Boretius and Krause, c. 4, 309; Nelson, *Charles the Bald*, 206.

[39] *Annales Bertiniani*, ed. Grat *et al.*, s.a. 859, p. 80. Charles himself may have encouraged non-aristocratic involvement in the army: Halsall, *Warfare and Society*, 100.

'peace' that the king demanded from his aristocrats was expressly defined as a commitment to dedicate all resources to communal defence against the Vikings, in the form of the bridge at Pont-de-l'Arche. Anything that smacked of self-help, whether that be forming a sworn association, organising a militia, or diverting resources to build 'castles, fortifications or hedges' other than the bridge, would be regarded by the king as a breach of that agreement. The tone of this demand was certainly threatening – but it was exhortatory and specific rather than legislative and general. Read in context, the king's prohibition on 'castles' was not intended as an injunction against the dilution of a royal right. The problem that exercised Charles was not the breach of a venerable royal prerogative, but the extreme difficulty of coordinating a particular infrastructure project. The powerful of the region had promised to focus their energies and resources on a collective effort against the Vikings, and they were not staying true to their word. In 864 Charles chided them in his speech not for encroaching on his rights, but for failing to stick to what they had promised.

If the six additional clauses recording the king's speech were not integral to the Edict itself, how did they end up in the MGH edition of the text? There are twelve manuscripts of the Edict (a reasonably substantial number for a Carolingian capitulary):

Heiligenkreuz, Stiftsbibliothek, 217 (late 10th C, SE Germany)
London, British Library, Add. 22398 (9th/early 10th C, France)
Munich, Bayerische Staatsbibliothek, Lat. 3853 (late 10th C, S Germany)
Munich, Bayerische Staatsbibliothek, Lat. 29555/1 (9th/10th C, N Italy)
New Haven, Yale University, Beinecke Rare Book and Manuscript Library, MS 413 (c.875, Rheims)
Paris, Bibliothèque Nationale, Baluze 94 (17th C, Paris)
Paris, Bibliothèque Nationale, Lat. 9654 (10th/11th C, Lotharingia)
Paris, Bibliothèque Nationale, Lat. 5095 (late 9th C, Laon)
**Rome, Biblioteca Vallicelliana, C. 16** (16th C)
Vatican, Biblioteca Apostolica Vaticana, Pal. Lat. 582 (late 9th C, Rheims area)
**Vatican, Biblioteca Apostolica Vaticana, Reg. Lat. 291** (late 16th C, N France)
**Vatican, Biblioteca Apostolica Vaticana, Vat. Lat. 4982** (late 16th C, N France)[40]

The majority of these manuscripts contain the thirty-seven-clause Edict text described in the *Annals of St-Bertin*. Although a couple are excerpted, most are complete, giving no sign that the text was transmitted in fragmentary or damaged form. Unfortunately we have no 'original' or 'official' manuscripts of any capitulary and we know much less than

---

[40] H. Mordek, *Bibliotheca capitularium regum Francorum manuscripta: Überlieferung und Traditionszusammenhang der fränkischen Herrschererlasse* (Munich, 1995), 168, 221, 301, 375–6, 389, 556, 575–6, 636, 795, 816, 874–5, 1041. See also http://capitularia.uni-koeln.de/en/mss/capit/ under 'Edictum Pistense [BK 273]'.

we would like about their production and early circulation, but in the case of the Edict it is significant that we have three ninth-century copies from Rheims and environs, including one seemingly made in Hincmar's lifetime, and all of them contain the thirty-seven-clause version.[41] The forty-three-clause version including the preamble and the epilogue is only transmitted in three manuscripts, highlighted in bold above. The manuscript history therefore indicates the existence of two distinct versions of the capitulary: one with only the core text of the Edict, the other with the king's speech added.

The three witnesses to the extended version all date from the sixteenth century, but it has been demonstrated that all derived from the same source: a now-lost capitulary manuscript which was used by a number of early modern scholars (including Pithou, Sirmond and Baluze) to create editions of Carolingian texts. This lost exemplar was most likely compiled in late ninth-century Beauvais, where it remained in the cathedral archive until at least the eighteenth century, and surviving descriptions indicate that it was a large and well-decorated manuscript. Via its later copies, the book remains an important source for the transmission of later Carolingian capitularies. In addition to both the major ninth-century collections of Carolingian legal material (by Ansegisus and Benedictus Levita), it seemingly contained a comprehensive set of Charles the Bald's capitularies from 843 to 876, arranged chronologically.[42] Such systematic organisation and copying of capitularies suggests that those who created it were sincerely invested in the idea of Carolingian authority, and that of Charles the Bald in particular.

The leading figure in Beauvais in this period was Odo, bishop from 859/61 to 881. Odo was not a common or garden bishop, but belonged to the top echelons of the ruling class. He spent the 850s as the abbot of the major royal monastery of Corbie, the kind of appointment only accessible to those with extremely powerful patrons, and in that capacity attended many of the decade's major synods and assemblies. In the 860s and 870s he was entrusted by King Charles with missions to Rome and close involvement in almost all the great disputes of the period, including the Lothar II divorce case and the prosecutions of the alleged heretic Gottschalk of Orbais and errant bishop Hincmar of Laon. Later, he helped ensure the succession of Charles's son Louis the Stammerer; and then his grandson Louis III. We also see him on numerous occasions

---

[41] On the Yale manuscript as a 'court-adjacent' compilation, see Mordek, *Bibliotheca*, 386–91. On questions of reception and originality in the history of the capitularies, see S. Patzold, 'Capitularies in the Ottonian Realm', *Early Medieval Europe*, 27 (2019), 112–32.

[42] Mordek, *Bibliotheca*, 631, 810–11, 865–7; L. Kéry, *Canonical Collections of the Early Middle Ages (ca. 400–1140): A Bibliographical Guide to the Manuscripts and Literature* (Washington, DC, 1999), 99.

working closely with the king's most prominent adviser, Archbishop Hincmar, who was also the chief drafter of many capitularies (including the Edict). Odo may have held the formal court position of archchaplain.[43]

Given all this, we might well suspect that Odo and his circle (like Hincmar and his) were exactly the type of people who harboured the kind of principled commitment to Carolingian authority implied by the grand Beauvais legal compilation. He was made bishop by the king in the face of opposition from the local community, and the first public test of his loyalties came at the Pîtres assembly in 862, where he was required to support the prosecution of the bishop of Soissons. He was also present at the 864 assembly.[44] Odo's unusual closeness to the royal court gives a possible context for why the scribes of Beauvais thought it worth preserving Charles's exhortatory speech as a preamble and postscript to their copy of the Edict of Pîtres. But there are also more immediate reasons to suspect that Odo had a personal interest in the speech's main topic, namely the completion of the building project at Pont-de-l'Arche. Beauvais is about 50 miles east of Pîtres, and can be seen as one point of a triangle with Paris and Rouen which defined the region terrorised by the Scandinavians in the middle of the ninth century. That threat was undoubtedly on Odo's mind in the early years of his tenure, for his predecessor had been killed by the Vikings in 859.[45] For someone in his position, constructing an effective defence was a matter of self-preservation as much as one of principle.

His appointment to the bishopric is even more intriguing in light of some tantalising evidence that Odo had expertise in military matters. The evidence comes in the form of two letters written to him in 859, when he was still abbot of Corbie, by Lupus, abbot of nearby Ferrières. In these, Lupus refers to 'some of your men seriously wounded in a battle against the barbarians' and implores Odo not to risk involvement in warfare himself since, as a monk, he could no longer legitimately use weapons. He had a reputation, according to Lupus, for 'rushing out heedlessly into the midst of danger unarmed, incited by youthful prowess and a desire to win'. He nonetheless congratulates Odo for defeating the 'barbarians' in the battle and putting them to death 'through your might, or rather God's'; and proclaims himself satisfied with Odo's decision about where to station his troops 'with their apparatus of battle'.[46] We also know from a charter of 902

---

[43] For a detailed study of Odo's career see P. Grierson, 'Eudes Ier, évêque de Beauvais', *Le Moyen Âge*, 45 (1935), 161–98.

[44] For Odo's movements in this period see *ibid.*, 166–72.

[45] *Annales Bertiniani*, ed. Grat *et al.*, s.a. 859, p. 81.

[46] Lupus, *Correspondance*, ed. L. Levillain (2 vols., Paris, 1964), II, nos. 106–7, pp. 134–45.

that Corbie was fortified with a 'castellum' before the end of the ninth century, though we do not know when – but Odo's abbacy, after the major Viking raid of the region in 857, is a strong candidate.

Another interesting window onto Odo's public persona is opened by a saint's biography he wrote not long after moving to Beauvais.[47] The subject was Lucien, a noble Roman reputed to have brought Christianity to the city in the third century. Odo turned him into the first bishop of Beauvais, in deliberate contrast to the existing eighth-century Life.[48] He also introduced a close association between Lucien and two other saints: Denis (who was regarded by Charles the Bald as his own special patron); and Rieul (who was associated with Hincmar's Rheims). One of the themes of the text is the warlike and ferocious nature of the people of Beauvais, and how difficult it had been for the Romans to master them. This was done partly by playing on the old word for the people of the region, Bellovaci, which was assumed to have derived from 'bellum' – 'war'. There is even a hint that the bishop's audience shared this association. Odo illustrates the warlike nature of the locals by relating an incident when 60,000 soldiers fought to defend Beauvais against Julius Caesar and the Roman army, 'as the public [or well-known] histories [*publiciis historiis*] say'.[49] This seems to be an allusion to the very long account of Caesar's struggle to control the region in his *Gallic War* (or to one of the later texts that transmitted the story). Among other things, the Bellovaci are referred to as 'the strongest people of the Belgae' and 'a people with a reputation for outstanding bravery', who dared to fight the Romans without help from others.[50] In referring to these events, Odo assumed that his audience were familiar with Caesar's work or with stories derived from it. Such stories about the warlike deeds of their ancient predecessors must therefore have been a resource for the formation of local identity in mid-ninth-century Beauvais. The value of this hagiography for present purposes is the way that it shows how Odo deliberately positioned Lucien as his episcopal predecessor and role model, and by extension presented himself as the leader of a ferocious, warlike community.

We are entitled to wonder whether these martial aspects of Odo's career might help us understand why the king was so keen to make him bishop of Beauvais, against local wishes, at a time of intense Viking activity in the region. Was he involved in some way in

---

[47] *Vita Auctore Odone Episc.*, in *Acta Sanctorum Jan. I*, 461–6.

[48] F. Vercauteren, *Étude sur les civitates de la Belgique Seconde: contribution à l'histoire urbaine du nord de la France de la fin du IIIe à la fin du XIe siècle* (Brussels, 1934), 268.

[49] *Vita Auctore Odone Episc.*, 463.

[50] Julius Caesar, *The Gallic War*, ed. H. J. Edwards (Cambridge, MA, 1917), 2.4, 7.59, 7.75, 8.6–7, 8.12–22, pp. 92–7, 462–5, 486–9, 522–7, 532–49.

coordinating the region's defence? His neighbour, Archbishop Wenilo of Rouen, was directly involved in the Pont-de-l'Arche bridge project, but we only know this thanks to a passing reference.[51] Either way, what we know about Odo's career gives us an important context in which to think about the additional clauses in the Beauvais version of the Edict. These extra chapters memorialised, above all, the king's exhortations to pull together against the Vikings; to maintain the agreed peace; and to drop, at least temporarily, any other projects that were distracting from the business of finishing the bridge. That is somewhat at odds with the emphasis of the Edict itself, which had very little to say directly about questions of fortification until its final chapter, where Charles signed off by complaining about damage done (by Franks) to the lodge used to accommodate men involved in building work. The Beauvais epilogue drew additional attention to this clause, and enhanced it, by reminding its readers that the assembly of Pîtres, if not the Edict itself, had been concerned above all with the collective organisation of regional defence. The addition of the framing exhortations created, in other words, a specifically Beauvaisian version of the Edict, reflecting the particular priorities of the city's leaders. The additional clauses afford us valuable insight into the discussions that took place among the orchestrators of the 864 assembly. Nonetheless, we should regard them less as an integral part of the Edict than as evidence for its reception.

## IV Castles and the Carolingian state

Whoever composed the forty-three-clause version, the argument presented above undermines the idea that the Carolingians enjoyed a formal right to authorise fortifications, the case for which is based primarily on a legalistic reading of the Edict's additional chapters. That is not to deny that ninth-century kings, like Charles the Bald in 864, might sometimes try to forbid or permit the construction of castles. Nor does it mean that the 'castles, fortifications and hedges' mentioned in the king's speech did not exist – obviously, the text provides clear evidence that they did. How, then, should we frame the history of these so-called 'private' Carolingian castles, and their relationship to Carolingian political order? What was the place of buildings called castles in the wider ecology of ninth-century fortifications against the Vikings, and why are they barely mentioned by contemporary authors? If we dispense with the notion of a royal right to license, then these questions require new answers. In the rest of this article, I will offer some preliminary reflections by interrogating two important concepts: the modern distinction

---

[51] Flodoard, *Historia*, ed. Stratmann, 3.18, 3.21, pp. 258, 279; Le Maho, 'Un grand ouvrage', 146, 157–8.

between public fortifications and private castles in the second half of the ninth century; and the Carolingian idea of the castle itself.

The framework traditionally used to explain the history of the empire from the 840s until its disintegration after 888 involves a narrative of decline and fall, accompanied by a shift of power from public to private. While many parts of this framework have been questioned in recent decades, the castle is still widely characterised as an incipient element of the private which indicates a fragmentation of the state and offers the first glimpse of the 'feudal' future. The most coherent articulation of this argument is a justly influential study published in 1936 by Fernand Vercauteren. He drew a sharp contrast between Charles the Bald's fortification programme in the 860s (which he saw as centrally coordinated), and the 'castella' which appear frequently in the narrative sources after the 880s (which he saw as examples of Pîtres-style 'private' castles built in spite of rather than in line with royal authority). Vercauteren concluded that this history 'confirms what we already know about the decomposition of royal authority at the end of the century'; and that the late Carolingian castles were 'one of the factors that contributed towards the development of *la féodalité*'.[52]

Vercauteren's thesis lays particular emphasis on the 885 entry in the *Annals of St-Vaast* (written at Arras, 80 miles north-east of Beauvais), which he saw as proclaiming the beginning of a 'new defensive policy': 'the Franks made preparations to withstand the Northmen, not in battle, but by building fortifications'.[53] Reading this extract in context, however, we can see that the annalist was not heralding the adoption of a new strategy writ large. The surrounding sentences make clear that the Frankish decision not to fight was a reaction to a recent defeat; and that the Vikings in question had recently moved to Rouen from their previous base in Leuven (some 230 miles to the east). This marked the return of a major Scandinavian presence on the Seine for the first time since the 860s. Moreover, the fortifications were not castles but riverside 'munitiones' intended 'to prevent their [the Northmen's] passage by ship'. These consisted of a reinforcement of the town of Paris and the construction of a new fortification at Pontoise, where the Seine met the Oise. There was nothing new about this strategy. It was, in fact, identical to the one pursued by Charles

---

[52] F. Vercauteren, 'Comment s'est-on défendu, au IXe siècle dans l'empire franc contre les invasions normandes?', *Annales du XXXe Congrès de la Fédération archéologique et historique de Belgique, Bruxelles* (1936), 132. See further A. D'Haenens, *Les invasions normandes, une catastrophe?* (Paris, 1970), 63–5; G. Koziol, *The Peace of God* (Leeds, 2018), 28–9.

[53] *Annales Xantenses et Annales Vedastini*, ed. B. Simson, MGH SRG 12 (Hanover and Leipzig, 1909), s.a. 885, p. 57; Vercauteren, 'Comment', 129.

the Bald in the same region twenty years earlier when the Vikings had last menaced the Seine.

Moreover, while it is certainly the case that the annalists of the late ninth century made many references to fortifications built against the Vikings in the most intense phase of activity between 879 and 892, none of these fortifications appear to be what we would understand as castles. In almost every case, they were reinforcements to existing towns, riverside installations and monasteries like St-Vaast itself, which the annalist referred to as 'stronghold-cum-monastery'.[54] Such sites were not insignificant, but they were not new defensive nodes which reconfigured the existing landscape. As Luc Bourgeois has pointed out, the fortification of towns and large monasteries, even if remarked upon by contemporaries at times of crisis, was rarely a unique event. All such sites were potentially defensible by their very nature, and went through constant but undocumented cycles of fortification, dilapidation and repair from the moment they were built until the day they were abandoned.[55] We cannot in any case be sure what authors meant when they said that such places were fortified. Many improvements were clearly made at very short notice: in 882 the walls of Mainz were repaired and additional defences added only when the Vikings were at Koblenz, a mere 60 miles downriver; in 894 Rheims was fortified even as an enemy army approached; and in 880 the Vikings themselves repelled a Frankish army by quickly encircling the captured palace of Nijmegen with an external rampart (a tactic known to have been used by the Franks on other occasions).[56]

Such improvised measures can hardly have been permanent, and may be what the drafters of the twelfth-century *Laws of Henry I* had in mind when they forbade unlicensed 'castellatio', glossed obtusely as 'fortifications of three walls' – not the building of castles, but the activation of a site for war by the addition of extra ramparts. The effectiveness of such improvements was variable. On the one hand, it was alleged that no field fortification improvised by the Vikings had ever been conquered; on the other, even heavy weather could be enough to destroy ancient city walls and newly refurbished buildings.[57] But whereas modern historians sometimes see fortification as a magic bullet, or at least as the key indicator of a coherent defensive strategy, contemporaries were aware that it was not in itself sufficient. 'Even those cities fortified with towers could not preserve the lives of their bishops', went one contemporary reflection on the deaths at Viking hands of three senior churchmen (including Odo's

[54] *Annales Xantenses et Annales Vedastini*, ed. Simson, s.a. 895, p. 77.
[55] Bourgeois, 'Les résidences', 120–1.
[56] *Annales Fuldenses*, ed. F. Kurze, MGH SRG 7 (Hanover, 1891), s.a. 880, 882, pp. 96, 97; *Annales Xantenses et Annales Vedastini*, ed. Simson, s.a. 894, p. 74.
[57] *Annales Fuldenses*, ed. Kurze, s.a. 858, 872, 891, pp. 48, 77, 120.

predecessor at Beauvais) in the late 850s.[58] Fortifications had to be staffed to be effective, so the king's ability to coordinate manpower was the fundamental factor. The giving of tribute and the gathering of armies to pursue war-bands were not inferior alternatives to fortification but – even in Alfredian Wessex – essential complements.[59]

The anti-Viking fortifications of the 880s were therefore not representative of a fundamental change in Frankish strategy, and they were not, generally speaking, castles. Nor, *pace* Vercauteren, were they purely private initiatives. Where we have enough information, the sources indicate that the people doing the building were collaborating in various ways with the king.[60] Insight into the nature of such collaboration is given by a handful of charters in which rulers granted fortifications to individuals and churches. For example, we have a charter of 884 in which Carloman II gave to the bishop of Châlons-sur-Marne the small abbey of St-Sulpicius, which sat at one end of a bridge over the Marne, on condition that he allow a royal 'vasallus' to occupy it in order to defend the kingdom 'from the infestation of the pagans'.[61] In 888, King Arnulf made a gift to one of his more powerful followers on condition that he and his men help the local count build a refuge fortification on the eastern frontier.[62] These kings were not dispensing licences to fortify so much as trying to incentivise their leading men to become actively involved in the communal defence of the kingdom.

These dynamics, of kings urging their implicitly reluctant magnates to collaborate in the creation of a coherent defensive strategy against an escalating Viking presence, were not substantially different from those of the 860s. The story of Charles the Bald's efforts to get his bridge built at Pont-de-l'Arche is a similar tale of persistent exhortation. Having threatened his audience in 862 with dire imprecations about the Vikings as a divine punishment for sin, his adoption in 864 of a neo-Theodosian pose was a change of tack intended to increase the pressure for action. A year later, he found that the Vikings were passing the site with impunity and got his leading men to agree that labour could be diverted from 'distant regions' to bridges on the Oise.[63] But in 866, the

---

[58] Hildegar, *Vita Faronis*, ed. B. Krusch, MGH SRM 5 (Hanover and Leipzig, 1910), c. 123, 200: 'Civitates vero quaedam turribus firmae non potuerunt episcoporum suorum servare vitam.'

[59] J. Baker and S. Brookes, *Beyond the Burghal Hidage: Anglo-Saxon Civil Defence in the Viking Age* (Leiden and Boston, MA, 2013).

[60] S. MacLean, 'Charles the Fat and the Viking Great Army: The Military Explanation for the End of the Carolingian Empire', *War Studies Journal*, 3 (1998), 74–95.

[61] *Recueil des actes de Louis II le Bègue, Louis III et Carloman II, rois de France (877–884)*, ed. F. Grat *et al.* (Paris, 1978), no. 76.

[62] *Die Urkunden Arnolfs*, ed. P. Kehr (Berlin, 1940), no. 32.

[63] *Annales Bertiniani*, ed. Grat *et al.*, s.a. 865, pp. 122–3.

Vikings were able to travel up the Seine to the Paris region and score a major victory, prompting yet another change of strategy: now Charles paid a ransom to win a Scandinavian retreat. This bought him time to take men to the building site himself, but when this too failed he formally devolved responsibility for the bridge to 'various men of his realm' by assigning them specific sections.[64] A final push in 869 saw him shift the obligation to ecclesiastical landowners. 'Bishops, abbots and abbesses' were now compelled to send 'young warriors' in proportion to their wealth to complete and then guard the fortifications.[65] The most striking thing about this sequence is that it suggests that Charles had extreme difficulty in getting his magnates to cooperate in the building of one bridge; and shows that he had to cycle through a variety of strategies to coax sufficient collaboration out of them, step by step.[66]

In the 860s and in the 880s, then, the defence of the realm was neither exclusively public nor private, but a matter for collaboration between royals and aristocrats. That collaboration was not achieved easily or automatically, but required persistent exhortation on the part of the king, dressed up in a variety of rhetorical postures. What the Edict shows us, therefore, is not the breakdown of the formal powers held by the high Carolingian state, but a glimpse of how that state normally operated: even at its most sophisticated, it worked through the co-opting of support by means of persuasion, threats and oaths. In the mid-ninth century the public sphere, and the magnates' duty to serve it, was not an objective fact about the Carolingian Empire, but something that kings had to constantly assert to conjure into being, time and time again. Even in the mid-860s, when Charles was at the height of his power and the kingdom faced a communal external threat, he was clearly unable to take it for granted. The Edict of Pîtres shows us the exhortatory mode of Carolingian public authority in full swagger, as Charles fought to bend the resources and priorities of his magnates towards his defence project. The 'castella' he complained about in his speech were clearly an impediment to that project, but it would be a category error to think of them as an affront to the integrity of the public sphere.

## V Ways of seeing Carolingian castles

This still leaves us wondering how Carolingian writers ordinarily thought about such buildings. Why were 'castella' mentioned in 864, but rarely in

---

[64] *Annales Bertiniani*, ed. Grat *et al.*, s.a. 866, 868, pp. 125–6, 127, 150.

[65] *Annales Bertiniani*, ed. Grat *et al.*, s.a. 869, pp. 152–3; *Capitula Pistensia*, ed. Boretius and Krause, MGH Capitularia Regum Francorum II, no. 275, 332–7. In general see C. Gillmor, 'The Logistics of Fortified Bridge Building on the Seine under Charles the Bald', *Anglo-Norman Studies*, 11 (1989), 87–106.

[66] Halsall, *Warfare and Society*, 98–101.

other ninth-century sources? Carolingian texts hardly ever mention the residences of secular aristocrats, but there are reasons to think that they could be quite grand. Charlemagne's advisor Alcuin refers in passing to 'the ceiling of a great man's house' being painted with 'the order of the stars'.[67] Some must have been defensible, like the 'strongly-fortified house [*casa firmissima*]' of Count Egfrid of Bourges mentioned by Hincmar in his annals for 868.[68] Thomas Kohl has identified a number of further examples, and shows that broadly castle-like buildings were a feature of the Frankish landscape.[69] We also have plenty of archaeological evidence (especially from northern and western France and the Low Countries) for fortified sites reflecting a variety of social strata in the ninth century and before. Most of these are unmentioned in the written sources from the ninth century, but some were described as castles in the tenth.[70] The main reason that the modern literature does not describe these sites as castles in their Carolingian phase is that the rise of the castle is seen as a post-Carolingian phenomenon by definition. That is at least partly a matter of perception. The written sources from which the paradigm is derived are not transparent and do not map neatly onto our modern categories: castle terminology was not technical, and the same building could be called different things at different times.[71] What is a castle? To some extent, it's in the eye of the beholder.

The question must therefore be: why did Carolingian authors themselves (in contrast to tenth-century writers) not behold such places as castles? The *Royal Frankish Annals*, the pro-Frankish account of the empire's eighth-century expansion, uses what we might call 'castle words' ('castrum', 'castellum', 'oppidum' and the like) when describing external landscapes, but when describing the Frankish heartlands its authors preferred terminology like 'villa' and 'palatium'. The distinction seems to indicate a perception of difference between the landscapes of the empire's interior and the world beyond its frontier.[72] Carolingian

---

[67] *Epistolae Karolini Aevi*, II, ed. E. Dümmler (Berlin, 1895), 176–7.

[68] *Annales Bertiniani*, ed. Grat *et al.*, s.a. 868, p. 141.

[69] Kohl, 'Befestigungen'.

[70] For examples see e.g. L. Schneider, 'De la fouille des villages abandonnés à l'archéologie des territoires locaux. L'étude des systèmes d'habitat du haut Moyen Âge en France méridionale (Ve–Xe siècle): nouveaux matériaux, nouvelles interrogations', in *Trente ans d'archéologie médiévale en France: Un bilan pour un avenir*, ed. J. Chapelot (Paris, 2010), 133–62; Creighton, *Early European Castles*; and the case studies collected in the journal *Château Gaillard*, 25 (2012).

[71] P. Dixon, 'The Myth of the Keep', in *The Seigneurial Residence in Western Europe, c.800–1600*, ed. G. Meirion-Jones *et al.* (Oxford, 2002), 9–13; A. Wheatley, *The Idea of the Castle in Medieval England* (Woodbridge, 2004).

[72] *Annales Regni Francorum*, ed. F. Kurze, MGH SRG 6 (Hanover, 1895). I hope to elaborate this argument elsewhere.

cultural distaste for societies organised round large fortifications is also detectable in ninth-century annals, as in the revulsion of one author for the 'unspeakable stronghold' of the Moravian Slavs.[73] One Carolingian vision of the afterlife even pictures hell as centred on a monstrous fortification where bad monks were sent to suffer.[74] A handful of sites on prominent outcrops and/or situated at strategic riverside places (notably Koblenz, at the confluence of the Rhine and the Moselle) were regularly classified as 'fortresses' by Carolingian authors, and there was open talk of fortifications in frontier regions.[75] But by and large, words like 'castrum' and 'castellum' were hardly ever used for sites in the Frankish heartlands except in descriptions of internal Frankish conflict. It appears, in other words, that fortified sites were perceived and identified as fortified sites only when they were functioning as such. Hincmar only referred to Egfrid's 'strongly fortified house' as part of a detailed description of an attack on it – but he also mentioned it was part of a 'villa'. In Hincmar's eyes, it was not architecture but context that made this Carolingian villa transmute into a fortified residence.[76]

The worldview implied by this pattern of vocabulary is fundamentally different from what we see in tenth-century texts from the same areas, in which castles appear to be everywhere. The contrast is so striking that it must reflect more than simply changing literary preferences. The perspective of ninth-century authors was generated by the political structures of the Frankish Empire itself. In contrast to those of later centuries, the family strategies of Carolingian aristocrats were not anchored to residences, but structured around other sources of identity such as the foundation and domination of monasteries or public offices.[77] This is why Hincmar mentioned Egfrid's fortified house only in passing but emphasised with some care his control of the important monastery of St-Hilary in Poitiers 'and many other rich benefices'.[78] Egfrid's antagonist Gerald also seems to have controlled several 'strongholds', but it was only when he was deprived of his offices by Charles the Bald that he vanished from the pages of the contemporary histories.[79] Another noble 'manor' is mentioned in a Bavarian charter of 839 which describes a count called Ratolt at the head of what may have

---

[73] *Annales Fuldenses*, ed. Kurze, s.a. 869, p. 69.

[74] *Heito und Walahfrid Strabo, Visio Wettini*, ed. H. Knittel (Heidelberg, 2004), 34–63; Kohl, 'Befestigungen', 191.

[75] *Annales Fuldenses*, ed. Kurze, s.a. 842, 857, 860, 882, pp. 34, 47, 54, 97.

[76] Other 'castles' mentioned in the context of conflict: *Annales Bertiniani*, ed. Grat *et al.*, s.a. 873, 878, pp. 193, 222.

[77] M. Costambeys, M. Innes and S. MacLean, *The Carolingian World* (Cambridge, 2011), 271–323.

[78] *Annales Bertiniani*, ed. Grat *et al.*, s.a. 867, p. 140.

[79] *Ibid.*, s.a. 871, pp. 178–9.

been a muster for a royal campaign. He is depicted posed in the court-yard of his house, 'manfully girded with his sword', surrounded by his own retinue and the political community of the region, including such luminaries as the bishop of Freising. In this highly stylised text, the count's house is merely a backdrop for his performance of Carolingian elite masculinity, which was public and needed an audience. Ratolt's eminence is expressed by the way he stood before and amongst this assembly of local worthies, not by any hint that he entertained them in his residence.[80]

The same set of values is reflected in Thegan of Trier's description of how Count Hugh of Tours, one of the most powerful figures in the empire in the 820s, became a figure of fun after failing in his leadership of an imperial campaign to defend Barcelona. According to Thegan, he was mocked when he attempted to leave his house. His presumably grand residence thus symbolised domesticity and was mobilised by Thegan as a source of shame rather than pride – it diminished Hugh's masculinity and enhanced his humiliation.[81] Another example comes from a dispute over ecclesiastical jurisdiction in central Europe in 900, when a group of Bavarian bishops wrote to the pope defending the royal status of King Louis IV 'the Child' by contrasting the virtues of the Carolingian line with the nefariousness of the neighbouring Moravian Slavs. Where the Carolingians fostered Christianity, the Moravians weakened it; where the Carolingians respected Rome, the Moravians despised it; and where the Carolingians were 'openly seen by the whole world', the Moravian rulers 'hid away in secret lairs and fortresses'.[82] In this highly polemical letter, the matter of openness vs closed-ness, visibility vs inaccessibility, was rhetorically elevated to one of the fundamental principles of Frankish rule. For Louis the Child as for Hugh of Tours, the proper place of an aristocratic or royal male in the ninth century was not resplendent and self-contained in his castle, like a later medieval lord, but out in public performing his status and engaging with the social world of the Carolingian ruling class.

The absence of castles in Carolingian sources is not, therefore, a simple reflection of the absence of castles in the Carolingian landscape. At least in part, it is indicative of a Carolingian way of seeing, generated by the political framework of the empire. With this in mind, the castles

---

[80] *Die Traditionen des Hochstiftes Freising*, ed. T. Bitterauf (Munich, 1905–9), no. 634; E. J. Goldberg, *Struggle for Empire: Kingship and Conflict under Louis the German, 817–76* (Ithaca, 2006), 92–3.

[81] Costambeys, Innes and MacLean, *Carolingian World*, 298.

[82] F. Lošek, *Die Conversio Bagoariorum et Carantanorum und der Brief des Erzbischofs Theotmar von Salzburg* (Hanover, 1997), 148: 'illi toto mundo spectabiles apparuerunt, isti latibulis et urbibus occultati fuerunt'.

we see in the Edict – though probably not built by figures quite as grand as Hugh of Tours or Egbert of Bourges – were most likely nothing much out of the ordinary. They were part of the background noise, rarely commented on and in 864 glimpsed in exceptional circumstances created by an intense phase of Viking pressure. The reason was not that those circumstances led to the proliferation of a previously rare type of structure, but that they prompted an abrupt shift of categories – a glitch in the Matrix. In the context of Charles's attempts to build his bridge, amidst a high-pitched and sustained discourse about public power and communal effort, the king and his drafters momentarily saw these structures as troubling irruptions from outside the normal political order: as castles.

## VI Conclusion

As I hope will be clear by now, my analysis of the additional clauses in Charles the Bald's 864 capitulary is significant in two respects. Firstly, recontextualising the Edict has consequences for how we conceptualise the grand narrative of the castle between the ninth and twelfth centuries. Charles's demand that fortifications be demolished was genuine and serious but it was not a legislative pronouncement intended to have general effect, and it was not understood as such by contemporaries or by posterity. It can no longer stand as the proof that the Frankish kings had once enjoyed a regalian monopoly on the right to authorise fortifications, and we can therefore no longer explain the developments of the post-Carolingian centuries simply with reference to the lingering persistence or disintegration of that supposed monopoly. Without the legalistic interpretation of the Edict of Pîtres to bind them together, the threads linking it to texts like the Norman *Constitutiones* of the 1090s, the *Laws of Henry I* of 1115, and the 1154 decree of Henry II begin to look very frayed.

Secondly, I am arguing that the above interpretation of the king's speech should prompt us to reconsider the history of fortifications in the ninth century itself. The traditional reading of the Edict underwrote a view of the Carolingian Empire as a prelapsarian era whose once pristine public sphere was gradually infiltrated and eventually overwhelmed by incipient lordships represented by 'proto-castles'. As we have seen, the underlying story cannot be that straightforward. Although there was a strong idea of the public sphere in the empire, it is too simple to imagine anti-Viking fortification as its private antithesis. Instead, the apparent absence and occasional presence of castles in ninth-century sources should draw our attention to some interesting aspects of Carolingian political structures and ideologies.

In short, the Edict can no longer be used as a skeleton key to unlock the early history of the medieval castle. But that does not mean that the castle did not have an early history. We need not throw the baby out with the bathwater. The castle certainly was a potent symbol of medieval society and its power structures, and there is no doubt that its proliferation between the tenth and thirteenth centuries went hand in hand with fundamental changes to society and politics in the post-Carolingian West.[83] Although there were probably a lot more fortifications pre-900 than those 'seen' by contemporary writers, it is absolutely not my intention to make an argument for full-spectrum 'continuity' across this period, as some have done, by implying that post-Carolingian conditions were somehow there all along in the ninth century, hiding behind the veil of the sources. There were clearly fundamental differences (as well as some similarities) between the Carolingian and post-Carolingian political landscapes. My point is that simple binaries like continuity vs change or public vs private are insufficient to explain them. This article does not aspire to definitively resolve questions of cause, effect and chronology in the early history of the castle, but to put those questions back on the table. The issue that needs to be addressed is not whether or not fortifications existed – it is what they meant, in different places and at different times, and what changing positions they held in the constantly changing political landscape. Castles, fortifications and walls of all types rich potential to tell us about the social and political environments that produced them. My suggestion is that they may still have much more to tell us than we previously thought.[84]

---

[83] R. Bartlett, *The Making of Europe* (London and Princeton, 1993), 65–70; L. Bourgeois, 'Castrum et habitat des élites: France et ses abords (vers 880 – vers 1000)', in *Cluny: Les moines et la société au premier âge féodal*, ed. D. Russo *et al.* (Rennes, 2013), 471–94; Koziol, *Peace of God*, 24–31.

[84] For discussion and feedback I am grateful to the members of the network 'The Castle and the Palace', funded by the Royal Society of Edinburgh and led by Stuart Airlie; and to Marios Costambeys, Mayke De Jong, Stefan Esders, Eric Goldberg, Guy Halsall, Thomas Kohl, Geoff Koziol, Jinty Nelson, Steffen Patzold and Charles West.

*Transactions of the RHS* 30 (2020), pp. 55–75 © The Author(s), 2020. Published by Cambridge University Press on behalf of the Royal Historical Society
doi:10.1017/S0080440120000031

# 'ACCEPTABLE TRUTHS' DURING THE FRENCH RELIGIOUS WARS*

## By Penny Roberts ⓘ

READ 20 SEPTEMBER 2019

ABSTRACT. This paper seeks to provide some historical perspective on contemporary preoccupations with competing versions of the truth. Truth has always been contested and subject to scrutiny, particularly during troubled times. It can take many forms – judicial truth, religious truth, personal truth – and is bound up with the context of time and place. This paper sets out the multidisciplinary approaches to truth and examines its role in a specific context, that of early modern Europe and, in particular, the French religious wars of the sixteenth century. Truth was a subject of intense debate among both Renaissance and Reformation scholars, it was upheld as an absolute by judges, theologians and rulers. Yet, it also needed to be concealed by those who maintained a different truth to that of the authorities. In the case of France, in order to advance their cause, the Huguenots used subterfuge of various kinds, including the illicit carrying of messages. In this instance, truth was dependent on the integrity of its carrier, whether the messenger could be trusted and, therefore, their truth accepted. Both sides also sought to defend the truth by countering what they presented as the deceit of their opponents. Then, as now, acceptance of what is true depends on which side we are on and who we are prepared to believe.

Truth for us nowadays is not what is, but what others can be brought to accept.[1]

Michel de Montaigne's wry comment on the fickleness of his sixteenth-century French contemporaries, written during and in response to the kingdom's religious wars, exposes the slippery nature of determining what is true in any period. Writing as he was in troubled times, Montaigne's observation also speaks to our current anxieties about a widening ideological division in society in which competing truths

---

*Many thanks to all those colleagues, from a variety of disciplines, who have passed on references and indulged my ideas. All misrepresentations remain my own. This article benefited from a fellowship at the Institut d'Études Avancées de Paris, with the financial support of the French state programme 'Investissements d'avenir' managed by the Agence Nationale de la Recherche (ANR-11-LABX-0027-01 Labex RFIEA+).
[1] M. de Montaigne, 'On Giving the Lie', in *The Complete Essays*, trans. and ed. M. A. Screech (1991), 756: 'Nostre verité de maintenant, ce n'est pas ce qui est, mais ce qui se persuade à autruy'.

appear to hold sway. It can prove instructive, therefore, to provide some historical perspective on contemporary preoccupations and on what constitutes 'acceptable truth'. The Protestant Reformation produced powerfully conflicted truths, for asserting one's own beliefs meant denying those of others. It became a theological schism impossible to bridge, with both sides believing that they were facing 'the enemies of truth'.[2] As divisions deepened, in France, the religious wars came to define the battle between what was true and what was false, who could be trusted and who might prove duplicitous. Yet, treachery might come from any quarter, not just openly declared enemies, but those previously thought to be friends and allies. Daily suspicions made neighbours increasingly unsure of who or what they could trust, who might deny them to the authorities or betray the local community.[3] In the sovereign courts, royal judges sought to establish the truth of plots and other illicit activities carried out in support of a religious cause and to condemn those responsible for them. However, the definition of justice, too, was changeable during times of peace and war. Thus, actions condemned in one circumstance might be vindicated in another, as successive edicts pardoned rebellious deeds on both sides, and property seized legitimately during conflict had to be returned.[4] The French religious wars are, therefore, a fruitful testing ground for thinking about how multiple truths can operate and coexist, jostling for attention within a complicated political, judicial and religious landscape. Contested truths were an inevitable outcome of confessional and other divisions, reflecting the fraught context in which they were propagated, for 'truth had many layers'.[5] The collision of judicial process and royal authority, on the one hand, with the various strands of opposition which served to undermine them on the other, demonstrates that truth was not just the first, but ultimately the principal, casualty of the wars.

# I

The pursuit of truth is central to many academic disciplines; its study is a source of fascination, too, in philosophy, psychology, theology, sociology

---

[2] A phrase frequently used by John Calvin, for example in a letter to Antoine de Crussol, 31 July 1563, in *Ioannis Calvini opera quae supersunt omnia* (59 vols., Brunswick and Berlin, 1879), XX, 112.

[3] J. Foa, 'Who Goes There? To Live and Survive during the Wars of Religion, 1562–1598', in Forum: 'Communities and Religious Identities in the Early Modern Francophone World, 1550–1700', *French Historical Studies*, 40 (2017), 425–38.

[4] P. Roberts, *Peace and Authority during the French Religious Wars c.1560–1600* (Basingstoke, 2013), 33–7, 94, 140.

[5] A. Pettegree, *The Invention of News: How the World Came to Know about Itself* (New Haven and London, 2014), 252.

and law, as well as history. Such studies reveal that, contrary to what we might expect and hope, truth can prove both unstable and destabilising. From an early age, children are encouraged by parents and teachers to tell the truth, although experiments have shown that even the very young practise deceit if they think that it is to their advantage and that they can get away with it.[6] While people may claim to value and desire the truth from others, they frequently justify concealing aspects of it themselves and tell white lies on a daily basis.[7] After all, while it is advantageous to be candid in some situations, telling the truth is not always the best policy and facing up to the truth can be inconvenient and uncomfortable for all concerned. To be brutally honest is to alienate and offend when most people rather seek to influence and persuade. Indeed, it is widely recognised that deception is a necessary survival strategy, but, while everyone depends on deception, no one wants to be deceived.[8] Concealing the truth can also be profoundly damaging and unjust for those harmed or misled thereby.

Above all, the centrality of trust is key to our willingness to believe and accept the truth of, or as told to us by, others.[9] The sociologist George Simmel claimed that all our relationships are predicated on the fine balance between expecting that our friends or spouses or relatives will be honest with us, and accepting that this will not always be the case: 'truthfulness and mendacity … form a scale that registers the ratios of the intensity of these relationships'.[10] If those with whom we are close prove to be more dishonest than is acceptable, then our trust in them, and often the relationship itself, will break down. Thus, the deceit of loved ones, in whom we place greatest trust, can prove almost impossible to bear. In our personal lives, and as historians, too, we tend to search for the truth in how people speak about themselves, both in the present and the past, but that is often not a reliable barometer. People pronounce reasoned and coherent narratives for why they act as they do which often rely on a degree of self-deception and creative thinking. They look to persuade others, and in the process often convince themselves, a position with which they may persist even in the face of evidence to the contrary. Much supposed truth relies, too, on the fallibility of memory, leading to the disputing of facts and the merging or blurring

---

[6]  A. D. Evans and K. Lee, 'Emergence of Lying in Very Young Children', *Developmental Psychology*, 49 (2013), 1958–63; A. D. Evans, F. Xu and K. Lee, 'When All Signs Point to You: Lies Told in the Face of Evidence', *Developmental Psychology*, 47 (2011), 39–49.

[7]  Discussed in A. Katwala, 'The race to create a perfect lie detector – and the dangers of succeeding', *The Guardian*, 5 September 2019.

[8]  S. Bok, *Lying: Moral Choice in Public and Private Life* (Hassocks, Sussex, 1978), 18–20.

[9]  *The Philosophy of Trust*, ed. P. Faulkner and T. Simpson (Oxford, 2017).

[10] G. Simmel, 'The Sociology of Secrecy and of Secret Societies', *American Journal of Sociology*, 11 (1906), 441–98, at 446.

of events that may be only feebly recalled or deliberately manipulated. As a result, it is entirely possible to mislead ourselves as well as others about what is true.

Nevertheless, it may seem as if the truth has never been as contested as it is today, with the widespread claims of fake news and alternative facts, and we have come to distrust what we are told by politicians and journalists perhaps more than ever.[11] Despite big data, instant communication and popular access to the means to livestream and record whatever events or incidents occur across the globe, the truth is not easily verifiable and remains deeply contested. Seeing is not believing; establishing the truth is not a simple process, for it is often in the eye of the beholder. Increasingly, it seems, subjectivity is dominant, objective thinking distrusted. 'Groupthink', but also individual truth, 'my truth', is all that counts. In this circumstance, 'truth is just a name for opinions', for what we 'can be brought to accept' or the declarations of whomever we think we can trust.[12] Put another way, the truth is an accumulation of received information, what we perceive to be true and what we wish to be so. For scholars who feel that some form of truth is still worth seeking out, even if it can never be absolute, this kind of relativism may be disconcerting. Yet, is this current 'crisis of truth' real, or indeed true, historically speaking? Hannah Arendt and Sissela Bok, writing in the 1960s and 1970s, provided forensic critiques of the strained relationship between truth and politics and the declining public trust and confidence in what politicians said.[13] Indeed, truth has always been contested, we might say 'in crisis', alongside a wider debate about whether, in certain circumstances, lying, or at least concealment of the truth, is permissible. Thus, on examination, truth is conceptually complex and elusive, and it proves challenging to encapsulate what it is at any time, in any place.

## II

What is truth? For Douglas Edwards 'answering this question is notoriously difficult'.[14] For moral philosophers, like Edwards, truth is

---

[11] W. Davies, 'Why can't we agree on what's true anymore?', *The Guardian*, 19 September 2019 (the day before I first gave this talk), which begs the question whether we ever did agree; M. Kakutani, *The Death of Truth* (New York, 2018); and 'The Decade of Distrust' presented by L. Kuenssberg on BBC Radio 4, 29 February 2020.

[12] F. Fernández-Armesto, *Truth: A History* (1997), 2.

[13] H. Arendt, 'Truth and Politics', *New Yorker*, 25 February 1967 (making a distinction between 'factual' and 'rational' truth and presented in a historical context from Plato and Hobbes onwards); H. Arendt, 'Lying in Politics: Reflections on The Pentagon Papers', *New York Review of Books*, 18 November 1971; Bok, *Lying*, xviii.

[14] D. Edwards, *The Metaphysics of Truth* (Oxford, 2018), 1. The philosophical literature on this question is extensive, for example, C. J. F. Williams, *What is Truth?* (Cambridge, 1976);

metaphysical, dependent on belief as much as reality, and thus 'elusive'. Its relationship to language and thought is key. Thus, truth is an abstract human construct of thought and speech rather than an objective fact or reflection of reality. Yet, establishing what is true is central, indeed, crucial, to systems of both belief and justice. Unsurprisingly, then, the establishment of the truth was and is the principal pursuit of theologians and judges and will be central to this discussion. In particular, it will focus on the views on truth and untruth held in the sixteenth century by thinkers such as Montaigne, but also others who lived through and commented on the French religious wars, as well as those who were tried in its courts and those who pronounced sentence on them. Particularly contested was the concept of religious truth, or 'Truth', capitalised by both sides to assert that its singularity was not open to challenge. Faced by prosecution, the upholding of religious truth might clash with the need to establish the judicial truth, itself framed in spiritual terms. In this way, both judge and accused sought to defend the truth, as they interpreted it, in the sight of God. Both believed that divine will would prevail to support justice by revealing the truth. Central here is the dichotomy between absolute truth and competing truths, the certainty of both sides that their truth would prevail even though that truth was often strategic and frequently partial.

The Renaissance scholar Desiderius Erasmus, in his *Adages*, when discussing 'In vino veritas', recalled that a 'proverb is still in common use today, to the effect that you never hear the truth from anyone, save only from three kinds of person: children, drunkards and madmen'.[15] Thus, the wise, experienced and sober are careful to be economical with the truth, to safeguard secrets as well as not to cause offence. Humanists such as Erasmus and Montaigne drew on classical learning for their comments on truth and lies, both subjects of lively discussion in ancient philosophy. At the risk of oversimplifying centuries of debate, a quick summary should be at least helpful here. Aristotle and other philosophers had debated whether truth was knowable or was simply a matter of interpretation. By the Middle Ages, these issues were particularly rehearsed in theological debate and, with the advent of the Reformation, became increasingly pertinent. Saints Augustine and Anselm and Thomas Aquinas focused on truth being essentially divine, but with differing shades of tolerance for its concealment, dependent on the circumstances. For Augustine, it was simple; to lie

---

*What is Truth?*, ed. R. Schantz (Berlin and New York, 2002). A. C. Grayling, *An Introduction to Philosophical Logic* (Brighton and Totowa, NJ, 1982), argues that 'The *wrong* question to ask about truth is "what is truth?"', 125, also cited by R. L. Kirkham, *Theories of Truth: A Critical Introduction* (Cambridge, MA, 1997), who states that 'there is little agreement about what the philosophical problem of truth is', 1.

[15] D. Erasmus, *Adages*, 1 vii 17.

was to sin against God, thus all lies were equally sinful and to be condemned, whereas Aquinas saw more gradations. He condemned all
lying as sinful, but wrote that 'the greater the good intended, the more
is the sin of lying diminished in gravity'.[16] Erasmus conceded, too, that
to tell a lie was unchristian, but that withholding or concealing the
truth was 'acceptable and in certain cases even prudent'. Humanists in
general asserted that they were 'strongly committed to the truth', and
rejected allegations that through their rhetorical flourishes they deliberately distorted it.[17]

While Alan Nelson claims that a 'potentially frustrating feature of
early modern philosophical theories is that truth is often taken to be com-
paratively unproblematic', Stefania Tutino concludes that the 'fragility
of the relationship between truth and language ... originated in the
early modern world', and it was then that thinkers perceived and
reflected on the 'cracks that started to appear in the system linking language, truth, and Truth'.[18] In particular, at the time of the Protestant
Reformation, and the greatest and most systematic challenge to the
authority of the Catholic Church, the battle for truth was at its most
fraught. In order to uphold that truth, however, its champions needed
to operate clandestinely. Maintaining this work became more important
than bearing witness to it. Secrets sometimes needed to be kept and,
therefore, the truth concealed, but a moral judgement had to be made
in what circumstances that behaviour was defensible before God. For
members of a religious minority, upholding the 'Truth' of their faith
could clash with the imperative to be truthful. As Tutino has argued,
'[u]nderstanding the early modern origin of this tension can give us a
better perspective as we try to reflect on the relationship between true,
false, and feigned'.[19]

With its vast historiography, many scholars have written extensively
and expertly on the notion of mental reservation or equivocation, effectively the concealment of truth, a phenomenon that became a crucial

[16] Quoted in J. P. Sommerville, 'The "New Art of Lying": Equivocation, Mental
Reservation, and Casuistry', in *Conscience and Casuistry in Early Modern Europe*, ed. E. Leites
(Cambridge, 2002), 159–84, at 161.

[17] T. van Houdt, 'Word Histories and Beyond: Towards a Conceptualization of Fraud
and Deceit in Early Modern Times', in *On the Edge of Truth and Honesty: Principles and
Strategies of Fraud and Deceit in the Early Modern Period*, ed. T. van Houdt, J. L. de Jong,
Z. Kwak, M. Spies and M. van Vaeck (Leiden, 2002), 1–32, at 11, 19; see also the essay
by J. Trapman, 'Erasmus on Lying and Simulation', in the same volume, 33–46.

[18] A. H. Nelson, 'Early Modern Theories of Truth', in *The Oxford Handbook of Truth*,
ed. M. Glanzberg (Oxford, 2018); S. Tutino, *Shadows of Doubt: Language and Truth in Post-
Reformation Catholic Culture* (Oxford, 2014), 190.

[19] S. Tutino, 'Nothing But the Truth? Hermeneutics and Morality in the Doctrines of
Equivocation and Mental Reservation in Early Modern Europe', *Renaissance Quarterly*, 64
(2011), 115–55, at 152.

safeguard for many during the Reformation period. The discussion to date has mainly focused on those brought before the inquisition in Italy and Spain, on the one hand, and the Jesuits' moral justification for how lying could be reconciled with its prohibition on the other. This was also the case for the recusants in England, attending Protestant services while continuing Catholic worship at home. Scholars have provided their own and contemporary definitions of what this meant in practice: 'inner qualification was believed to preserve an apparently untrue spoken expression from being a lie'.[20] For instance, by making a distinction between mental and spoken language, 'it is not lying to make a spoken assertion which you believe to be false ... provided that you add in thought some words which make the whole truthful'.[21] In particular, it allowed someone to 'reconcile the prohibition on lying with the obligation of keeping a secret', and as such it was a 'more or less ethically acceptable, way to allow a certain course of action ... in the name of a different, and higher, moral principle'.[22] This was the case for the confessor torn between 'the moral imperative of keeping the confessional seal intact ... [and] the other moral imperative of not lying'.[23] It was essential, too, for those brought before the courts on accusations of heresy or dissent, for 'equivocation was a necessary resource against interrogation in a world of strong convictions, when deponents were not in any serious doubt about the truth or falsehood of what they said'.[24] Such certainty cemented the belief in where truth lay and how best it could be protected by being concealed from its detractors.

The Augustinian dilemma that lying could never be justified remained, however. Largely associated with the Jesuits, so-called casuistry later came to be seen as amoral, or morally reprehensible, especially for a committed Jansenist like Blaise Pascal. Yet, recent scholars have sought to defend it. Braun and Vallance define it as 'a theory of practical reasoning developed for dealing with cases in which particular courses of action provoked moral doubt', whereby the conscience acted as intermediary between God and man, and the resulting strictures were stringent and rigorous, not lax.[25] To some extent, what we are looking at here is a distinction between the position of ecclesiastical and secular courts, or perhaps, more precisely, between ecclesiastical and secular judges, or, rather, which side of the judicial process the accused was

[20] Van Houdt, 'Word Histories and Beyond', 11.

[21] Sommerville, 'The "New Art of Lying"', 160.

[22] Van Houdt, 'Word Histories and Beyond', 11; Tutino, 'Nothing But the Truth?', 115–16.

[23] Tutino, 'Nothing But the Truth?', 121.

[24] Fernández-Armesto, *Truth*, 163–4.

[25] *Contexts of Conscience in Early Modern Europe, 1500–1700*, ed. H. E. Braun and E. Vallance (Basingstoke, 2004), x.

on. From the inquisitors' perspective, 'truth was one' and the Church saw itself as the only channel through which it was revealed, thus heresy undermined the 'unity of the truth' and heretics were 'lacking in both truth and in virtue' and were, above all, 'untrustworthy'.[26] By contrast, in the late sixteenth century, the Jesuit Gregory of Valencia, sought to question the legitimacy of the court system itself that challenged God's truth, 'such as the case of a man *unjustly* interrogated'. In those specific circumstances, he argued, a man could use both ambiguous speech and forms of mental reservation, 'for the judge in this case is *illegitimate*'.[27] Truth was central to the judicial process that framed these encounters, but its interpretation and understanding remained deliberately elusive.

## III

The phenomenon of mental reservation has been less extensively explored in the case of France. Its inquisitorial system of examination by the judges of the secular *parlements*, and the emphasis on sedition rather than heresy in the courts, has clear parallels, however. Furthermore, it was not just the Huguenots, but their coreligionists from foreign states, who had to face this challenge when they operated in the French kingdom. Traditionally, though, scholars of the French Reformation have tended to focus rather on the Calvinist condemnation of both deceit and dissent, more specifically the practice of so-called Nicodemism, with believers urged to openly confess their faith, not keep it secret in their hearts.[28] There was much soul-searching, too, among Calvinist authors about the internal torments of acting against one's conscience. Yet, as with their covert support for political rebellion, it is demonstrable that Geneva was central to the clandestine organisation of the French Reformed churches and their networks. While asserting that 'God is truth', and quick to condemn Nicodemites for concealing their faith, John Calvin and Theodore Beza made extensive use of deceptive practices to further their cause while repeatedly denying that they were doing so. As Jon Balserak puts it, 'Geneva's systematic employment of falsehood and dissembling in their ministry to France must be recognized and acknowledged ... to uncover the true character of the French Reformation.'[29] Thus, at the highest levels of the Reformed Church

[26] N. S. Davidson, '"Fuggir la libertà della coscienza": Conscience and the Inquisition in Sixteenth-Century Italy', in *ibid.*, 49–55, at 52–3, 55.

[27] Tutino, 'Nothing But the Truth?', 136.

[28] On more positive views of Nicodemites, C. Koslovsky, *Evening's Empire: A History of the Night in Early Modern Europe* (Cambridge, 2011), 49.

[29] J. Balserak, Geneva's Use of Lies, Deceit, and Simulation in Their Efforts to Reform France, 1536–1563', *Harvard Theological Review*, 112 (2019), 76–100.

these practices were commonplace, if not openly condoned in the cause of a higher principle, upholding 'the truth of Scripture'.

A tendency to dissimulation was, thus, a result of the religious controversies arising from the Reformation, when concealing your faith and illicit activities was particularly necessary to avoid prosecution. As Alexandra Walsham argues, '[a]gainst a back drop of coercion and violence, dissimulation might be a legitimate short-term solution, a prudent strategy'.[30] As a member of a minority religion, it was dangerous to admit and speak openly about one's faith or beliefs, as was true for those brought before the inquisition in the Middle Ages. The vexed relationship between inner conviction and outward conduct, private belief and public behaviour, and the separation between physical and spiritual self, had a profound effect on individual perceptions of truth. Indeed, whatever the religious drivers for concealment and deception, contemporary and modern authors, such as Perez Zagorin and Jon Snyder, have emphasised the extent to which the early modern period should be viewed, in its entirety, as an age of dissimulation.[31] Summed up most succinctly, once again, by Montaigne, 'dissimulation is one of the most striking characteristics of our age'. He also declared, 'what man are we to trust when he speaks of himself, seeing there are few, perhaps none, whom we can trust when they speak of others, where they have less to gain from lying' which 'is an accursed vice'.[32] The implication of such a position was that almost no one was trustworthy and everyone had a reason to conceal the truth.

Furthermore, many observers claimed that it had become the fashion of the time to dissemble, to conceal your true feelings, to play a part or to present a manufactured self, as advocated by Renaissance authors such as Niccolò Machiavelli and Baldassare Castiglione. According to Snyder, the discourse on dissimulation prevailed among dominant social groups especially in Italy, creating a 'culture of secrecy', as well as the opportunity for 'self-expression and self-representation', and revealing the tension between 'the concern to publish the truth and that of protecting it'.[33] Erasmus commented that '[t]ruth however is not always opposed to falsehood; sometimes its opposite is pretence. A man can speak sincerely and what he says may be false; and what he says can be true though he

---

[30] A. Walsham, 'Ordeals of Conscience: Casuistry, Conformity and Confessional Identity in Post-Reformation England', in *Contexts of Conscience*, ed. Braun and Vallance, 32–48, at 47.

[31] P. Zagorin, *Ways of Lying: Dissimulation, Persecution and Conformity in Early Modern Europe* (Cambridge, MA, 1990) and 'The Historical Significance of Lying and Dissimulation', *Social Research*, 63 (1996), 863–912; J. R. Snyder, *Dissimulation and the Culture of Secrecy in Early Modern Europe* (Berkeley and London, 2009).

[32] Montaigne, 'On Giving the Lie', 756; 'On Liars', in *The Complete Essays*, 35.

[33] Snyder, *Dissimulation and the Culture of Secrecy*, xvi–xvii.

does not speak the truth.'[34] Appearances could be deceiving. In particular, to appear what you were not, or to have your reactions be so inscrutable that no one could be sure what you were thinking, became à la mode at the French court, including wearing masks both actual and metaphorical. Henri III of France developed a particular reputation for being adept at concealing his true feelings, a trait which his opponents exploited, and which reinforced a sense of distrust that was one of the contributory factors in the failed promise of his reign.[35] Montaigne even claimed that such deception was a peculiarly French vice and that lying 'at the present time is for them a virtue' and 'more commonplace among us than any of the others'.[36] The religious wars brought with them a particular dilemma, as Frenchman was pitted against Frenchman, not just on the battlefield and in the streets, but also in the courtroom. Avoiding capture and prosecution to safeguard one's faith might involve physical disguise as well as mental dissimulation, in order to carry out illicit and potentially seditious acts. But there was a necessity in doing so, for the enemies of truth needed to be defeated and, as such, a degree of deception could serve God's cause.

## IV

As is evident, much of the scholarship on truth and falsehood looks at the various debates from the philosophical or theological point of view. Interesting as it is to know what humanist scholars and other elites of the period thought about these issues, it does not tell us much about the lived experience, the real risks and practical dangers, as well as moral dilemmas, which individuals faced in negotiating this world. One place to look for these encounters, as we have seen, is in the courtroom, but this lens, too, is problematic. Thomas Weigend pronounces, rather starkly, that '[f]inding the Truth is a difficult task under any set of circumstances, but finding the truth in the context of crime and punishment is almost impossible'.[37] He argues further that the criminal process provides 'a strong incentive for … concealing relevant facts' and 'a vested interest in concealing the truth'. Tension between the judge's quest for truth and the accused's motivation to prevent its discovery results in the need to seek a credible judgement based on substantive truth and resulting in 'natural justice', for 'truth and justice are intimately

---

[34] Erasmus, *Adages*, I vii 17.

[35] X. Le Person, *"Practiques" et "practiqueurs". La vie politique à la fin du règne de Henri III (1584–1589)* (Geneva, 2002).

[36] Montaigne, 'On Giving the Lie', 756; note his switch between 'them' and 'us'.

[37] T. Weigend, 'Is the Criminal Process about Truth?: A German Perspective', *Harvard Journal of Law & Public Policy*, 26 (2003) (special issue on 'Law & Truth'), 157–73, at 157.

intertwined'.[38] Torture, too, in Weigend's judgement, 'turns out to be less than effective in producing the truth'.[39] Montaigne, himself a judge in the *parlement* at Bordeaux, echoes this:

> Torture is a dangerous innovation; it would appear that it is an assay not of the truth but of a man's endurance. The man who can endure it hides the truth: so does he who cannot. For why should pain make me confess what is true rather than force me to say what is not true?[40]

Yet studies of the use of early modern torture show that it was often carefully calibrated and judges were '[a]ware that torture did not always yield the truth but anxious to ensure that it did so'.[41] The role of God in the early modern court and the torture chamber was significant, for both the judges and the accused. In the heightened atmosphere of French witchcraft trials, the confession was key to a conviction, but its refusal could also be damning for the accused, since the truth needed to be heard.[42] This imperative was crucial, too, in the case of other so-called moral crimes. In Geneva, according to Sara Beam, 'truth, conscience and sin were concepts constantly evoked by the interrogators during torture sessions' aiming for 'unadulterated truth produced by a purified soul'.[43] The spiritual intent might be less explicitly evoked in Catholic France than it was in Calvinist Geneva, but that does not mean that God was not believed to be present in the chamber, through his judicial representatives, as we will see.

Truth is difficult to pin down, therefore, particularly when we look at it historically, and religious confrontation exacerbates its fragility. Furthermore, our interest should not be so much in determining what was true from what was not, but how contemporaries talked about, and conceived, the role of truth. This concerns both the judges and the accused. The role of truth in judicial procedures was freighted by expectations on both sides. The judges' openly declared pursuit of truth, articulated in interrogations and court procedures, is a good example. In the inquisitorial system of Roman law that prevailed in France and elsewhere, dominated by the assessment by judges, truth needed to be measured and not directed too much by what the judicial

---

[38] *Ibid.*, 157, 160, 172.

[39] *Ibid.*, 160–1.

[40] Montaigne, 'On Conscience', in *The Complete Essays*, 414.

[41] S. Beam, 'Rites of Torture in Reformation Geneva', in *Ritual and Violence: Natalie Zemon Davis and Early Modern France*, ed. G. Murdock, P. Roberts and A. Spicer (Oxford, Past & Present Supplement, 2012), 197–219, at 201.

[42] V. Krause, *Witchcraft, Demonology, and Confession in Early Modern France* (Cambridge, 2015): 'The truth must be spoken – or rather, to take the standpoint of the inquisitor and then demonologist, it can only be *heard*.' Krause also asserts that, during this period, hearing rather than vision was held to be the most spiritual sense.

[43] Beam, 'Rites of Torture', 201, 210.

perception was of what that truth might be. Equally, those before the courts were often guided by what they thought the judges wanted to hear, or rather what version of the truth might be most likely to secure their release.[44] Judicial truth had to be palatable as well as procedural. It was valorised, but judges actually needed to show restraint in its exercise as with the use of torture. So we have to be careful with our reliance on the veracity of court papers, compounded by the fact that we have relatively few of the sort of documents surviving which would tell us about these procedures in the French courts in any detail.

Truth be told, the survival of interrogation documents for the sixteenth century is sparse, particularly from the early decades of the wars, the 1560s and 1570s, and often involves high-profile cases.[45] Much of it is dependent on chance or circumstance, and the diligent copying out after the event can be crucial to interpret the original scrawl. Those documents that do survive are often related to the importance of the case, or how unusual it was, so again we have to be careful about what we can extrapolate from these 'exceptional norms'. On the other hand, they can still tell us a great deal about the operation of truth in the 'courtroom' in sixteenth-century France. The truth was used in two ways during interrogations, and stock phrases and judicial formulae recur in many documents. Under oath, the accused was admonished, sometimes repeatedly, 'to tell the truth' (*dire la vérité*); at other times they were put under pressure to respond in a particular way by a confrontational assertion regarding what was 'the truth'. So that they could not purport that what was written down was other than the truth they had given, they were asked to sign (if they could do so) at the end, or even sometimes on every page, of the account, which was most likely read to them. In response to the appeals of those subject to it, the use of torture was also defended in these terms, as a way of determining or 'knowing the truth' and 'to find out and extract the truth from [the accused's] mouth'.[46] Similarly, 'false testimony' was to be severely punished, that is, what was 'falsely and contrary to the truth, deposed against' someone.[47] In many cases, the judges

---

[44] For a German example, see J. F. Harrington, 'Tortured Truths: The Self-Expositions of a Juvenile Career Criminal in Early Modern Nuremberg', *German History*, 23 (2005), 143–71, and on 'the early modern axiom that pain always produced truth, and thus revealed the true voice of the interrogated' (147).

[45] The vital work of A. Soman, who has done so much to open our eyes to the riches of the archives of the *parlement*, including 'The Parlement of Paris and the Great Witch Hunt (1565–1640)', *The Sixteenth Century Journal*, 9 (1978), 30–44, is focused mainly on the period from the 1580s when the sources are more abundant.

[46] Some examples: Archives nationales, Paris (hereafter AN), X/2a/129, 492v, 17 March 1562, 'savoir la verité'; X/2b/80, 31 July 1574, 'pour scavoir et tirer par sa bouche la verité'.

[47] AN, X/2b/85, 30 June 1575, 'faulx tesmoignaige … faulement et contre verité desposé alencontre de'.

chose to believe or dismiss what they heard, determining the truth as they saw fit. The necessity of determining what was 'véritable' also led to confrontations between prisoners and/or witnesses with conflicting testimonies. As they stood face-to-face with one another, and before the judges, they were under pressure to defend and uphold their statements in order to see whose version of the truth would prevail. This process will be explored here with reference to a few specific, but very different, case studies from the 1570s, and what they can tell us about the uses of truth. In particular, it is important to consider how the judges and the accused responded in the court and if this suggests that they were aware or not of the wider debate on the role of truth and the status of lying for the fate of the soul.

## V

The first case is an unusually detailed treason trial from 1574 and a contemporary cause célèbre.[48] It involved accusations against close associates of the king's youngest brother, the duke of Alençon. They were accused of plotting with Protestant nobles and their international allies, and even an Italian astrologer, to place Alençon on the throne. Although there was a confessional element, the principal charges were political rather than religious; nevertheless, spiritual concerns played a central role for both the accused and their prosecutors. We are fortunate to have the complete transcript of all the depositions and interrogations because they were published a few years afterwards by the Calvinist pastor Simon Goulart in his *Mémoires de l'estat de France*.[49] Those tried were repeatedly asked to tell the truth, particularly in the latter stages of the trial when torture was introduced. The account of their interrogations demonstrates the vivid escalation in the pressure put upon them to speak truthfully and, thereby, to incriminate themselves and their accomplices. Meanwhile, rumours swirled around the case, with Sigismondo di Cavalli, the Venetian ambassador, declaring that 'no one knows the truth of all this'.[50] The principal suspects, Joseph de Boniface, sieur de La Molle, and Annibal de Coconat, took very different approaches to their predicament. La Molle chose outright denial. He repeatedly 'said that he knew nothing' in response to the twenty-one questions he was asked, and of which he had sight the evening before, extrapolating only occasionally to declare a statement as 'false' or an event as never

---

[48] I have recently discussed this trial in more detail, and from a different perspective, in P. Roberts, 'Violence by Royal Command: A Judicial "Moment" 1574–1575', *French History*, 33 (2019), 199–217.

[49] S. Goulart, *Mémoires de l'estat de France sous Charles Neufiesme*, III (1577), 208–81.

[50] Quoted in M. P. Holt, *The Duke of Anjou and the Politique Struggle during the Wars of Religion* (Cambridge, 1986), 41.

having happened.[51] He was probably trusting in his master's protection to come to his rescue, while his alleged accomplice, Coconat, went for full and frank disclosure, probably in the hope that he might be granted a royal pardon. Neither strategy served them well. After three weeks of questioning, both men were condemned and swiftly executed.

La Molle and Coconat defended themselves as having been loyal and obedient to the young prince to counter accusations of their disloyalty and disobedience to the crown. Alençon and his brother-in-law, Henri de Navarre, were also forced to testify, with the former declaring 'in the word of a prince that the above is the truth', while Navarre complained that the crown chose not to trust him, but only the lies of his enemies 'and the malice of those who have lied about me'.[52] Aristocratic privilege protected the princes of the blood, but did not prevent them from being held under suspicion through effective house arrest. For the nobility, in particular, truth and trustworthiness were tightly bound up with a sense of honour. To be dishonest was to be dishonourable. Truth was a matter of honour, and to give someone the lie was to dishonour them, as we know from several high-profile instances.[53] When the accused were confronted with those who had testified against them, it was to test the resolve as well as the conscience of both parties that they had told the truth, as well as providing the opportunity for them to impugn each other's reputation or honour. Often these confrontations concluded with the accuser persisting with the truth of what they had asserted and the accused declaring it to be untrue.[54] When confronted by the testimonies of others which challenged his claims to know nothing, La Molle declared that he was only answerable to the truth and then only in his master the duke's presence. Coconat also sought to bring in the duke of Guise as a 'truthful (or trustworthy) prince' to argue his case.[55]

The judges in the trial, which was expedited outside the timetable of normal or ordinary justice, explicitly tied the declaration of the truth to service to the king, saying that there was 'no service more agreeable to the king than to tell the truth'.[56] Once torture began, the condemned were repeatedly asked to confess the truth, but they were more

---

[51] Goulart, *Mémoires*, III, 208–10: 'dit qu'il n'en sait rien'. Declarations of knowing nothing were contrary to the guidance on mental reservation.

[52] *Ibid.*, 219, 220, 224: 'en parole de prince que ce que dessus est la vérité'; 'la meschanceté de ceux qui peuvent avoir menty de moy'.

[53] For instance, Bibliothèque Nationale de France (Paris) (hereafter BNF), MS Dupuy 755, 'Mélange des divers titres et mémoires', 143, dispute between Lieutenant-Governor Blaise de Monluc and Marshal Montmorency-Damville, February 1570.

[54] For examples, see Goulart, *Mémoires*, III, 235–6, 240–1, 260–1.

[55] *Ibid.*, 248: 'prince véritable'.

[56] *Ibid.*, 256: 'il ne sauroit faire service plus agréable au Roy que de dire vérité'.

concerned with the fate of their souls, making it clear that to persist in a denial or untruth made no sense. François de Tourtay, as his torture continued, asked in desperation, 'what do you want me to tell you? I promise you that I know only what I have said', and 'what use would it be for me to deny it, since you have condemned me to death?'[57] Furthermore, he declared that God should damn him if he knew anything more and, despite the urging of his judges, stayed firm in this assertion right up to his execution.[58] La Molle also continued to resist through several rounds of torture. While the judges told him that he would 'never enter paradise unless he discharged his conscience', he asserted that he sought nothing more than 'to pray to God for the rest of my life'. La Molle eventually broke down, admitting that he had not told the truth before because his master the duke had 'obliged him a hundred thousand times, on my life and all that I hold dear in this world to say nothing'.[59] Thus, his fidelity to his master, to keep his secret, had trumped La Molle's obligation to tell the truth. As the judges put it, he had thus committed 'his heart to the world and to the service of great lords, and had forgotten God', and the Jesuits would probably have agreed. Like Tourtay, once he had confessed, La Molle declared that God should 'damn his soul if he knew any more', and 'I know no more on the damnation of my soul' and by the 'True eternal God'.[60] Nevertheless, right up until the moment that he was beheaded, the judges continued their demands that he tell the truth, not only so as to determine who was culpable for the plot against the king, but in the interests of La Molle's salvation.

In this, as in other trials, it was not at all unusual for a suspect to declare as 'true' or 'véritable' certain aspects of the accusations made, while denying others, perhaps so as to deflect suspicion that they were concealing something. The language of truthfulness and lying permeated both the judges' rhetoric and the defendants' discourse. The accused were urged not to lie and they, in turn, pleaded their innocence. During the La Molle/Coconat trial, Catherine de Medici and others enquired directly from the procurator-general of the Paris *parlement* what the truth was in regard to the supposed threat to Charles IX's

---

[57] *Ibid.*, 256–7: 'Que voulez-vous que je vous die? Je vous promets que je n'en say que ce que j'en ay dit'; 'Que me serviroit-il de le nier, puisque vous m'avez condamnez à la mort?'.
[58] *Ibid.*, 259, 262.
[59] *Ibid.*, 267–9: 'n'entrera jamais en paradis s'il ne descharge sa conscience'; 'ne demande autre chose que d'estre enfermé en un couvent, pour prier Dieu le reste de ma vie'; 'm'ayant obligé cent mille fois, me commanda sur ma vie et sur ce que j'avois le plus cher en ce monde que je ne disse rien'.
[60] *Ibid.*, 270, 272–3, 279: 'son cœur au monde et aux service des grands seigneurs, et a oublié Dieu'; 'damne son ame s'il en sait aucunes'; 'je ne say autre chose sur la damnation de mon ame', 'Vray Dieu éternel'.

life, 'the truth of the king's illness' and the enchantment of Alençon by La Molle.[61] Directly afterwards, the king himself asked the judges to tell him what lessons could be learned. Royal justice and, by extension, divine justice had to be upheld, especially when the life of the monarch was under threat. The judicial pursuit of the truth aimed to stabilise the French polity threatened by the deception of those of the king's subjects who sought to destroy him and, thus, his kingdom.

## VI

The worst of these wars is that the cards are so mixed up, with your enemy indistinguishable from you by any clear indication of language or deportment, being brought up under the same laws, manners and climate, that it is not easy to avoid confusion and disorder.[62]

As the conflict progressed, this sense of confusion that Montaigne describes was intensified. In such circumstances, the Protestant minority in particular had no choice but to rely on the trustworthiness of their co-religionists, forming new associations through faith as well as reinforcing some already established bonds. This spiritual solidarity clearly strengthened the sense of common endeavour and shared risk, at a time when lives were endangered for holding a particular view or belief and everyday activities reinterpreted as suspect and threatening.[63] The establishment of religious 'Truth', whatever one's faith, was incontestable and brought certainty. Religious dissent encouraged the promotion of this truth through subterfuge. One striking example is the illicit carrying of messages and correspondence by the Huguenots. This practice involved deceit in the service of 'Truth', 'the truth of God's word', as the Huguenots saw it, with the carriage of letters to facilitate communication between the leadership, including nobles and ministers, the end therefore justifying the means. The concealment of activities was defensible because it allowed the true religion to be perpetuated, to flourish, to triumph, in the face of temporal power. This, of course, brought those carrying out such actions before the courts, which were defending truth of another sort.

Discerning the true from the false was even more vital at a time of contested belief. It was important to know whom you could trust, that some sources of news were more reliable than others, as were some messengers if they were to give a truthful account since, for the sake of secrecy, many messages were transmitted orally. The trouble involved in getting

[61] BNF, MS Dupuy 590, 'Recueil des pièces', 24 and 26, letters from Catherine and the sieur de Lanssac to Jean de La Guesle, 26 and 29 April 1574, regarding the need to 'scavoir la verité' and to check 'la verité du mal du roi'.
[62] Montaigne, 'On Conscience', in *The Complete Essays*, 410.
[63] Foa, 'Who Goes There?'.

reliable news is reflected in contemporary correspondence. Thus the Huguenot sieur de Montjay wrote from England in January 1569, requesting an update on how his coreligionists were faring, as he suspected that the French ambassador 'often silenced the most truthful [reports] and [those] at which we would most rejoice'.[64] This transport across borders caused problems for ambassadorial messengers too. Edmund Mather, who worked as a courier for the English ambassador to France, commented from Boulogne that, '[a]s troubled waters be … furthest from the frontier, so are news bruited in remote places oft times furthest from the truth'.[65] Mather came to know more about the hazards of circulating news than most as the English authorities arrested, interrogated and executed him for treason, in 1572, for acting as a double agent in collusion with Spain. Furthermore, from prison, after his condemnation, he wrote that because of his 'error', and with nothing to lose, he might be expected 'more plainly to discourse the truth'.[66] Thus, Mather asserted that he was a more reliable source precisely because he had previously proved untrustworthy!

Someone who almost certainly crossed paths with Mather at the English ambassador's house was the merchant Jehan Thivignat. The account of his arrest and interrogation at Dieppe in May 1570, for smuggling concealed correspondence to England, survives because officials subsequently sent it to Paris for scrutiny by the crown.[67] Thivignat was three times asked to 'dire la vérité' and twice challenged on the truth of his testimony. Despite the danger he was in, he did not appear to dissemble at all. It would seem that he was open and honest about his activities, his acquaintances and even his faith. We can compare his experience with that of Henri Fléel, arrested between Saint-Omer and Calais in the same year for carrying correspondence between the Netherlands and England.[68] Here, the focus was on the religious beliefs of the accused which probably resulted in a death sentence before the Council of Troubles. By contrast, Thivignat mentioned attending Protestant services in the French church in London as well as his frequent carriage of correspondence to and from Protestant

---

[64] BNF, MS Cinq Cents Colbert 24, fo. 363: 'bien souvent luy taizent les plus véritables et dequoy nous serions les plus resjouiz'. More broadly on this issue, see Pettegree, *The Invention of News*.

[65] Calendar of State Papers Foreign (hereafter CSPF), 70/107, 52–3, May 1569.

[66] British Museum, Harleian Manuscripts 0/6991, fo. 11 (undated), Mather to the Earl of Leicester and Lord Burghley.

[67] BNF, MS français 15551, fos. 272–7 (10 May 1570); I am currently writing a full-length study centred on this incident.

[68] A. L. E. Verheyden, 'Une correspondance inédite adressée par des familles protestantes des Pays-Bas à leurs coreligionnaires d'Angleterre (11 novembre 1569–25 février 1570)', *Bulletin de la Commission Royale d'Histoire*, 120 (1955), 95–257.

exiles in England. In another surviving case, including a detailed interrogation and prepared questions, the royal sergeant, Claude Boursier, was sentenced to death for having evaded his majesty's justice by escaping from the Conciergerie prison in Paris.[69] He had originally been condemned for blasphemy, rather than heresy, against which he had appealed. However, his interrogators showed no interest in his religious views, focusing rather on the veracity of the account he gave of his escape and the contacts he had with others outside the prison. While they were at pains to point out the 'véritable' details of the accounts given by witnesses, Boursier's story was not believed by the judges and he was subsequently executed.

Significantly, although his interrogation does not survive, and we know that he was tortured and said to have confessed to having plotted to kill the king, Jehan Abraham was arrested for much the same offence as Thivignat in July 1575.[70] Partly this was due to his closeness to a high-ranking rebel, as Abraham was secretary to Henri, prince of Condé, then in exile in the Empire. Timing was equally important though. When Thivignat was arrested, the crown was negotiating peace. When Abraham was seized, the crown was still fearful of Protestant reprisals for the St Bartholomew's Day massacre of 1572 and other plots.[71] Thus, the type of truth extracted by the royal judges in these circumstances was also shaped by the prevailing political climate. Abraham's account (which does not survive), extracted under torture, was incriminating, whereas Thivignat's was much more about information-gathering. Furthermore, Thivignat was a small cog in a much wider network and he was forthright about his role, that he did this as a favour and was not paid to do so. It seemed to be a matter of honour for him that this 'truth' was understood, although he certainly knew that what he was doing was illicit in view of the deliberate measures he took to conceal the letters he was carrying.

The network around Thivignat included not only those who supplied him, but others charged with carrying correspondence for the English ambassador to France. The 'distinction between spies and official couriers', as seen with Mather, was a fine one; many ambassadorial messengers were regularly detained and, therefore, their communications disrupted.[72] In September 1568, an Englishman charged with carrying

---

[69] AN, X/2b/1174, 'Chambre criminelle ou de la Tournelle'; Archives historiques de la Préfecture de Police (Paris) (hereafter AHPP), Conciergerie, A$^B$ 3, 102v (31 October 1569), judgement (18 February 1570).

[70] AHPP, Conciergerie, A$^B$ 5, fo. 10r (19 July 1575), judgement (13 August).

[71] Roberts, 'Violence by Royal Command', esp. 210.

[72] V. Groebner, *Who Are You? Identification, Deception, and Surveillance in Early Modern Europe*, trans. M. Kyburz and J. Peck (New York, 2007), 166.

letters from Paris to England was arrested by the authorities at Rouen.[73] Their suspicions had been aroused, they told the king, by his 'disguises, variations and lies, while trembling', and the fact that he had tried to dispose of several packets of the letters in question. As a result, they had opened one and were sufficiently concerned about their contents, and the ill will expressed therein to the crown, to send them on and to imprison the courier. We know from other correspondence that this was one of the English ambassador's men and Queen Elizabeth was outraged by both the detention and confiscation.[74] The French ambassador to England faced similar problems with getting his dispatches through, including deliberate obstruction and interception. In addition, ambassadorial disputes regarding the truth or otherwise of each other's reports were commonplace.

The suspicion with which ambassadors were viewed by the courts in which they were resident intensified at a time of confessional conflict. They were suspected of subterfuge and the conscious distortion of events. Catherine de Medici decried the 'fine opinions ... customarily' expressed by the English ambassador, Henry Norris, as 'so false, malicious and contrary' and 'entirely false'.[75] In the fraught circumstances of the religious wars, the need to establish the truth and counter the false claims of adversaries could prove vital. Thus, in January 1569, the young prince Henri of Navarre wrote to Elizabeth's chief minister, William Cecil, regarding the Huguenots' military position, so that 'you have truly understood the state of our arms ... without disguising anything as readily as do our enemies who, in all sorts of ways, hunt down the truth'.[76] Following defeat at the battle of Jarnac a couple of months later, Henri once again sought to downplay to their allies the seriousness of the Huguenot losses and the rumours spread by the other side, for 'our enemies publish as they please', whereas this messenger 'will not disguise nor conceal any of it'.[77] His mother, the queen of

---

[73] BnF, MS fr 15548, fo. 10r (3 September 1568), president of the *parlement* at Rouen to the king: 'les desguisemens, variations et menteries avec un tremblement'.

[74] CSPF, 70/101, 30 (6 September 1568), English ambassador in Paris, Henry Norris, to Cecil.

[75] *Lettres de Catherine de Médicis*, ed. H de La Ferrière, III (Paris, 1887), 261 (9 July 1569), Catherine to the French ambassador to England, Bertrand de Salignac de La Mothe-Fénélon, 'beaux advis ... selon sa coutume ... sy faulx, malicieux et controuvez ... entierement faulx'.

[76] CSPF, 70/105, fo. 48 (10 January 1569), Navarre to Cecil, 'vous ayez véritablement entendu l'estat de noz armes ... sans vous desguiser aucune chose comme voluntiers font noz ennemys qui chassent la vérité en toutes sortes'.

[77] CSPF, 70/106, fo. 43 (18 March 1569), Navarre to Cecil, 'noz ennemys publient ainsi que bon leur semble ... n'en desguisera ne dissimulera chose quelconque'.

Navarre, wrote in similar vein 'au vray' ('in truth/truthfully') regarding these events, also endorsing the credibility of the messenger as 'worthy of trust'.[78] In this, as in other situations, good news was more readily accepted than bad; reports of defeats and deaths were received with scepticism until more fully verified, whereas victories and survivals were celebrated. The death of the Huguenot commander, Louis de Bourbon, prince of Condé, at Jarnac, for example, was not fully accepted by the English court until a month after it was first reported.[79] Some circumspection was justified, however, as the deaths of leaders on both sides were often falsely relayed during the wars.[80]

## VII

The upholding of truth in sixteenth-century France was more complex in practice than it appeared in theory. Returning to Montaigne's observation that truth is what others can be brought to accept, we can see that this is a fair assessment of what occurred when those accused of secretive practices came before their judges. What judges were prepared to accept was dependent on context as the events of the wars played out and the crown was more or less concerned about what those around it were able to conceal. So the truth was caught somewhere between the judges' determination to seek it out and the accused's willingness to reveal it. Some were prepared to take considerable risks to uphold a higher or absolute 'Truth' and, thus, to be answerable to divine rather than royal justice. The myriad responses that individuals might have to the circumstances in which the wars placed them shaped their attitudes to the reconciliation of their consciences with deception and concealment, conviction and condemnation, and were as complex as truth itself. By anchoring cases in royal justice, seeking consensus while refuting the assertions of others, the crown and its judges looked to establish an acceptable truth that they could present to a wider audience. Likewise, leaders on both sides sought to counter the falsehoods disseminated by their opponents, and their coreligionists were more inclined to believe what they were told by trusted intermediaries. In some cases, however, the truth was unavoidable, as with the death of Condé, but

---

[78] CSPF, 70/106, fo. 50 (21 March 1569), Jeanne d'Albret to Cecil, and fo. 110 (13 April 1569), to Queen Elizabeth; 'digne de foy'.

[79] *Correspondance Diplomatique de Bertrand de Salignac de la Mothe-Fénélon, ambassadeur de France en Angleterre de 1568 à 1575*, I (Paris and London, 1838), 302–5, 308–9 (12 & 17 April 1569).

[80] In the case of Jarnac, both the sieurs de Téligny and Montgomery were falsely reported dead. Téligny was killed during the St Bartholomew's Day massacre in 1572, but Montgomery survived until his execution in 1574.

the context was open to interpretation and distortion, and a version of events which was acceptable and, therefore, in some sense 'true'. The evident contemporary parallels with the way that truth is constructed and manipulated today reinforce the need for us to continue to challenge and interrogate which truths we, too, are prepared to accept.

*Transactions of the RHS* 30 (2020), pp. 77–96 © The Author(s), 2020. Published by Cambridge University Press on behalf of the Royal Historical Society
doi:10.1017/S0080440120000043

# MONARCHS, TRAVELLERS AND EMPIRE IN THE PACIFIC'S AGE OF REVOLUTIONS*

*Prothero Lecture*

## By Sujit Sivasundaram

READ 5 JULY 2019

ABSTRACT. The Pacific has often been invisible in global histories written in the UK. Yet it has consistently been a site for contemplating the past and the future, even among Britons cast on its shores. In this lecture, I reconsider a critical moment of globalisation and empire, the 'age of revolutions' at the end of the eighteenth century and the start of the nineteenth century, by journeying with European voyagers to the Pacific Ocean. The lecture will point to what this age meant for Pacific islanders, in social, political and cultural terms. It works with a definition of the Pacific's age of revolutions as a surge of indigeneity met by a counter-revolutionary imperialism. What was involved in undertaking a European voyage changed in this era, even as one important expedition was interrupted by news from revolutionary Europe. Yet more fundamentally vocabularies and practices of monarchy were consolidated by islanders across the Pacific. This was followed by the outworkings of counter-revolutionary imperialism through agreements of alliance and alleged cessation. Such an argument allows me, for instance, to place the 1806 wreck of the *Port-au-Prince* within the Pacific's age of revolutions. This was an English ship used to raid French and Spanish targets in the Pacific, but which was stripped of its guns, iron, gunpowder and carronades by Tongans. To chart the trajectory from revolution and islander agency on to violence and empire is to appreciate the unsettled paths that gave rise to our modern world. This view foregrounds people who inhabited and travelled through the earth's oceanic frontiers. It is a global history from a specific place in the oceanic south, on the opposite side of the planet to Europe.

How might the Pacific be brought alive to an audience in central London and at the Royal Historical Society? It is an ocean that spans one-third of the surface of the Earth but which is so often seen as far away and as a definitive other. It is important to begin with the argument that the

*I am especially grateful to the audience at the Royal Historical Society for their questions. This paper was also presented at the University of Edinburgh and I also thank the audience there for comments. The anonymous reviewer made astute and deeply constructive observations. Margot Finn read the paper carefully. Andrew Spicer edited and commented on the paper very helpfully.

Pacific unsettles our sense of what counts as History or even how we plot History on the globe.[1]

Through the long past, Pacific islanders have narrated their histories not as texts but as oral performances or genealogies, charting their descent down generations and linking their selves and their rulers to stories of their arrival across the sea to their islands.[2] These histories disorient Western conceptions of time as an evenly measured background for the writing of history. Pacific genealogies also disrupt divisions between nature and humankind, for seas and islands are alive and changing. The perspective from which a genealogy is narrated in the Pacific is dynamic in relational terms: not simply an account of the dead but rather an organic relation between ancestors and descendants which is intensely embodied in the act of telling. I'm not a genealogist or a Pacific islander, but in the Pacific it is said that you walk backwards into the future while facing the past, and it is in this sense too that to write from the Pacific is to adopt a different practice; a decolonised practice.

Among those who led the way in decentring the European Pacific was Epeli Hau'ofa, the Tongan and Fijian anthropologist who has been inspirational for Pacific historians.[3] Hau'ofa, who died in 2009, sought to dislodge a view of the Pacific as a chain of islands in a faraway sea, a place which silently bore the brunt of Western invasion or global transformation. Instead he insisted that the Pacific was a 'sea of islands', a site of intense energy and connection which is indigenous. Meanwhile, recently deceased Fijian, Chinese, British and Australian historian Tracey Banivanua Mar persuasively argued that indigenous processes of decolonisation have persisted over a long period.[4] These scholars, among others, have challenged the invisibility that is imposed on the Pacific by historians in gatherings like ours. Thinking with the Pacific provides another lens for debates afoot in this country today about what it takes to decolonise the historical curriculum and research programme, especially as there are so few Pacific historians in the UK.[5]

---

[1] In making this claim I follow a rich vein of Pacific critique and historiography. See for instance, as a starting point, *Pacific Futures: Past and Present*, ed. Warwick Anderson, Miranda Johnson and Barbara Brookes (Honolulu, 2018). This collection is very useful on the nature of Pacific genealogies and has informed the following paragraphs.

[2] For more on this see Sujit Sivasundaram, 'Materialities in the Making of World Histories: South Asia and the South Pacific', in *Oxford Handbook of History and Material Culture: World Perspectives*, ed. Ivan Gaskell and Sarah Carter (Oxford, 2020), 507–28.

[3] Epeli Hau'ofa, 'Our Sea of Islands', *The Contemporary Pacific*, 6 (1994), 148–61.

[4] Tracey Banivanua Mar, *Decolonisation and the Pacific: Indigenous Globalisation and the Ends of Empire* (Cambridge, 2016).

[5] For a recent piece in a UK journal on what this means, see Matthew Fitzpatrick, 'Indigenous Australians and German Anthropology in the Era of "Decolonization"', *Historical Journal*, 63 (2020), 683–709. See also the very important work of Linda Tuhiwai-Smith, *Decolonising Methodologies: Research and Indigenous Peoples* (New York, 2012).

## I The Pacific's age of revolutions

Rather than a Pacific genealogy, what follows is an account of the age of revolutions in the Pacific Ocean. Accordingly, I propose in this lecture to reconceptualise and even repopulate a central analytical term of Western historiography and Western modernity: the age of revolutions.[6]

The uneven and transformative meetings between invaders and islanders which occurred and accelerated at the end of the eighteenth and start of the nineteenth centuries radically altered the Pacific. From the Pacific, the age of revolutions might be defined, following European historiography, as an age of empirical knowledge-gathering which birthed new kinds of sciences and ethnologies in this sea.[7] Simultaneously, a form of colonial history was born here too as an account of migration and relatedness between Europeans and islanders which was plotted on a linear calendar. This recontextualised prior ways of thinking about the past, exemplified by genealogies. In this age of revolutions, the Pacific also saw extensive exploration, settlement and disease; the arrival of new bodies and the dispossession of Islanders. The region saw the advent of new kinds of imperial alliances and takeovers.[8]

If all this cannot be denied, in critical engagement with these perspectives, the starting premise of this lecture is that it is important to attend to the creative agency of Pacific islanders, steeped in other ways of telling history. The age of revolutions in the Pacific was characterised first and foremost by a vibrant and surging indigeneity. Pacific peoples took ideas, material culture and structures from invaders and cast them anew in light of their own traditions, for instance of legitimacy, descent and rule, to mount a transformation in their politics, culture and society.[9] Invaders sought in turn to mount a counter-revolutionary imperialism. This never outdid indigenous creativity. The history that follows braids Western and indigenous agents, Outlanders and Islanders as they are called in the Pacific, textual and visual archives, and the indigenous as much as possible.

---

[6] The classic work on this period is E. J. Hobsbawm, *The Age of Revolution, 1789–1848* (New York, 1962). For the need to widen the compass and geography of this period see *The Age of Revolutions in Global Context, c.1760–1840*, ed. David Armitage and Sanjay Subrahmanyam (Basingstoke, 2010); and *The Routledge Companion to the French Revolution in World History*, ed. Alan Forrest and Matthias Middell (London and New York, 2016).

[7] For the history of science in the global age of revolutions see *Global Scientific Practice in an Age of Revolutions, 1750–1850*, ed. Patrick Manning and Daniel Rood (Pittsburgh, 2016).

[8] For surveys of Pacific history in this era see Nicholas Thomas, *Islanders: The Pacific in an Age of Empire* (New Haven, 2010); and David Igler, *The Great Ocean: Pacific Worlds from Captain Cook to the Gold Rush* (New York, 2013).

[9] This follows my forthcoming book, *Waves across the South: A New History of Revolution and Empire* (2020).

In arguing like this, the paper joins a vast literature on the age of revolutions.[10] Many of these works focus in on the Atlantic, and this dominant emphasis is in keeping with the sentiment of the Atlanticist and early historian of the age of revolutions R. R. Palmer, who wrote as long ago as 1959 that '[a]ll revolutions since 1800, in Europe, Latin America, Asia and Africa, have learned from the eighteenth-century Revolution of Western Civilization'.[11] Yet more recently, there is the work of Kate Fullagar and Mike McDonnell. They, together with a band of mostly Australian historians, have shown that in this revolutionary age what it meant be indigenous was pushed forward.[12]

A surge of indigeneity occurred through declarations of independence and definitions of sovereignty that reverberate until the present. This surge was then met with a counter-revolutionary imperialism. The meeting of these separate manoeuvres constituted the transformative intersections of this period at the end of the eighteenth century and the start of the nineteenth century, in the oceanic South, outside the Atlantic. The next section considers how to approach the history of European exploration in the Pacific through the lens of the age of revolutions.

## II  French voyages to the Pacific and the tumult of Europe

In October 1793, the French ships the *Recherche* and *Espérance* lay moored 25 miles outside the Dutch foothold of Surabaya, now the second largest city of Indonesia.[13] With two-thirds of the crew ill, mostly with scurvy,

---

[10] For critical commentary on the shape of the field of the Atlantic age of revolutions see Sarah Knott, 'Narrating the Age of Revolution', *The William and Mary Quarterly*, 73 (2016), 3–36. For some work on the Atlantic age of revolutions see Peter Linebaugh and Marcus Rediker, *The Many-Headed Hydra: Sailors, Slaves, Commoners, and the Hidden History of the Revolutionary Atlantic* (London and New York, 2000); Nathan Perl-Rosenthal, *Citizen Sailors: Becoming American in the Age of Revolution* (Cambridge, MA, 2015); Gabrielle Paquette, *Imperial Portugal in the Age of Atlantic Revolutions: The Luso-Brazilian World, c. 1770–1850* (Cambridge, 2013); and Paul E. Lovejoy, *Jihad in West Africa during the Age of Revolutions* (Athens, OH, 2016); and on Europe see Janet Polasky, *Revolutionaries without Borders: The Call to Liberty in the Atlantic World* (New Haven, 2015).

[11] R. R. Palmer, 'The Age of the Democratic Revolution', in *The Historian's Workshop: Original Essays by Sixteen Historians*, ed. L. P. Curtis (New York, 1970), 169–86, at 170.

[12] *Facing Empire: Indigenous Experiences in a Revolutionary Age*, ed. Kate Fullagar and Michael A. McDonnell (Baltimore, 2018).

[13] For details of the stand-off outside Surabaya and for detail which has fed into this section see John Dunmore, *French Explorers in the Pacific* (2 vols., Oxford, 1959–65), I, 328–31; Frank Horner, *Looking for La Pérouse: D'Entrecasteaux in Australia and the South Pacific, 1792–1793* (Carlton, Vic., 1995), ch. 14; Bruny d'Entrecasteaux, *Voyage to Australia and the Pacific 1791* (Carlton, Vic., 2001), trans. Edward Duyker and Maryse Duyker, introduction, xxx–xxxix; Roger Williams, *French Botany in the Enlightenment: The Ill-Fated Voyages of La Pérouse and his Rescuers* (Dordrecht, 2003), ch. 13; Seymour L. Chapin, 'The French Revolution in the South Seas: The Republican Spirit and the d'Entrecasteaux Expedition', *Proceedings of the Western Society for French History*, 17 (1990), 178–86; and Dianne Johnson, *Bruny*

they longed to be received into Surabaya. Alexandre d'Auribeau, now the commanding officer, very sick from an unknown ailment, sent out another boat, this time flying a white flag as a sign of peace. Eventually a Javanese chief brought out the latest supplement of news of the European age of revolutions: Louis XVI had been executed and France was at war with its European neighbours, including the Dutch. A republic had been declared. The way ahead for these ships was thus uncertain. All the men – and tellingly for the operation of gender, one disguised woman – were Dutch prisoners of war. The European family had been torn apart, and the diplomatic etiquette surrounding the provisioning of ships in the Pacific no longer held.

Months had to pass before the final fate of this expedition – which had left Europe under the command of Bruni d'Entrecasteaux in 1791, with the sanction of the National Assembly – was sealed. But when it finally happened it was dramatic proof of the impact of the European age of revolutions on a particular Pacific voyage. In the interim, the commanding officer had weighed up the possibility of sailing to republican Mauritius; there was the prospect of ship-board commotion and conflict between republican and royalist camps; and there was the rumour that the National Assembly had sent secret orders to some of the crew. As the Frenchmen's debts mounted, the *Recherche* and *Espérance* were sold at auction in Batavia at the end of 1794.[14]

The royalist d'Auribeau died of dysentery before republican envoys from Mauritius could take him captive as a traitor. Yet the workings-out of the age of revolutions in the specific conditions of this voyage continued further. After d'Auribeau's death the papers of the d'Entrecasteaux expedition were seized in St Helena by the British and were eventually kept in London under the protection of the final commander of the expedition, Élisabeth-Paul-Édouard de Rossel.[15] Rossel was a royalist. He based himself in London in these tumultuous years until the Treaty of Amiens in 1802, after which he returned to France. The republican Jacques-Julien Houtou de La Billardière, one of the surviving naturalists from the d'Entrecasteaux expedition, returned to Paris and ingeniously arranged for the expedition's natural history cases to be transferred there.[16]

---

*d'Entrecasteaux and His Encounter with Tasmanian Aborigines: From Provence to Recherche Bay* (Lawson, NSW, 2012), ch. 14. Most recently, *Collecting in the South Seas: The Voyage of Bruni d'Entrecasteaux, 1791–1794*, ed. Bronwen Douglas et al. (Leiden, 2018).

[14] Johnson, *Bruny d'Entrecasteaux*, 72.

[15] D'Entrecasteaux, *Voyage to Australia*, xxxvi.

[16] See M. La Billardière, *An Account of a Voyage in search of La Pérouse, undertaken by order of the Constituent Assembly of France and Performed in the Years 1791, 1792 and 1793 translated from the French* (2 vols., 1800), I, xix. For the intriguing and diverse paths taken by the collections of this expedition, see *Collecting in the South Seas*, ed. Douglas et al.

Despite this example of the impact of the Western age of revolutions in the Pacific, there has barely been any discussion in the historical literature of what the age of revolutions looks like from the Pacific. One could argue that French Pacific voyages nicely illustrate the phases of the European age of revolutions. The d'Entrecasteaux expedition that ended in Surabaya was sandwiched between two others: on one side was an expedition under the command of Comte La Pérouse (1785–8) and with the authority of an absolute monarch, Louis XVI; and on the other was the expedition of Nicolas Baudin (1800–3), under instruction by Napoleon.[17] As well as the change in patrons, the transition from La Pérouse and d'Entrecasteaux to Baudin is itself revealing: unlike the two aristocrats who went before him, Baudin was the first French captain not of noble birth to sail through the Pacific. Another path through which the politics of the European age of revolutions is apparent is in a key aim that drove the d'Entrecasteaux voyage, and in which it failed too. This was to solve the puzzle of the lost voyage of La Pérouse which preceded it. Unfounded rumours spread in France that it had gone missing because of the action of the anti-republican English, who had just formed a convict settlement in Port Jackson – Sydney.[18]

The disappearance of this official French voyage served as a much-repeated tale, an affront to French glory. In the end, the mystery was solved not by a Frenchman but by an Irish private trader in the 1820s, Peter Dillon, who took news not to London but to Calcutta.[19] It later became clear that the expedition had come to its end in the midst of a hurricane. The fact that it was Dillon, rather than d'Entrecasteaux, who found the first inklings of the evidence points to the rise of the British and ports like Calcutta over the oceanic South by the second decade of the nineteenth century.

### III  To be a king in Tonga

Let us then return to the d'Entrecasteaux voyage but with a different footing; a footing in what is now Tonga. Captain Cook had been here in the 1770s. In Tonga, while in search of the lost La Pérouse, explorer

---

[17] For analysis of the relationship between these three voyages see Nicole Starbuck, *Baudin, Napoleon and the Exploration of Australia* (2013), introduction.

[18] Leslie R. Marchant, 'La Pérouse, Jean-François de Galaup (1741–1788)', *Australian Dictionary of Biography*, National Centre of Biography, Australian National University, http://adb.anu.edu.au/biography/la-perouse-jean-francois-de-galaup-2329/text3029, accessed 4 October 2013.

[19] For Peter Dillon see J. W. Davidson, *Peter Dillon of Vanikoro: Chevalier of the South Seas*, ed. O. H. K. Spate (Melbourne, 1975); and J. W. Davidson, 'Peter Dillon: The Voyages of the *Calder* and *St. Patrick*', in *Pacific Islands Portraits*, ed. J. W. Davidson and Deryck Scarr (Canberra, 1970), 9–30.

d'Entrecasteaux had some of his most charged ethnographic encounters.[20] And d'Entercasteaux was particularly interested in political arrangements. European voyagers like him – and this includes both the British and the French, and both republican and royalist observers – sought to theorise Tonga's politics. D'Entrecasteaux wrote, for instance: 'I believe, like Cook, that this government has a lot in common with the old feudal regime, where the inconveniences increase in proportion to the weaknesses of the principal chief.'[21] D'Entrecasteaux held to the view that anarchy was especially evident in the prevalence in Tonga of theft, which arose from the insecurity of property. For the chiefs owned all the property and could demand from their inferiors anything that they wished. Yet the riddle which plagued d'Entrecasteaux was this: who was the monarch of Tonga?

Between Cook's visit and his own, he would have expected that the throne would have passed to Fuanunuiava, the son of the man denoted as sovereign by Cook.[22] Perhaps it was because of Fuanunuiava's youth, he pondered, that this had not occurred. D'Entrecasteaux also puzzled over the fact that Tiné, whom he now took to be the head of state and called queen, could not confer the throne on her death to her immediate relations. For d'Entrecasteaux the complicated rules of succession were part of the problem. There was too much confusion in 'distinguishing men who exercise power and to whom respect is given'.[23] Here was a man who wished for authority – but for the kind of authority upheld by rules and constitutions and hemmed in by a market in trade, land and familiar gender norms. D'Entrecasteaux's naturalist, La Billardière, wrote, in similar terms to d'Entrecasteaux, of 'King Tuoobou' or Tupou of Tonga.[24] Tupou was in fact the Tu'i Kanokupolu, one of three paramount titles in Tonga; the highest ranking however held another title, Tu'i Tonga. Fuanunuiava was named as Tu'i Tonga in 1795. La Billardière also observed how Queen Tiné was conscious of her privileges as the paramount authority on Tonga. Inferior chiefs including Tupou were obliged to pay their respects by taking her right foot to their heads.[25]

Europeans, who themselves were reworking politics sought to work out politics in this island world by searching for monarchs and trying

[20] For a perspective from Tongan historiography see *Essays on the History of Tonga*, ed. Peter Suren (3 vols., Nuku'alofa, Tonga, 2001–6), II and III.

[21] D'Entrecasteaux, *Voyage to Australia*, 186.

[22] For Cook's interest in the royal line of Tonga see Robert Langdon, 'The Maritime Explorers', in *The Friendly Islands: A History of Tonga*, ed. Noel Rutherford (Melbourne, 1977), 50–1.

[23] D'Entrecasteaux, *Voyage to Australia*, 184.

[24] La Billardière, *An Account*, II, 116.

[25] *Ibid.*, 128.

to fit Pacific societies against categorisations of feudalism or royalism. Yet d'Entreacasteaux's portrait of Tonga reveals more about his culture and its paradigms than of the Tonga of this period.[26] Until the arrival of Europeans, there were no European-style kings and queens. In Tonga, chiefly status was determined by a rank prescribed by society, on the basis of descent from a chosen ancestor, where age and gender were valued as in Europe, but where sisterhood was ranked as a higher privilege than brotherhood in questions of succession. The differences between chiefs and others did not lie in questions of what labour they undertook, if any, and so the language of class that d'Entrecasteaux used to observe Tonga was misplaced. Objects were not marketised and did not retain a value on the basis of the work that had been put into making them. Rather, value was determined primarily by the rank and status of the creator of the object; it was no wonder that Tongans wished to possess European objects. Yet those whom the Tongans called *papālangis*, or men from the sky, brought to these islands a new language of politics and organisation and this was creatively adopted. In this region, these changes counted as a consolidation of monarchy whereas elsewhere the period could see monarchies torn down. European weapons in particular made early nineteenth-century Tonga a place characterised by intense wars. Chiefs quarrelled over the arrival of European ships, trying to attract them to their harbours. And those who resided at ports inevitably did better than those based elsewhere. As Europeans sought for kings and queens, islanders reinvented their politics.

In Tonga, with the arrival of a range of European settlers in the 1790s, including traders, evangelical missionaries as well as those who had escaped from the convict station in Australia, there came a long civil war between rival chiefs. The investiture of the paramount chief, Tu'i Tonga, was laid aside and there was a conflict between the lineages of the Tu'i Tonga and Tu'i Kanokupolu.[27] Chiefs fought over tribute and connections to missionaries and other Europeans. The wars between chiefs were attended by the spread of European diseases and weapons, and the fleeing of many chiefs to neighbouring Fiji or Samoa. One chief fled with his wife to British Sydney.[28] In the midst of these radical changes, there was a loss of cohesion and the chiefly system of rule was in crisis. It was in this context that a new monarchic ideal was firmed up.

---

[26] This paragraph relies on Christine Ward Gailey, *Kinship to Kingship: Gender, Hierarchy and State Formation in the Tongan Islands* (Austin, TX, 1987).

[27] *Ibid.*, 178ff. For the history of this period in Tonga, and for further discussion of material below, see I. C. Campbell, *Island Kingdom: Tonga, Ancient and Modern* (Christchurch, 1992).

[28] See *Essays*, ed. Suren, III, 187ff.

The work of Protestant missionaries is notable here. A new age dawned in Tonga with the conversion of the uninstalled paramount chief Taufaʻahau to Protestantism through the work of Wesleyan missionaries who arrived in 1822. Taufaʻahau changed the political make-up of Tonga, transforming it from a competitive set of chiefdoms into a united monarchic polity. Taufaʻahau took the name George I at his baptism in 1831 and used the support of British missionaries to unify Tonga. The change in religion signified a drastic change in political organisation: for where chiefs had received their sanction from lineages tied to gods, the spread of Christianity now brought a different relationship between political and sacred authority. Now the missionaries were the purveyors of the Word, and George I was the keeper of the law. Taufaʻahau's opponents feared that soon the missionaries themselves would become chiefs. Many of George I's followers adopted Christianity, though there continued to be a great deal of wavering and movement in and out of Christian faith and church attendance. George I boasted: 'I am the only Chief on the Island … When I turn they will all turn.'[29] He was right: his monarchical line has survived till today, priding itself on never being formally colonised. This shows how indigenous reworkings of politics in the age of revolutions were successful. Tonga is a microcosm of changes afoot elsewhere in an Pacific where monarchy was also consolidated.

## IV Tongans raiding Europe

As the argument is deepened further, attention is paid in what follows to the specific material and cultural dynamics that attended this moment of political transformation. There were mutual exchanges but also blockages and creative reinventions which allowed Pacific peoples to craft the modern in light of the old and within the context of the age of revolutions. Tongans raided the ships of Europe, quite literally at times, to find their own path. This is especially evident in an iconic moment in Tonga's history which is often retold.

Fifteen years had passed since d'Entrecasteaux's time in Tonga when William Mariner was taken captive in the Tongan islands, at the age of fifteen, and to the north of where d'Entrecasteaux had made his observations. The vessel in which he arrived in 1806 was rather different to the state-owned French and British vessels used by d'Entrecasteaux and Cook. The *Port-au-Prince* was an English privateer-whaler, which was formerly French, and which was now deployed to raid French or Spanish vessels. The ship was 'nearly 500 tons, 96 men, and mounting 24 long nine and twelve pounders, besides 8 twelve-pound carronades

---

[29] Gailey, *Kinship to Kingship*, 179.

on the quarter-deck'.[30] The sailors on board the *Port-au-Prince* were allowed to keep their booty. In the words of recent historians from Tonga, the crew of this vessel behaved 'like pirates and robbers'.[31] It is important to first establish that these Europeans were raiders of an unprecedented kind.

Yet this vessel the *Port-au-Prince* was taken over by about 300 Tongans who went aboard the ship and attacked the surprised crew. They eventually grounded it. Gunpowder, carronades and stripped iron were taken ashore, and after the ship had been summarily looted of everything that was deemed valuable it was burnt.[32] About half of its crew were massacred by the Tongans in what followed. According to Mariner, the attack was led by a Hawai'ian, who had probably arrived in Tonga on an American ship.[33] And it was in this way that William Mariner's time in Tonga began. Mariner wrote of the noise let off by the guns on board:

> In the evening they set fire to her, in order to get more easily afterwards at the iron work. All the great guns were loaded, and as they began to be heated by the general conflagration they went off, one after another, producing a terrible panic among all the natives.[34]

The survivors, their skills and what were looted were recycled by Tongans in the wars ravaging Tonga, before the consolidation of George I's monarchical state.[35] So even the people on board became goods in Tonga. The story that was later told in Tonga is that the future George I, then about nine years old, was himself involved in the raid on the *Port-au-Prince* and nearly drowned in the whale oil in the hold of the vessel.[36] Mariner was to become a key asset. He was very much liked by the chief Finau 'Ulukalala II, who had raided the ship, and he was adopted by one of 'Ulukalala's wives, marking his incorporation into Tongan society. Another of the survivors of the *Port-au-Prince* was serving as 'prime minister' to a chief on Vava'u as late as 1830.[37]

---

[30] William Mariner, *An Account of the Natives of the Tongan Islands in the South Pacific Ocean* (2 vols., London, 1817), I, xx, footnote. For some details of Mariner's time in Tonga see also I. C. Campbell, *Gone Native in Polynesia: Captivity Narratives and Experiences from the South Pacific* (Westport, CT, 1998), 52–9.

[31] *Essays*, ed. Suren, III, 71. See also, Nelson Eustis, *The King of Tonga* (Adelaide, 1997), 20–1.

[32] Mariner, *An Account*, I, 58–62.

[33] *Ibid.*, I, 46 and see also *Essays*, ed. Suren, III, 67.

[34] Mariner, *An Account*, I, 61.

[35] See N. Gunson, 'The Coming of the Foreigners', in *Friendly Islands: A History of Tonga*, ed. N. Rutherford (Melbourne, 1978), 90–113, at 102.

[36] Campbell, *Gone Native in Polynesia*, 54; *Essays*, ed. Suren, III, 69–70.

[37] See J. Orlebar, *A Midshipman's Journal on Board H.M.S. Seringapatam during the Year 1830*, ed. Melvin J. Voigt (San Diego, 1976), 72. Gunson estimates that there were 'eighty aliens' from Europe and 'the more distant Pacific islands' who resided in Tonga from 1796 to 1826: 'Coming of the Foreigners', 90.

From his base in the Ha'apai islands 'Ulukalala, wished to attack the political centre of these islands in Tongatapu. In seizing the *Port-au-Prince* he was arming himself for his wars with the ruling powers in the main island. Mariner together with fifteen other Britons participated in the raid that followed on Tongatapu, undertaken using a fleet of canoes and the carronades looted from the *Port-au-Prince*.[38] In the end, one of the most important forts at Nuku'alofa, now the capital of Tonga, fell into the hands of 'Ulukalala's forces. Mariner described the fort as constructed of wickerwork supported by posts, to make 9-foot-high fences; it had stood for eleven years but was now ravaged. It was a truly awful rout: 'The conquerors, club in hand, entered the place in several quarters and slew all they met, men, women and children.'[39] The inhabitants were awestruck by the new weapons used by their assailants. They described balls as if they were alive, entering houses, going around their dwellings looking for someone to kill, rather than exploding straight away. While the battle was in progress, 'Ulukalala sat himself in an English chair taken off the *Port-au-Prince* and surveyed the scene from the reef.[40] After this attack, his further attempt to take the fort in Vava'u harbour was not as successful.

When at peace, 'Ulukalala took the opportunity to learn about the outside world from Mariner, and one topic that was particularly interesting was that of politics. 'Ulukalala wished to be the king of England. This again highlights the central argument that this period saw an assertion of indigenous political agency in Islanders' adoption of the new in light of the old:

'Oh, that the gods would make me king of England! [T]here is not an island in the whole world, however small, but that I would then subject to my power: the King of England does not deserve the dominion he enjoys; possessed of so many great ships, why does he suffer such petty islands as those of Tonga continually to insult his people with acts of treachery? Where [*sic*] I he, would I send tamely to *ask* for yams and pigs? No, I would come with the *front of battle*; and with *the thunder of Bolotane* [the noise of the guns of Britain].'[41]

Mariner finally escaped in 1810. In 1832, Mafihape, Mariner's alleged adoptive mother in Tonga, sent him an intriguing letter now in an Australian archive.[42] In her letter, written or probably transcribed for her by someone very familiar with Tonga, she asks Mariner to send a ship with a son whom she could adopt:

---

[38] For an account of the other survivors from the *Port-au-Prince* see *Essays*, ed. Suren, III, 74. There were twenty-six survivors, excluding the Hawai'ians.

[39] Mariner, *An Account*, I, 101.

[40] *Ibid.*, 100.

[41] *Ibid.*, 420.

[42] For discussion of this, see Nigel Statham, 'Mafihape's Letter to William Mariner (1832)', *Journal of Pacific History*, 43 (2008), 341–66.

> If you have genuine affection [for me] it would be wonderful if you could send your younger brother, if you have one – or your son, if you have one, so I can see him, and also so that you be shown, in the Lord, to be manly – if you are so determined not to come yourself and see me. He can come and live here instead.[43]

Mafihape herself had by this time converted, but wanted Mariner to know that she was 'very poorly off'. Despite the spread of Christianity, and its associated trappings of paper and writing, as also new conceptions of behaviour, Mafihape still hoped to utilise the customs of chieftaincy, where chiefs adopted powerful sons, to circumvent her lowly situation.

Mariner could not read Mafihape's letter, having forgotten most of his Tongan. He complained that its 'orthography' was in too unfamiliar a form, indicating the impact of the English missionaries perhaps.[44] After returning to England, he gave up his life of adventure, became a stockbroker in London, married and fathered eleven children and, rather unfittingly, drowned in Surrey Canal at the age of fifty-three.[45] In the Pacific, meanwhile, there are also still people who claim the name Mariner. As for Mariner's own end in the canal, a speculative Tongan theory that I heard when I was there is that Mariner committed suicide, being unable in the end to come to terms with his life in England.[46]

Mariner's account of his travels was published for him by a doctor John Martin. The image facing the title page is a full-length view of Mariner dressed in Tongan clothes and bare-bodied above the waist (Figure 1). Mariner had thus straddled worlds. A product of the European age of revolutions, and its commitment to global war at any price, he had been taken captive to fight in a series of other wars, which were Tongan tussles for a monarchy and indigenous political assertion. The dispersal of European weapons was critical to the story around the *Port-au-Prince*; it is appropriate that three of the cannons from the *Port-au-Prince* are today placed in front of the site of the British High Commission in Tonga (Figure 2).

## V Aotearoa and monarchy before Waitangi

Once monarchism had been articulated like this by islanders across the Southern Pacific and in the context of prior cultures of descent, it was an

---

[43] From the translation in *ibid.*, 353.

[44] In a letter dated London 8 May 1837 to J. H. Cook who brought him the letter he writes: 'I regret that I have been able to translate very little of my kind Mother's Epistle – partly from having forgotten the language, but principally from the orthography differing materially from that used by me.' This letter is pasted at the front of Mariner, *An Account*, I; a copy is at the Mitchell Library, Sydney (hereafter MLS), C 797 v.I.

[45] Campbell *Gone Native in Polynesia*, 59.

[46] See also *Essays*, ed. Suren, III, 144.

Figure 1 'Mr Mariner in the Costume of the Tonga Islands', from William Mariner, *An Account of the Natives of the Tonga Islands* (London, 1817) (E.30.3). Reproduced by kind permission of the Syndics of Cambridge University Library.

idea that was open to political use. Islanders could manipulate monarchy in a contest with the invaders who were becoming increasingly familiar on these shores. These invaders, and the British in particular, wished

Figure 2 Cannons from the *Port-au-Prince* at the British High Commission, Tonga. (Author's photograph)

in turn to overtake monarchism with an authoritarian imperialism; they wanted to be bigger kings. In this manner, as the period wore on, the debate about political organisation opened up a space for the rise of the British Empire and an Islander response to it which was creative and at times anti-colonial. If the age of revolutions is defined as indigenous assertion meeting European invasion, this dynamic carried on in this next phase as British government tightened and as indigenous peoples fought and organised themselves. The argument is now illustrated from a different site, from Aotearoa or New Zealand.[47]

Māori were mobile peoples who undertook war in order to restore their integrity and status.[48] If war could not be undertaken against offenders it could be conducted against distant non-kin, to this end of

---

[47] The broad outline of the history of New Zealand which follows draws on Keith Sinclair, *The Oxford Illustrated History of New Zealand* (Auckland, 1990) and M. N. Smith, *New Zealand: A Concise History* (Cambridge, 2005). It has also been heavily influenced by the revisionist reading of this period and the 'musket wars' in Angela Ballara, *Taua: 'Musket Wars', 'Land Wars' or Tikanga?: Warfare in Maori Society in the Early Nineteenth Century* (Auckland, 2003), as well as the work of Judith Binney, for instance *The Legacy of Guilt: A Life of Thomas Kendall* (Wellington, 2005) and *Stories without End: Essays, 1795–2010* (Wellington, 2010). Among more recent works, see Tony Ballantyne, *Entanglements of Empire: Missionaries, Maori, and the Question of the Body* (Durham, NC, 2014), and *New Zealand and the Sea: New Historical Perspectives*, ed. Frances Steel (Wellington, 2018).

[48] This follows the argument in Ballara, *Taua*.

restoration. The arrival of Europeans expanded these customary forms of politics in new directions, making wars more intense and wider in their radius. As in Tonga, the appropriation of European weapons was significant. Newer styles of war, sometimes termed 'muskets wars', unified and concentrated power. They generated an unprecedented number of fatalities and a decline in population. But they transformed what already existed by way of conflict, rather than giving rise to a simple fatal impact with no room for indigenous response.

The physical power of muskets was not the sole determining factor in these wars. Some historians have cast the new culture of the potato as being equally significant, in providing the means to keep long-range war parties fed.[49] In the opinion of the first British Resident of New Zealand in 1837, 'there seems to be good reason to doubt whether their wars were less sanguinary before Fire Arms were introduced'.[50] Established military tactics involving close combat evolved in order to accommodate the new long-distance weapons.[51] The symbolism of these muskets was critical too. Particular chiefs who acquired weapons were cast as great leaders and warriors even though they were operating within pre-existent modes of righting wrongs. As an example of the attribution of monarchy, the artist Augustus Earle drew 'King George' or 'Shulitea' (Te Uri-Ti), who served as his friend and protector in New Zealand.[52]

Gradually, over the decades that followed, and beyond the signing of the Treaty of Waitangi in 1840, the concept of the Māori monarch appeared as a result of this entanglement between old and new, the Pacific and Europe. The 'King Movement', or Kīngitanga, appointed the first Māori king in the late 1850s and opposed the take-up of ancestral land by the British Empire. It declared the boundaries of the Kīngitanga, or kingdom, in 1858. The movement expected to govern alongside the settler state. Yet it is possible to trace the longer ancestry of this commitment to monarchy. Missionaries reported how the concept of monarchy was already being discussed by Māori prior to the 1840 Treaty of Waitangi.[53] Iconic fighters also show the evolution of notions of leadership and monarchy.

---

[49] See James Belich, *The New Zealand Wars and the Victorian Interpretation of Racial Conflict* (Auckland, 1986).

[50] James Busby, British Resident at New Zealand, to the Secretary of State, dated the Bay of Islands, 16 June 1837, MLS: MLMSS 1668 (typescript copy), 206.

[51] Ballara, *Taua*, 400ff.

[52] See Augustus Earle, *A Narrative of a Nine Months' Residence* (n.p., 1832), 53–4. For Earle's images of 'King George' see 'King George, N Zealand costume', watercolour, 1828, National Library of Australia: PIC Solander Box A37 T122 NK 12/84 and 'The residence of Shulitea, chief of Kororadika, Bay of Islands', watercolour, 1827, National Library of Australia: PIC Solander Box A36 T109 NK 12/71.

[53] Samuel Marsden was a key figure in the origins of the missionary movement in New Zealand. For some context about his ideology, see Andrew Sharp, *The World, the Flesh*

The so-called 'Māori Napoleon', Hongi Hika (1772?–1828), was an early initiate to the power of European muskets and utilised them in wars in the Bay of Islands district of North Island.[54] Hongi arrived in London in 1820 and created quite a stir, accompanied by the evangelical Thomas Kendall and an aide, Waikato. Tellingly he was presented to the British monarch, George IV. According to one mid-nineteenth-century chronicler, he is said to have observed: 'There is only one king in England, there shall be only one king in New Zealand.'[55] When he returned to New Zealand, he came with gifts and patronage and a personal bond with the British Crown. This allowed him to immediately mount a series of campaigns to consolidate his power. He traded many of his presents in Sydney on the way back to New Zealand, preferring muskets, powder and shot. (He had hundreds of muskets in his hands when he returned to New Zealand.) He retained a suit of armour which was presented to him.[56] His journey to Britain was in a sense a validation of his kingship. A similar story might be traced in relation to another iconic figure of this period, Te Rauparaha, where once again contact with Europeans expanded the reach of existent customs of politics and war.[57]

To move one step further with this analysis, the arrival of British bureaucracy and legislation took the guise of an attempt to protect Māori from the Europeans' depredations against them. However, in practice these modes of governance aimed at overtaking extant notions of chieftaincy and monarchism. The flux in concepts of rule and monarchy is evident in the following sequence of evidence. The British appointed a Resident to New Zealand, the Tory James Busby, in 1833. Busby was seen by Māori as the British 'king's man', just as men-of-war were called the 'king's ships' and their sailors the 'king's warriors'.[58] Busby arranged for a Māori flag, previously used by the missionaries, to be flown by vessels built in New Zealand entering Sydney, as 'the Flag of

---

*and the Devil: The Life and Opinions of Samuel Marsden in England and the Antipodes* (Auckland, 2016).

[54] Details of Hongi's biography draw from Angela Ballara, 'Hongi Hika', in *Dictionary of New Zealand Biography, Te Ara – The Encyclopaedia of New Zealand*, www.teara.govt.nz/en/biographies/1h32/hongi-hika, accessed 10 September 2014.

[55] *Memoirs of the Life and Labours of the Rev. Samuel Marsden*, ed. J. B. Marsden (Cambridge, 2011), 142.

[56] From Ballara, 'Hongi Hika'; also Smith, *New Zealand*, 33–4.

[57] *Life and Times of Te Rauparaha by His Son Tamihana Te Rauparaha*, ed. Peter Butler (Waiura, Martinborough, 1980). For a critique of the iconic status of Te Rauparaha see Ballara, *Taua*, 34.

[58] For references to the king's ships and king's warriors see Earle, *Narrative of a Nine Months Residence*, 164–5. For another reference to the king's ships see Richard A. Cruise, *Journal of a Ten Months' Residence in New Zealand, 1820*, ed. A. G. Bagnall (Christchurch, 1957), 27.

an Independent State'.[59] A declaration of Māori independence was also signed by fifty-two chiefs by the end of the 1830s in the name of 'The United Tribes of New Zealand'.[60] This was conceived by Busby as a 'Magna Carta of New Zealand Independence'.[61]

The scene was set for the controversial Treaty of Waitangi of 1840. A change in the language of politics had come to pass in slow motion. This happened through the evolution of established concepts such as *iwi* (denoting people of common descent), *hapu* (meaning groups subordinate to chiefs, fighting as units) and intra-tribal identity and war and Māori attempts to respond to British ideas. It also involved attempts, not fully successful, at British control of the structures of Māori organisation and independence.

## VI On the age of revolutions

The argument may now be summarised. Pacific cultures had long-established customs of political arrangement around hereditary chieftaincy, notions of kinship, genealogy, historical memory and ceremonial decision-making. It was into this world that European voyagers arrived. In an age of 'democratic' revolutions, these travellers sought out the monarchs of Tonga, for instance, and their discussion of the politics of the Pacific was supercharged by the political changes in Europe.

Yet, the intent of this lecture instead was to highlight the space that then opened up between Pacific islanders and Europeans in the age of revolutions – making it possible for the Pacific and its peoples to craft this period of transition. Pacific islanders asserted their agency, and this response characterises the Pacific's age of revolutions. The spread of weapons – for instance, think of Hongi's muskets – the skills brought by settlers – for example, William Mariner as an asset himself – or the dispersal of other sorts of material culture – think about flags – all generated a crisis point in chiefly systems of organisation, and in turn the opportunity to consolidate newer monarchic lines out of the old. This change was not a smooth or unidirectional one – as is evident in the way the *Port-au-Prince* was physically raided or how Hongi travelled to Britain and then came back to orchestrate war.

---

[59] For the process of choosing the flag see Extract of a Letter from the British Resident of New Zealand to the Colonial Secretary, 22 March 1834, MLS: Governors' Despatches and Correspondence, A1267/13 (typescript copy), pp. 1417–18. For commentary on the flag and on a possible constitution see James Busby, British Resident at New Zealand, dated 16 June 1837, Bay of Islands to Secretary of State, MLS: MLMSS 1668 (typescript copy), 207.

[60] For the 1835 treaty see 'A Declaration of Independence of New Zealand', in Claudia Orange, *The Treaty of Waitangi* (Wellington, 1976), app. 1, 256.

[61] James Busby to Alexander Busby, 10 December 1835, Waitangi, MLS: MLMSS 1349 (typescript copy), 97.

The arrival of Christianity in turn provided an ideological foundation for consolidating newer forms of politics in the Pacific, though the relics of older ideas of chieftaincy, encompassing notions of kinship as much as military custom, were never obliterated – as is evident for instance in Mafihape's letter. The gaps, ignorances and at times wilful misconstruals were politically useful for the ascent of the British Empire, even as treaties were made with indigenous peoples, allowing Britons to become the dominant authorities over the Pacific's kings; the bigger and more militarily powerful kings. If islanders' characteristic agency counts as definitive of the age of revolutions, this imperial manoeuvre was a counter-revolution. Yet the relics of older ideas of chieftaincy, now become kingship, were still evident in the later nineteenth century and could serve as a ground of resistance – for instance in the Kīngitanga movement which became violent by the early 1860s.

If this is the argument about the Pacific's age of revolutions, it is important to return to the wider claims at the start of my lecture on decolonising history. It is worth noting here that this very transition between old and new, between different kinds of materials, oral and printed, and between indigenous peoples and Western writers characterised the making of History itself at the end of this age of revolutions.

## VII  History in the Pacific age of revolutions and decolonisation today

Among a series of histories of the Māori that appeared in the later nineteenth century was John White's six-volume *Ancient History of the Maori* (1887–90), which was sponsored by the colonial state in New Zealand, and which followed White's having been editor of a Māori newspaper.[62] White asked Māori to fill the books that he provided with information about Māori knowledge; he paid £5 for a full book and £3 for one which was partly full.[63] Aperahama (or Abraham) Taonui wrote his genealogy in such a notebook of forty-three pages for White.[64] In

[62] John White, *The Ancient History of the Maori: His Mythology and Traditions* (6 vols., Wellington, 1887–90).

[63] D. R. Simmons, *The Great New Zealand Myth: A Study of the Discovery and Origin of the Traditions of the Maori* (Wellington, 1976), 113.

[64] The biographical information here is taken from Ruth Miriam Ross, 'Taonui, Aperahama (c.1815–1882)', in *An Encyclopaedia of New Zealand*, ed. A. H. McLintock (3 vols., Wellington, 1966), III, 347–8 and also Judith Binney, 'Aperahama Taonui', in *Dictionary of New Zealand Biography* II (1993), republished www.teara.govt.nz/en/biographies/2t7/taonui-aperahama, accessed 10 April 2014. On one telling, which is unreferenced, Taonui was the first to write down a genealogy in 1843; see Rāwiri Taonui, 'Whakapapa – genealogy – What is whakapapa?', in *Te Ara – The Encyclopaedia of New Zealand*, www.teara.govt.nz/en/whakapapa-genealogy/page-5, accessed 10 June 2015. For the manuscript see D. R. Simmons, 'The Taonui Manuscript', *Record of the Auckland Institute and Museum*, 12

corresponding with White, Tanoui showed an eagerness for the stuff of writing, asking for ink on a couple of occasions: 'As I have no ink to write Genealogy books with this is why there has been nothing for you.'[65] He came to terms with the lack of materials in the context of why access to Māori cultural traditions was confined to the initiated: 'It is impossible to write the explanations and meanings of the many waiata and the whaka-tauki and the other things which you have requested.'

This letter, dated 8 September 1856, is composed of shreds of torn paper with uneven edges. Taonui's coming to terms with the materiality of writing was thus occurring side by side with his coming to terms with how to integrate Māori cosmology and genealogy alongside and within Judaeo-Christian History, within empiricist Western history. It is through processes like this that came at the end of the age of revolutions that the colonial printed history of Māori was born, and yet within it and within White's confused text one can see the stamp of the oral. White cut and pasted genealogies to construct linear time.

The making of History alongside the tussle over the concepts of the age of revolutions is also apparent in how Taonui called in 1855 for a 'Mekana Tata', changing his sense of customary authority and possession of land and resources in the light of British political thought. 'Mekana Tata' is a transliteration of Magna Carta and here is his explanation of what this means:

> The Barons of England (that is the chief of those days as we are now in New Zealand) met and demanded of this King certain terms which they required him to sign, some of which were that every man should enjoy his own property, and that the Chiefs of the King should not take anything by force, unless the law allowed it. This document which the King signed was called 'Magna Carta'. From this has come all England's good. Now, if the Chiefs agree to any thing this night in the assembly, we might call it 'Mekana Tata'.[66]

The interlocking of imperialism and monarchy is a story of counter-revolution that followed indigenous creativity and agency; an account of how the possibilities of this period, the age of revolutions, had opponents who were elites and imperialists. Following the story of White and the agenda of decolonising history, it might be added that the opponents were colonial historians too. Such an argument is in keeping with a broader literature on the global history of this period which stresses

---

(1975), 57–82. A more recent piece on Taonui is Laura Kamau, 'Mekana Tata: Magna Carta and the Political Thought of Aperahama Taonui', in *Magna Carta and New Zealand: History, Politics and Law in New Zealand*, ed. Stephen Winter and Chris Jones (Auckland, 2017), 153–60.

[65] Letter dated Waima, 8 September 1856, from Taonui to White, 'Letters in Maori from Aperahama Taonui', MS-Papers-0075-008A, Alexander Turnbull Library, Wellington, New Zealand. Translation as in the archive. I discuss this whole episode further in Sivasundaram, 'Materialities'.

[66] Cited in Kamau, 'Mekana Tata', 153.

the contradictory results of this age, with its differing articulations of what counts as revolution and the differing outcomes of revolutions. Yet there is a specific feature to this history: for most writers and observers of the time and for pretty much the whole of the vast historiography of the age of revolutions today, the Pacific does not count. It is not a place of significant political, cultural and intellectual agency at this critical period of transition around 1800. It is instead a place to authorise the West's history and its invention of the politics of the modern; and for White it was a place to gather myths.

Where Mariner came ashore in Tonga, when I visited at the end of 2017, there was nobody on the beach. A monument to the *Port-au-Prince* massacre was being overtaken by tropical vegetation; in the water lay the carcass of a dead pig and along the shoreline were some plastic bottles. If this lecture has been about an age which saw unprecedented change in the Pacific, another time of unprecedented change awaits. Weather patterns and changes in vegetation are a topic of constant conversation in Tonga. There are now more Tongans who live overseas than in the islands. If the Pacific shaped the age of revolutions in the late eighteenth and early nineteenth centuries, my prediction is that it is a place to watch once again for the human future. To decolonise history today is to respond to indigenous creativity. Additionally, now more than ever before, at a time of climate emergency it is important to take account of both the land and the sea and how they are changing. Such a perspective is vital for the Pacific's next age of revolutions.

*Transactions of the RHS* 30 (2020), pp. 97–117 © The Author(s), 2020. Published by Cambridge University Press on behalf of the Royal Historical Society
doi:10.1017/S0080440120000055

# CHILDREN AGAINST SLAVERY: JUVENILE AGENCY AND THE SUGAR BOYCOTTS IN BRITAIN

By Kathryn Gleadle
and
*The Whitfield Prize Winner*
Ryan Hanley

ABSTRACT. In late eighteenth- and early nineteenth-century Britain, many contemporaries observed a striking phenomenon: that children were especially active in the boycotts of sugar produced by enslaved people. First-hand accounts often suggested that children's activism was unilateral and unmediated, whereas historians of British abolitionism have tended to assume that children were passive recipients of antislavery literature and adult influence. Engaging with both the historiography on British abolitionism and the new histories of childhood, this article examines the nature of juvenile engagement within the sugar boycotts. Collecting together some of the extensive but dispersed evidence of juvenile antislavery across the country, and focusing upon a case study of the Plymley household of Shropshire during the early 1790s, we explore the intricacies of children's involvement. Children's agency, we argue, needs to be understood as a specific, historicised phenomenon. Adults often chose to represent children's abolitionist activities as self-determined, for their participation in the boycotts affirmed both adult positions and their own child-rearing practices. However, whilst adults frequently solicited particular types of juvenile response, children often responded independently and in unexpected ways, negotiating their own positions in relation to their parents, siblings, and peers. We situate juvenile antislavery as a recursive process, operating within complex, intergenerational interactions.

## I

In her 1839 *A History of the Slave Trade and its Abolition*, Esther Copley made an extraordinary claim: 'in some instances, children, having heard the sufferings endured by Africans in cultivating the sweet cane, … resolutely abstained from it, and introduced into whole families the system of abstinence'.[1] This dramatic declaration – that the young unilaterally initiated boycotts of slave-produced sugar – remains largely unexamined

---

[1] Esther Copley, *A History of Slavery and its Abolition*, 2nd edn (1839), 295. We thank Richard Huzzey for this reference.

by historians. This is surprising given that the role of young people was, as we shall see, widely acknowledged by contemporaries.

The boycotts of slave-produced sugar in Britain and Ireland in the 1790s were among the first examples of mass consumer protest. They were popularised by the unprecedented success of William Fox's *Address to the People of Great Britain, on the Propriety of Refraining from the Use of West India Sugar and Rum* (1791). Probably 'the most widely read pamphlet in British history',[2] it evidently enjoyed a juvenile as well as an adult audience. When William Dickson undertook a tour of Scotland for the Committee for the Abolition of the Slave Trade in 1792 he noted, among a number of instances of juvenile mobilisation, that the ten-year-old grandson of the Rev. Alice at Paisley 'won't take sugr. Since he read Fox's tract'.[3] The boycotts sought both to raise awareness of the brutality of slavery and to undermine it economically through consumer pressure. Participation was widespread; abolitionist Thomas Clarkson claimed that some 300,000 families had joined the boycott by the end of 1791 – a figure Seymour Drescher has described as 'not an unreasonable guess'.[4] This number was even greater in the later boycotts of the 1820s, when women's leadership was more formally organised under the auspices of the new Female Antislavery Societies, notably the large provincial societies in Birmingham and Sheffield.[5] Often conflated with the 1791–2 campaign, this second phase of boycotts related to a distinct phase in the antislavery movement, with its own blockbuster pamphlet in the form of Elizabeth Heyrick's *Immediate, Not Gradual Abolition* (1824).[6]

The domestic nature of the campaign, and its roots within home-based consumption, has been seen to constitute a form of lifestyle politics which facilitated an inclusive form of political activism.[7] It was, in James

---

[2]  William Fox, *An Address to the People of Great Britain, on the Propriety of Abstaining from West India Sugar and Rum* (1791); John Barrell and Timothy Whelan, 'Introduction', in *The Complete Writings of William Fox: Abolitionist, Tory, and Friend to the French Revolution* (Nottingham, 2011), ix.

[3]  William Dickson, 'Diary of a visit to Scotland on behalf of the Committee for the Abolition of the Slave Trade', 24 January 1792, Friends House Library, Temp MSS. Box 10/14, also cited in John R. Oldfield, *Popular Politics and British Anti-Slavery: The Mobilisation of Public Opinion against the Slave Trade, 1787–1807* (Manchester, 1995), 158.

[4]  Seymour Drescher, *Capitalism and Antislavery: British Mobilization in Comparative Perspective* (Oxford, 1987), 79.

[5]  See Clare Midgley, *Women against Slavery: The British Campaigns, 1780–1870* (1992), ch. 3.

[6]  Elizabeth Heyrick, *Immediate, Not Gradual Abolition; or, an Enquiry into the Shortest, Safest, and most Effectual Means of Getting Rid of West Indian Slavery* (1824); Clare Midgley, *Feminism and Empire: Women Activists in Imperial Britain, 1790–1865* (2007), ch. 2, especially 55–60.

[7]  Midgley, *Feminism and Empire*, ch. 2; Clare Midgley, 'Slave Sugar Boycotts, Female Activism and the Domestic Base of British Anti-Slavery Culture', *Slavery & Abolition*, 17 (1996), 137–62; Elizabeth Kowaleski-Wallace, *Consuming Subjects: Women, Shopping, and Business in the Eighteenth Century* (New York, 1997), 37–51; Julie L. Holcomb, 'Blood-Stained Sugar: Gender, Commerce and the British Slave-Trade Debates', *Slavery & Abolition*, 35

Walvin's words, 'female-led'.[8] Clare Midgley's landmark contributions have established the significance of women's actions, noting the huge potential for a 'feminised anti-slavery culture' to enable women to exert political influence without transgressing gendered expectations of propriety.[9] The proliferation of antislavery literature for juvenile consumption is also well known, with a huge number of tales, poems and tracts dedicated to a young audience.[10] Family-based studies, which have illuminated the significance of the home as a site of global activism, have, to date, provided the most in-depth insights into these issues. Most notably, Alison Twells has explored how the Read family of Sheffield were acculturated to 'missionary domesticity' through a range of family activities.[11] British children's support for missionary causes has received scrutiny[12] and there is now welcome attention to the resistance of enslaved children.[13] However, historians of slavery rarely examine in depth how and why adults solicited children's active support for abolitionism in Britain.[14] As Sarah Richardson has argued, the late Georgian and Victorian household formed a crucial incubator for children's political awareness. Richardson is one of the few historians to note children's decisions to abstain from sugar in response to familial education.[15]

(2014), 611–28; Seymour Drescher, *Abolition: A History of Slavery and Antislavery* (Cambridge, 2009), 248–51.

[8] James Walvin, *Questioning Slavery* (1996), 164.

[9] Midgley, *Feminism and Empire*, 51; *Women against Slavery*; 'Slave Sugar Boycotts'.

[10] Julie L. Holcomb, *Moral Commerce: Quakers and the Transatlantic Boycott of the Slave Labor Economy* (Ithaca, 2017), 115–22; Johanna M. Smith, 'Slavery, Abolition, and the Nation in Priscilla Wakefield's Tour Books for Children', in *Discourses of Slavery and Abolition: Britain and Its Colonies, 1760–1838*, ed. Brycchan Carey, Markman Ellis and Sara Salih (Basingstoke, 2004), 175–22; John R. Oldfield, 'Anti-Slavery Sentiment in Children's Literature, 1750–1850', *Slavery & Abolition*, 10 (1989), 44–59.

[11] Alison Twells, *The Civilising Mission and the English Middle Class, 1792–1850: The 'Heathen' at Home and Overseas* (Basingstoke, 2009), ch. 3. See also Zoë Laidlaw, '"Aunt Anna's Report": The Buxton Women and the Aborigines Select Committee, 1835–37', *Journal of Imperial and Commonwealth History*, 32 (2004), 1–28; and Kathryn Gleadle, *Borderline Citizens: Women, Gender and Political Culture in Britain, 1815–1867* (Oxford, 2009), ch. 7.

[12] F. K. Prochaska, *Women and Philanthropy in Nineteenth-Century England* (Oxford, 1980), ch. 3; Brian Stanley, '"Missionary Regiments for Immanuel's Service": Juvenile Missionary Organisations in English Sunday Schools', in *The Church and Childhood*, ed. Diana Wood (Oxford, 1994), 391–403; Hugh Morrison, 'British World Protestant Children, Young People, Education and the Missionary Movement, c. 1840s–1930s', *Studies in Church History*, 55 (2019), 468–78.

[13] Manisha Sinha, *The Slave's Cause: A History of Abolition* (New Haven, 2017), 254–6; Paula T. Connolly, *Slavery in American Children's Literature, 1790–2010* (Iowa City, 2013), 13–90; Colleen Vasconcellos, *Slavery, Childhood, and Abolition in Jamaica, 1788–1838* (Athens, GA, 2015).

[14] A notable exception is Oldfield, *Popular Politics*, 16–20, 142–8. For brief allusions in classic accounts, see Drescher, *Abolition*, 221; Midgley, *Women against Slavery*, 61; David Turley, *The Culture of English Antislavery, 1780–1860* (1991), 89–90.

[15] Sarah Richardson, *The Political Worlds of Women: Gender and Politics in Nineteenth Century Britain* (New York, 2013), ch. 1, especially 23–5.

This article builds upon these contributions through engaging with the insights of the new childhood history which seeks to excavate children's voices.[16] This provides an opportunity to revisit the phenomenon of British antislavery through the lens of its juvenile actors. Kathryn Gleadle has suggested there was a 'juvenile enlightenment' in the late eighteenth century which, through rational education, social practices and juvenile literature, created 'highly aware, often politicized, children with the ability to question and critique their own positions, their family's politics, and the world around them'.[17] A detailed consideration of children's involvement in the sugar boycott allows us to further explore this phenomenon, excavating the complex layers of influence, socialisation and education which variously produced juvenile anti-saccharists.

There was no static and universal definition of what constituted a 'child' in the period, and the transition to adulthood was always defined in relation to gender, class, 'race', ability, location, religion and personal maturity. Any assignation of child status is therefore bound to be arbitrary. While influential contributions from writers such as Mary Birkett (aged seventeen) and Maria and Harriet Falconar (aged seventeen and fourteen, respectively) indicate the significance of interventions from young people, in this article we focus especially upon those below the age of twelve.[18] Most of our subjects are considerably younger. In so doing, we hope to capture the experiences of those who might reasonably have been acknowledged as 'children' by modern readers as well as contemporaries. Legal definitions of childhood in this period varied considerably from one context to another, but in focusing upon those under the age of twelve, we are also mindful of the lowest age at which children were deemed to have attained the 'age of discretion' (meaning they could consent to marriage and issue a statement concerning personal property).[19] It is notable that most accounts of juvenile anti-saccharism relate to middle-class children. While the

---

[16] For example, William A. Corsaro, *The Sociology of Childhood* (Thousand Oaks, 1997), ch. 4; Kristine Moruzi, Nell Musgrove and Carla Pascoe Leahy, 'Hearing Children's Voices: Conceptual and Methodological Challenges', in *Children's Voices from the Past: New Historical and Interdisciplinary Perspectives*, ed. Kristine Moruzi, Nell Musgrove and Carla Pascoe Leahy (Cham, Switzerland, 2019), 1–25.

[17] Kathryn Gleadle, 'The Juvenile Enlightenment: British Children and Youth during the French Revolution', *Past & Present*, 233 (2016), 143–84, at 144.

[18] Mary Birkett, *A Poem on the African Slave Trade. Addressed to Her Own Sex* (Dublin, 1792); Maria Falconar and Harriet Falconar, *Poems on Slavery* (1788). See also the anonymous 'On the Slave Trade, by a Young Lady at School', *Manchester Mercury*, 4 March 1788.

[19] Girls were deemed to attain the age of discretion at twelve years, although boys not until fourteen. Anna-Christina Giovanopoulos, 'The Legal Status of Children in 18th-Century England', in *Fashioning Childhood in the Eighteenth Century: Age and Identity*, ed. Anja Müller (Aldershot, 2006), 47. In her study of eighteenth-century childhood, Alysa Levene chose to treat those under the age of thirteen as children, noting, for example, this was

sugar boycotts, particularly in the 1820s, boasted extensive cross-class popular support, they reflected broader trends within abolitionism in that they were formally organised by middle-class activists.[20] While some evidence tentatively suggests that the children of the poor were targeted as potential activists,[21] their responses were not usually recorded, particularly within the domestic settings at the core of our analysis.[22] As such, our focus is largely upon middle-class households.

Clearly, family dynamics of socialisation did not occur in isolation from the broader political climate, but at the same time, a nuanced understanding of how children's agency operated demands a forensic and tightly delimited focus. Thus, we look first to the broad contours of how children's engagement with the antislavery movement was publicly represented, drawing on the fragmentary reports of juvenile activity. We then turn to a detailed case study of how this played out within the home during the 1791–2 boycott. Juvenile engagement with the slavery question needs to be understood as a dynamic and complex phenomenon that defies easy categorisation. We seek to explore what children's contribution to abolitionism, and its representation, reveals about the complex interplay between adult influence and juvenile agency. We follow recent critiques of historians' consideration of childhood agency, understanding it, in the words of Mona Gleason, to be 'relational and complicated'.[23] However, we hope to contribute further to this conversation, by exploring how conceptions of juvenile agency are in themselves a historically specific phenomenon. In this case, it requires close attention not only to the political specificities of the antislavery campaign, but to

---

the age at which children were generally bound out as apprentices. Alysa Levene, *The Childhood of the Poor: Welfare in Eighteenth-Century London* (Basingstoke, 2012), 16–17.

[20] See Oldfield, *Popular Politics*, ch. 1.

[21] See, for example, John Rylands Library, University of Manchester, Rawson/Wilson Anti-Slavery Papers, GB 133 Eng MS 742, 'Minute Books of the Sheffield Ladies' Antislavery Society, 1825–1833', ff. 38–9.

[22] During the 1820s and 1830s, children working in factories were themselves increasingly likened to slaves. This was one facet of an increasingly complex and troubled relationship between working-class reform and abolitionism during this period. Understanding how these contexts affected representations of juvenile antislavery among the poor demands dedicated attention to the dynamics of class, labour, radicalism and reform, which is regrettably beyond the scope of the present article. See Robert Gray, *The Factory Question and Industrial England, 1830–1860* (Cambridge, 2002), 21–47; Kathryn Gleadle, '"We *Will* Have It": Children and Protest in the Ten Hours Movement', in *Childhood and Child Labour in Industrial England: Diversity and Agency, 1750–1914*, ed. Nigel Goose and Katrina Honeyman (Farnham, 2013), 215–30; Ryan Hanley, 'Slavery and the Birth of Working-Class Racism in England, 1814–1833', *Transactions of the Royal Historical Society*, 26 (2016), 103–23; Marcus Wood, *Slavery, Empathy, and Pornography* (Oxford, 2002), 141–80.

[23] Mona Gleason, 'Avoiding the Agency Trap: Caveats for Historians of Children, Youth, and Education', *History of Education*, 45 (2016), 446–59, at 457.

contingent understandings of childhood development, specific emotional cultures and distinctive family dynamics.

## II

Scholars of abolitionism, where they have discussed children's participation, have generally characterised it as adult-led. Drescher, for instance, suggests that children in some schools were 'not allowed' to consume sugar.[24] Sympathetic observers, however, were more likely to emphasise children's initiative. In 1792 educationist Maria Edgeworth asserted, 'Twenty-five thousand people in England have absolutely left off eating West Indian sugar, from the hope that when there is no longer any demand for sugar the slaves will not be so cruelly treated. Children in several schools have given up sweet things, which is surely very benevolent.'[25] In 1792, *The Times* published a letter supposedly from a young boy concerning his anti-saccharism, but the veracity of its authorship is impossible to verify.[26] Indeed, questions concerning agency are inherent in many of the scattered references to children's participation in the antislavery campaign, providing a crucial context for understanding juvenile sugar abstention. Within individual households, it is evident that the very young sometimes made striking efforts to express their antislavery sympathies. Nine-year-old Mary Ann West's 'LIBERTY and SLAVERY' sampler, completed in 1828, painstakingly cross-stitched over 1,000 words from Laurence Sterne's *A Sentimental Journey*, decrying the moral corrosion of colonial slavery.[27] This, and other examples of children's antislavery needlework samplers, seems to indicate at least the exercise of a negotiated form of political agency in producing them, but without understanding the family dynamics involved, it is difficult to assess.[28]

John Oldfield points out that schools and teachers were likely to have been prominent in negotiating and encouraging children's public engagement with antislavery.[29] While their influence over syllabi and day-to-day teaching was not always clear, several abolitionists, notably Hannah More and James Cropper, were involved in establishing and

---

[24] Drescher, *Capitalism and Antislavery*, 216 n. 46.

[25] *A Memoir of Maria Edgeworth, with a Selection from Her Letters*, ed. Frances Edgeworth (1867), 33.

[26] 'Letter to the Editor', *The Times*, 30 March 1792.

[27] Carol Humphrey, *Friends. A Common Thread: Samplers with a Quaker Inheritance* (Witney, 2008), 60.

[28] Other examples include Temperance Fisher's wool sampler, 'Jubilee Hymn for the First of August, 1834', and Esther Stewart's 1836 coloured wool sampler 'The African Slave'. Pamela Clabburn, *Samplers*, 2nd edn (Princes Risborough, 1998), 21, 24. We are grateful to the late Prof. Malcolm Chase for bringing these samplers to our attention.

[29] See Oldfield, *Popular Politics*, 147.

running schools.[30] After the Slavery Abolition Act had passed Parliament in 1833, antislavery was often appropriated within schools as a non-partisan moral issue which reflected well on British identity. Indeed, schoolchildren were frequently foregrounded in public celebrations of emancipation. In Methodist, Baptist and Anglican-affiliated schools around the country, festivals and celebratory meals were held to mark abolition.[31] It is harder to tease out from extant reports of these events how the children responded. It was noted in the *Bradford Observer*, for instance, that following the municipal celebrations of emancipation day on 1 August 1834, pupils at the local Eastbrook Quaker school returned to their schoolroom with their teachers, where they 'subscribed twenty shillings ... for the black population in the colonies'.[32] While we cannot recover the dynamics of the event, it is apparent that the children were positioned in this account as active recipients of the antislavery message. This tendency of representation is crucial when assessing retrospective narratives which stressed juvenile activism.

Those below the age of fourteen were discouraged from signing antislavery petitions.[33] However, direct appeals to children changed over time. The first sugar boycott predated the widespread production of antislavery literature for children, which was especially a feature of the 1820s and 1830s in Britain.[34] Most of this literature encouraged merely affective responses.[35] In contrast, some campaigners solicited more decisive involvement, for instance by exhorting children to contribute financially to the cause, especially after the boycotts of the 1820s.[36] The annual reports of the Female Society for the Relief of British Negro Slaves in Birmingham detailed a number of donations from children. Sometimes these were mediated through schoolteachers or parents,[37] although other small donations purported to be from children acting

---

[30] Anne Stott, *Hannah More: The First Victorian* (Oxford, 2004), ch. 5; National Museums Liverpool, Cropper Family Archives, Henry Brougham to James Cropper, 6 November 1833, D/CR/11/73.

[31] Turley, *The Culture of English Antislavery*, 89–90, 107–8.

[32] *Bradford Observer*, 7 August 1834.

[33] Plymley Notebooks, Shropshire Archives (hereafter SA), 1066/9 (1792), f. 18. Our thanks to the owners of the Plymley archive and to Shropshire Archives for their kind permission to use the Plymley material.

[34] Scholars have only identified sporadic publications prior to this. For the increase in antislavery literature from the 1820s, see Oldfield, 'Anti-Slavery Sentiment', 50–1.

[35] See, for example, Susanna Moodie, 'The Vanquished Lion (1831)', in Susanna Moodie, *Voyages: Short Narratives of Susanna Moodie*, ed. John Thurston (Ottawa, 1991), 31–42.

[36] E.g. Frances Rolleston, 'Anti-Slavery Hymn for Children', GB/133/Eng MS 742/30, University of Manchester, John Rylands Library, Rawson/Wilson Anti-Slavery Papers, Letters and Papers.

[37] *The Fifth Report of the Female Society, for Birmingham ... for the Relief of British Negro Slaves* (Birmingham, 1830), 68.

independently. The records sentimentally emphasised the donor's young age, for example listing 'a little boy' and a 'little girl' as donating one shilling apiece.[38] This suggests the figure of the self-motivated child activist could be mobilised to prompt adults into taking action. In a similar vein, a poem written by Sarah Read in the mid-1820s featured a young boy who resolved to urge his father to relinquish slave-produced sugar after seeing an advertisement for an antislavery meeting.[39] In exploring claims of children's unilateral sugar abstention, therefore, it is important to be alert to the wider discursive resonance such an image held, and the functions it might be hoped to serve.

This is especially apposite when considering retrospective accounts, such as autobiographies. The antislavery movement provided a significant point of reference for many nineteenth-century autobiographers when describing their childhood development.[40] Tracing juvenile engagement through the lens of such sources poses methodological challenges. Narrative shaping occurred through the lens of subsequent collective memories and often projected a teleological construction of a coherent self.[41] Thus, like contemporary adult observers, many autobiographers presented their juvenile involvement in the sugar boycott as unmediated and spontaneous. Recalling her childhood in Bristol during the 1820s, the pioneering physician Elizabeth Blackwell (1821–1910) claimed the 'children voluntarily gave up the use of sugar, as a "slave product"'.[42] Similarly, the famous scientist Mary Somerville (1780–1872) recalled:

> when I was a girl I took the anti-slavery cause so warmly to heart that I would not take sugar in my tea, or indeed taste anything with sugar in it. I was not singular in this, for my cousins and many of my acquaintances came to the same resolution.[43]

Writer Lucy Aikin (1781–1864), niece to the author Anna Letitia Barbauld, paid greater attention to the wider political agenda of the adults around her, recounting the personal impact of a 1788 vote in the Commons for the abolition of the slave trade alongside the

---

[38] *Ibid.*, 68; *The Third Report of the Female Society, for Birmingham … for the Relief of British Negro Slaves* (Birmingham, 1828), 35.

[39] Twells, *The Civilising Mission*, 97.

[40] See, for example, Roxanne Eberle, '"Tales of Truth?" Amelia Opie's Antislavery Poetics', in *Romanticism and Women Poets: Opening the Doors of Reception*, ed. Harriet Kramer Linkin and Stephen C. Behrendt (Lexington, 1999), 71–98, at 76.

[41] See Kathryn Gleadle, 'Playing at Soldiers: British Loyalism and Juvenile Identities during the Napoleonic Wars', *Journal for Eighteenth-Century Studies*, 38 (2015), 335–48.

[42] Elizabeth Blackwell, *Pioneer Work in Opening the Medical Profession to Women: Autobiographical Sketches* (1895), 7.

[43] Mary Somerville, *Personal Recollections, from Early Life to Old Age, of Mary Somerville, with Selections from her Correspondence* (1874), 124.

unsuccessful motion for the repeal of the Test and Corporation Acts.[44] Yet Aikin was keen to portray the striking commitment of children to the sugar boycott: 'I should scarcely be believed were I to recount the bitter persecutions we poor children underwent in the children's parties which we frequented, for the offence of denying ourselves *on principle* the dainties which children most delight in.'[45] A similar narrative emerges in the autobiography of Mary Anne Schimmelpenninck (1778–1856) (née Galton), who came from a Birmingham Quaker family of gun manufacturers. She too noted the significance of adults whilst continuing to emphasise juvenile initiative in the face of persecution. She described how she and her female cousins read antislavery pamphlets, examining 'in detail the prints of slave ships and slave treatment'. Despite delineating a variety of adult abolitionist influences (including the inspiring presence of family friend Thomas Clarkson), she presented her sugar abstention as a positive decision made by herself and her peers: 'both my cousins and I resolved to leave off sugar'. Her emphasis upon juvenile agency was enhanced by her account of the difficulties she faced in continuing with her resolve on returning to her nuclear family. Her governess, in particular, mocked the practice. It was thanks to the antislavery literature which her (adult) cousin Lizzie Forster lent her that she was able to abstain 'more zealously than ever, though alone in my family, from using sugar', despite being 'subject to daily ridicule and taunts'.[46] The parliamentary abolitionist Thomas Fowell Buxton claimed he was first 'made to think' about the issue of slavery during his childhood years because his sister Anna 'refused to eat sugar because it was produced by the enforced industry of slaves'.[47] A common thread throughout these accounts is the significance of peer-to-peer socialisation of young people in affecting their stance on sugar consumption and the place this held in their narratives of moral development into adulthood.

Representations of children's involvement in the antislavery campaign therefore raise complex questions concerning the nature and scope of juvenile agency, and open up further layers to investigate within the micro-ecologies of abolitionist families. To understand why many contemporaries categorised children's involvement in the sugar boycott as a decision taken independently of adults, we now turn to a specific case study.

---

[44] *Memories of Seventy Years by One of a Literary Family*, ed. Mrs Herbert Martin (1884), 18.
[45] *Ibid.*, 18 (emphasis in original).
[46] Mary Anne Schimmelpenninck, *Life of Mary Anne Schimmelpenninck: Autobiography*, ed. C. C. Hankin (1858), 51, 166, 180–1, 285.
[47] T. Wemyss Reid, *The Life of the Right Honourable William Edward Foster* (2 vols., 1888), I, 21.

## III

The notebooks and diaries of Katherine Plymley (1758–1829) provide one of the most detailed insights into children's socialisation in, and responses to, the British antislavery movement. Plymley was a member of the Shropshire gentry and sister of the local archdeacon, Joseph Corbett.[48] When Corbett's wife died in 1787, Katherine and her younger sister, Ann (born 1761), took on the responsibility of caring for their children: Panton (bap. April 1785), Josepha (born 1786) and Jane (born 19 November 1787).[49] The Plymley household combined an evangelical Anglicanism with sympathy for the cosmopolitan ideals of the French Revolution. Corbett was a key figure in the antislavery movement, heading up local petitions throughout Shropshire and working closely with the London committee of the Society for Effecting the Abolition of the Slave Trade (SEAST) and its successor organisations. The family was in close contact with prominent abolitionists, and Thomas Clarkson, the pre-eminent extra-parliamentary figure of the movement, was a frequent house guest.[50] Plymley and the children revered him.[51] It was Clarkson's first visit to the household in 1791 that inspired Plymley to begin her copious diaries detailing her brother's involvement in the campaign.[52] These notebooks included transcripts of correspondence, accounts of parliamentary proceedings, philosophical digressions, and narratives of family conversations and encounters. Taken together, they comprise an unofficial, highly partial history of the antislavery movement.

[48] Joseph Corbett (formerly Plymley) changed his surname to Corbett in 1806, having inherited his uncle's estate in 1804. Johanna Dahn, 'Women and Taste: A Case Study of Katherine Plymley, 1758–1829' (Ph.D. thesis, University of Wales, Aberystwyth, 2001), 153. For the sake of clarity, Joseph will be referred to as Corbett.

[49] Corbett married Matty Dansey in 1790. They had further children, but it was agreed that Katherine and Ann would continue to care for the three eldest children. For detailed discussions of Katherine Plymley, see Kathryn Gleadle, '"Opinions Deliver'd in Conversation": Conversation, Politics and Gender in the Late Eighteenth Century', in *Civil Society in British History: Ideas, Identities, Institutions*, ed. José Harris (Oxford, 2003), 61–78; Kathryn Gleadle, 'Gentry, Gender, and the Moral Economy during the Revolutionary and Napoleonic Wars in Provincial England', in *Economic Women: Essays on Desire and Dispossession in Nineteenth-Century British Culture*, ed. Lana L. Dalley and Jill Rappoport (Columbus, 2013), 25–40; Dahn, 'Women and Taste'.

[50] Corbett's sons, Panton and his half-brother Uvedale, were later elected directors of the antislavery African Institution. As a Member of Parliament, Panton supported the antislavery campaign. *The History of Parliament: The House of Commons 1820–1832* (Cambridge, 2009), ed. D. R. Fisher, www.historyofparliamentonline.org/volume/1820-1832/member/corbett-panton-1785-1855; SA 1066/90 (1812), f. 40.

[51] See, for example, SA 1066/48 (1797), f. 18. The family's opinion of him later cooled, regretting, amongst other things, his move towards Unitarianism. See SA 1066/131–4 (1825–8).

[52] SA 1066/1 (1791), f. 1.

Plymley's first decisive claim as to children's initiative in the sugar boycott was a reference to a local Shrewsbury printer, Mr Eddowes: 'His family have left off the use of sugar & the little people were the first to wish it.'[53] However, her wider narrative pointed to the organised sugar boycott campaign within which such decisions were located. Earlier, in autumn 1791, she had visited the family of the famous abolitionist Josiah Wedgwood at their home in Etruria, Staffordshire. Here she presented sugar abstention as a family, rather than a children's, issue: 'Mr. Wedgewood's [*sic*] family wou'd not have any West India sugar', noting they had ceased all sugar consumption whilst waiting for a consignment of East India-grown product. When she described this visit to Clarkson, he informed her of the emerging impact of Fox's *Address*.[54] Clarkson subsequently suggested that campaigners should induce their local booksellers to bulk-buy Fox's pamphlet for distribution. Her own brother, Plymley recorded, ordered 500 copies from Eddowes. It was only at this point, by which time Plymley had laid out Corbett and Eddowes's roles in a coordinated strategy to promote the sugar boycott, that she suggested Eddowes's children had been 'the first to wish it'.[55] This stark declaration of juvenile agency therefore belied the multiple influences which, as Plymley was aware, underpinned these actions.

Her complicated positioning of children's decisions is underlined by comparing Plymley's contemporaneous to her retrospective accounts of the same events. In April 1792, she recorded the family's early history of sugar abstention through a conversation with Clarkson:

> My Br. mention'd to Mr Clarkson his little people's zeal in the disuse of sugar & that little Jane had said she wou'd not use any till it came from Sierra Leone. Mr. C observed the virtue of little Children was wonderful. I have before noticed in this particular instance as among those children who are inform'd on the subject I have heard of more readiness to give up the use of sugar than among grown people.[56]

Looking back in 1797, Plymley recounted these events slightly differently:

> Mr Clarkson observed, at the time that it was thought advisable to abstain from West India Sugar, & we had mentioned to him that Panton, Josepha and Jane, then very young, were the first to leave off its use among us. 'It is wonderful the virtue of little children, I have known numbers of such instance'.[57]

These two accounts were substantially similar, suggesting that the children's abstention was a repeated, shared narrative within the family's circle.

---

[53] SA 1066/4 (1792), ff. 10–12.
[54] SA 1066/1 (1791), ff. 12–13. Timothy Whelan, 'William Fox, Martha Gurney, and Radical Discourse of the 1790s', *Eighteenth-Century Studies*, 42 (2009), 397–411.
[55] SA 1066/4 (1792), ff. 10–12.
[56] SA 1066/9 (1792), ff. 10–11.
[57] SA 1066/46 (1797), ff. 9–10.

However, in the later account, the balance between unilateral juvenile action and adult influence had shifted. It was implied that the children pioneered the family's anti-saccharite activity, while references to adult influences over this decision had been excised. By contrast, in the 1792 account, the significant qualifier 'among those children who are inform'd on the subject' acknowledged that childhood anti-saccharism could be a negotiated, if nevertheless deliberate, response to adult expectations.

Plymley's diaries therefore illuminate how a specific narrative of juvenile determination was favoured. In order to understand her account, it is necessary to excavate the views of childhood which circulated in her network, and the interconnected ideas on consumption, gender, morality, and education, through which the children's actions were both enabled and interpreted.

The particularities of the family's emotional culture were especially important. They served to cohere an investment in the values of bodily restraint and sensibility to suffering, whilst also affirming affective expression as an appropriate means to demonstrate concurrence with stated ideals. Hester Barron and Claire Langhamer have observed that recent histories of emotion, despite sensitivity to the 'power dynamics of emotional learning', tend to position children somewhat passively within adult-dominated models.[58] Emphasising instead the significance of intersubjective behaviour and responses, they argue, reveals that children can be highly cognisant of their potential to influence adult emotions. Our understanding of the Plymley children is mediated through adult-authored sources, limiting the potential to explore their own subjectivities or the likelihood of teasing out diverse emotional responses beyond the purview of their aunt, father or Clarkson. Nevertheless, this does not necessitate viewing them as simply responsive to the emotional demands of the adults around them. Plymley's approving accounts of her nieces' and nephew's behaviour include indications of the children's agentic conduct as well as the ways in which their responses affirmed and shaped adult identities.

Writing a retrospective account of Panton's childhood around 1800, Plymley recalled fondly his tenderness of disposition.[59] She was particularly proud of the then six-year-old's imaginative response to Clarkson's *Essay on the Slavery and Commerce of the Human Species*: 'when he read the part which mentions that the kidnappers lie conceal'd in the long grass to catch slaves, he wish'd a flight of locusts wou'd come there & eat up the grass that they may not have it to hide in'.[60] Panton's imaginary

[58] Hester Barron and Claire Langhamer, 'Feeling through Practice: Subjectivity and Emotion in Children's Writing', *Journal of Social History*, 51 (2017), 104.

[59] SA 1066/56 (1800–1), f. 22.

[60] SA 1066/9 (1792), f. 4.

rescue of the hunted Africans by divine intervention signified an appropriately interior, self-reflective response that confirmed his socialisation into the evangelical-political nexus occupied by his family and their circle.

Panton's emotional sensitivity was praised in other political contexts. Plymley reported he was left inconsolable after hearing of Lafayette's mistreatment in a Prussian jail. With evident satisfaction at his precocious sensibility, she added, in parentheses, 'He is not 8 years old.'[61] Plymley's approval of Panton's tears of sympathy evinced the positive valorisation of the 'masculine sensibility' which, as Catherine Hall and Leonore Davidoff have suggested, was endorsed within the evangelical middle-class family.[62] Many scholars have observed that sentimental responses to African suffering could act as moral palliatives, allowing metropolitan onlookers to indulge a sense of sympathy without motivating meaningful action.[63] It may well be that for many adults the 'solipsistic' nature of antislavery sensibility represented an ideal juvenile response.[64]

Encouraging the children to interact with the antislavery movement, then, was woven into an intricate web of ideological assumptions and family pressures. Their ready response to the sugar boycott was probably enhanced by the fact that the family already encouraged close reflection on the politics of food and its consumption. Another document authored by Plymley dating from this period discussed the waste of food in elite households; and the virtues of controlling 'intemperate passions' were recurring themes in her notebooks.[65] She quoted with evident gratification a letter sent from Theophilus Houlbrooke to her brother in which he expressed his delight with the children's anti-saccharism: 'they do well to abstain from Sugar, it is giving them a habit of self denial & from the best motives'.[66] Sugar abstention was valued not simply as an abolitionist strategy, but also for inculcating morality and personal discipline.

---

[61] SA 1066/14 (1792–3), ff. 17–18.

[62] Leonore Davidoff and Catherine Hall, *Family Fortunes: Men and Women of the English Middle Class, 1780–1850* (1987), 111.

[63] George Boulukos, *The Grateful Slave: The Emergence of Race in Eighteenth-Century British and American Culture* (Cambridge, 2008), 201–32; Jamie Rosenthal, 'The Contradictions of Racialized Sensibility: Gender, Slavery, and the Limits of Sympathy', in *Affect and Abolition in the Anglo-Atlantic, 1770–1830*, ed. Stephen Ahern (Farnham, 2013), 171–88; Brycchan Carey, *British Abolitionism and the Rhetoric of Sensibility: Writing, Sentiment, and Slavery, 1760–1807* (Basingstoke, 2005).

[64] See Stephen Ahern, 'Introduction: The Bonds of Sentiment', in *Affect and Abolition*, ed. Ahern, especially 6–9; Marcus Wood, *Slavery, Empathy, and Pornography* (Oxford, 2002), 23–36.

[65] SA 567/5/5/1/33, 'Thoughts Written At Lyth' (1792); Gleadle, 'Gentry, Gender, and the Moral Economy'.

[66] SA 1066/9 (1792), f. 20.

That the children's father was a prominent abolitionist further ensured that the affective culture of the family was intertwined with a commitment to the cause. Children had an emotional and psychological investment in identifying with the antislavery politics of their father. Autobiographers often referenced the significance of their fathers (rather than their mothers) in explaining their commitment to antislavery and other campaigning causes. This enabled them to align themselves with the social and cultural privileges accorded to fathers.[67] Within the Plymley family, the affective contours of the antislavery issue were reinforced through the children's relationship with Clarkson, with whom they were encouraged to interact with great intimacy. Plymley wrote approvingly of his holding the children's hands and their readiness to kiss him. 'They seem'd to win his affection & whilst he was conversing yesterday & today he wou'd hold their hands & play with their hair.'[68] This affectionate relationship gave the children the confidence to converse with Clarkson on the antislavery question; 'they had all ask'd him when he thought the Slave Trade wou'd be put a stop to', Plymley noted approvingly in October 1791. In turn, Clarkson 'had condescendingly taken pains to answer them in such a manner as he thought they wou'd best understand'.[69] During his many visits to the household during the early 1790s, he continued to spend time with the children, combining child-centred activities with delivering the antislavery message. In the autumn of 1792, Plymley described him helping them with a jigsaw puzzle:

> The children were putting a dissected map of Africa together. He [Clarkson] observ'd it, said it was not an accurate one, but that no accurate map of Africa cou'd be had ... He had the goodness to mark with a pen a dot for the [Sierra Leone] company's settlement & for the territories of Naimbana, Samie and Domingo which has render'd the map very valuable to us.[70]

While nominally educating the children about African geography, Clarkson could not help but campaign to them by centring the abolitionist-backed settlement at Sierra Leone (his brother John was at that time governor of the settlement).[71] Later, he continued to engage the children in the project by sending them Sierra Leonean coins as gifts.[72] The Plymley children were therefore explicitly encouraged to learn more

[67] For example, Josephine E. Butler, *Memoir of John Grey of Dilston* (1874), 127; Catherine Marsh, *The Life of the Rev. William Marsh, By His Daughter* (1868), 72–3; Gleadle, *Borderline Citizens*, 101–3.

[68] SA 1066/13 (1792), f. 2

[69] SA 1066/2 (1791), ff. 22–3.

[70] SA 1066/13 (1792), ff. 2–3.

[71] See Padraic X. Scanlan, *Freedom's Debtors: British Antislavery in Sierra Leone in the Age of Revolutions* (New Haven, 2017), ch. 1.

[72] SA 1066/21 (1793), 19.

about the antislavery movement through their emotional connection to Clarkson. This is borne out by young Jane's well-informed declaration in 1792, when she was four or five years old, that she would cease to consume sugar until it came from Sierra Leone.[73] Later, her older sister Josepha, then aged six or seven, made a sweet bag for Clarkson, with Plymley emphasising this was 'at her own desire'.[74] Plymley's endorsement of Josepha's wish to please Clarkson, and to make an affective gesture of her own accord, speaks to the emotional dynamics of Clarkson's presence in the house.

The creation of an atmosphere in which the children were eager to gratify Clarkson provides a vital context in understanding their responses to antislavery messages. In a diary entry dating from 1801, Plymley looked back on Panton's childhood reading habits, noting that 'in consequence of a conversation with Mr. Clarkson he wish'd to read his prize essay, & he did read it in the Decr. before he was seven years old'.[75] However, at the time in 1792, Plymley's account was more precise as to the nature of Clarkson's influence:

> He ask'd Panton yesterday what he wou'd do to put a stop to the slave trade & he prettily answer'd, I wou'd do anything I cou'd. Mr. C told him as he was so young the best thing he cou'd do was to read on the subject that he may grow up with a just detestation of it. Panton was eager to begin & this morning by his own desire began Mr. Clarkson's first Essay. When Mr. C returned from Coalbrooke Dale he ran to him eager to tell him of it.[76]

In this instance, observe the pressure that was put upon the child to respond, with Clarkson asking the six-year-old how he proposed to stop the slave trade. Panton's keen reaction did not reflect simply a desire to assist the movement, but was a juvenile decision to conform to a specific interpersonal dynamic. Pleasing Clarkson and responding to him with alacrity gained him praise in this environment.

Plymley's narrative concerning the children's abolitionism was also the product of a highly gendered form of female life writing. Plymley appeared unwilling to position herself as an antislavery advocate in her own right. She did not present the sugar boycott of the early 1790s as a woman-centred discourse, but drew attention to the responses of her nieces and nephew, as well as continuing to reference the lead taken by her brother. In a later summary of Jane's biography, Plymley established a narrative arc between Jane's life and that of the antislavery movement. Jane, she asserted, had known of the antislavery cause all her life, adding that she was born on

[73] SA 1066/9 (1792), ff. 10–11.
[74] SA 1066/21 (1793), ff. 18–19. A sweet bag is a small cloth bag containing herbs.
[75] SA 1066/56 (1800–1), ff. 4–5. Clarkson's prize-winning student dissertation was translated from Latin into English as *An Essay on the Slavery and Commerce of the Human Species, Particularly the African* (1788), and marketed extensively by SEAST.
[76] SA 1066/2 (1791), f. 22.

19 November 1787, and that the first committee for abolition had been formed earlier that year.[77] Situating the children within the antislavery movement was, for Plymley, a way of validating the family identity. She conveyed developments in the antislavery movement through the lens of the children in her care, erasing her own voice.

Nonetheless, she did have strongly held views on the importance of the domestic environment for children's moral development. This had significant implications for her representation of their antislavery sentiments. In 1797, Plymley noted a discussion arising from William Wilberforce's latest publication, *A Practical View of the Prevailing Religious System of Professed Christians*.[78] Wilberforce contended that people were born sinful and that only strict moral education could lead to grace. He brought attention to 'the perverse and froward disposition perceivable in children, which it is the business and sometimes the ineffectual attempt of education to reform'.[79] In the margin beside this passage in the household's copy of Wilberforce's tract, Plymley's brother wrote,

> the easy reception that good sentiments find in children not taught evil, shows how much man is formed for virtue tho' he may have, or rather has some contrary propensities; but these, as education is managed, are the seeds that are nurtured into action ninety nine times out of an hundred.[80]

While Wilberforce and Joseph Corbett shared an emphasis on the importance of education, they evidently differed on children's natural propensity towards good or evil. Ideological views on children do not necessarily relate simply to practice, and the Plymley family later commented approvingly on child-rearing within the Wilberforce family.[81] Nonetheless, these contrasting perspectives exemplify divisions in late Georgian attitudes towards childhood. The evangelical precepts of children's original sin contrasted with two distinct Enlightenment perspectives: firstly, John Locke's view of the child as a blank slate, and hence the power of the environment to shape the individual; and secondly Rousseau's emphasis upon humans' natural state of innocence and the importance of allowing children to develop without constraint. From the end of the eighteenth century, the latter perspective gained in credence due to an emergent, romantic ideal of childhood innocence.[82]

---

[77] SA 1066/147 (n.d.), ff. 34–5.

[78] William Wilberforce, *A Practical View of the Prevailing Religious System of Professed Christians, in the Higher and Middle Classes in this Country, Contrasted with Real Christianity* (1797).

[79] *Ibid.*, 34.

[80] SA 1066/46 (1797), f. 9.

[81] SA 1066/90 (1812), ff. 10–12.

[82] Hugh Cunningham, *Children and Childhood in Western Society since 1500* (1995), 61–72; Alan Richardson, *Literature, Education, and Romanticism: Reading as Social Practice, 1780–1832* (Cambridge, 1994), ch. 1.

One of Plymley's closest friends, Archibald Alison, who mixed in radical Edinburgh circles, insisted to her that children would be 'naturally good' providing they were not exposed to evil examples. Plymley appeared to align with her brother in generally preferring a slightly different emphasis – suggesting the key to moral education was to 'form the disposition' in children to do good.[83] In so doing, she emphasised the importance of the domestic sphere as a site for the training of moral citizens. As a result, she was firmly of the view that boys should be educated at home. In this she was joined by Clarkson who, she reported, proclaimed that Parliament would have voted to abolish the slave trade had not most of its members been educated in public schools.[84] Her brother, like many contemporaries, was increasingly concerned that a home-based education might expose boys to too great a female influence.[85] Not so Plymley. Her glowing appraisal of Panton as a young adult emphasised his upbringing at home, 'at a distance from all the vices and follies too often acquired at great schools'.[86] Her accounts of children's antislavery sensibilities were part of a rich interplay of discourses concerning juvenile development. An affection towards her charges combined with a sentimentalism towards the nature of childhood meant that the figure of the innocent child held considerable traction for her. As such, she did not adhere to a strict, Lockean or associationist view of the child; yet she did believe that children's potential for moral purity could be carefully cultivated by the adults, including by implication the women, around them.[87]

The antislavery cause was therefore not an isolated campaign to which the children were exposed, but part of a deeper, multifaceted nexus of messages and practices. As a result, it was more likely to gain credence for children as it affirmed other aspects of their education and upbringing. The additional emotional pressures placed upon the young to react in specific ways to the antislavery message and its campaigners created a highly charged environment in which dissent from abolitionism would have been experienced as dissent from the family's affective culture. Given this, it is hardly surprising that children chose to positively endorse the antislavery line. But this does not mean to say that the

[83] SA 1066/46 (1797), ff. 9–10.
[84] SA 1066/3 (1791), ff. 5–6.
[85] SA 1066/58, f. 19. Michèle Cohen, 'Gender and the Private/Public Debate on Education in the Long Eighteenth Century', in *Public or Private Education? Lessons from History*, ed. Richard Aldrich (2004), 2–24.
[86] SA 1066/53, f. 15.
[87] Christoph Houswitschka, 'Locke's Education or Rousseau's Freedom: Alternative Socializations in Modern Societies', in *Fashioning Childhood*, ed. Müller, 81–8; Mary Hilton, *Women and the Shaping of the Nation's Young: Education and Public Doctrine in Britain, 1750–1850* (Aldershot, 2007), chs. 1–4.

children were passive pawns of an intense socialisation process. As Susan Miller has observed, juvenile agency can be located in the historical record on a 'continuum' of relations to parental wishes, and could incorporate elements of compliance or assent as well as resistance.[88]

The Plymley notebooks provide an insightful commentary upon the ways in which the children reimagined the ideas and wishes of their father and aunts. Plymley later recalled that when Jane was a little girl, her father so enjoyed hearing her attempts to reason that he would often venture unexpected remarks to see what she would make of them.[89] This warns against conceptualising the influence of adults upon children in simple, direct terms. Rather, we might conceive of domestic relations consisting of a 'recursive loop' in which parental and juvenile interventions were continually responding to and building upon each other dialogically.[90] There are many instances in the Plymley archive in which the children reinterpreted the ideas to which they were exposed. For example, Plymley recorded of her teenaged niece Jane that her religious sensibilities became so finely developed that not only would she not read novels or plays – a common evangelical position – but that she 'carries it to such an extreme that the interesting moral stories of which there are now so many for young people, she objects to'.[91] Such decisions served to enhance the family's mythology of Jane as a uniquely godly young woman. Jane died in her twenty-first year, following a prolonged period of obsessive fasting which had originated in a decision to support the family's attempts to ensure greater foodstuffs for the poor.[92] Despite her fast's broad alignment with the family's stated values, their heartbreak at Jane's actions means that it can hardly be interpreted straightforwardly as compliance.

Similarly, notwithstanding Corbett and Plymley's encouragement of the children's antislavery activities, they were still occasionally surprised by unexpected responses. In April 1792, shortly after the children had begun to abstain from West India sugar, Plymley noticed that seven-year-old Panton's shoes looked 'very brown' and had not been polished. Upon enquiring with the servants, she found that 'he had given orders that they shou'd not be black'd because he understood sugar was used

[88] Susan A. Miller, 'Assent as Agency in the Early Years of the Children of the American Revolution', *Journal of the History of Childhood and Youth*, 9 (2016), 48–65.

[89] SA 1066/148 (n.d.), ff. 5–6.

[90] We follow Karen Sánchez-Eppler in adopting Elizabeth Maddock Dillon's formulation. Karen Sánchez-Eppler, 'Practicing for Print: The Hale Children's Manuscript Libraries', *Journal of the History of Childhood and Youth*, 1 (2008), 188–209; Elizabeth Maddock Dillon, *The Gender of Freedom: Fictions of Liberalism and the Literary Public Sphere* (Stanford, 2004), 35–6.

[91] SA 1066/56 (1800–1), f. 18.

[92] Gleadle, 'Gentry, Gender, and the Moral Economy', 30.

in the composition'.[93] This was an unusual form of abstention, not mentioned in any of the prominent campaigning literature. Thus, the children sometimes responded to the question of transatlantic slavery in ways that, while in broad accordance with their father and aunt's wishes, were nevertheless unanticipated and not explicitly encouraged. Young people could be innovative in participating in popular antislavery, in ways that navigated the tensions between obeisance to parental authority and their own intentionality.

This negotiation was at the heart of an exchange between the children and another famous abolitionist. Gustavus Vassa, better known today by his pen-name Olaudah Equiano, dined at the Plymley house during one of his national 'book tours' in June 1793.[94] Equiano had been looking to meet with Corbett, to whom he had been introduced in London, but he was not home at the time of the visit and so he dined instead with Corbett's sister Ann. He stayed to talk with the children afterwards. As Plymley recorded it,

> the little people, though they had not been accustomed to blacks, immediately went to him, offered their hands & behaved in their pretty friendly way. Whilst my sister was out of the room he gave Panton one of the little pamphlets against the use of sugar. When Ann return'd & Panton said, see what this gentleman has given me, she told him what warm friends they were to the abolition, & that they had long left off sugar. He gave Panton one of his memoirs & wrote his name in it himself, & desired him to remember him. He asked Panton if he should like to travel. P— said he did not know – Should he like to go to Africa – Yes – Will you go with me – just as my Papa pleases – Josepha on being asked made the same answer & he made many professions of the care he would take of them. Ann, Mrs. Plymley and the little people were much pleased with him.[95]

Having given Panton an antislavery pamphlet while his aunt was out of the room, Equiano may have inadvertently committed a minor social infraction by circumventing familial authority, precipitating Ann's gentle response that they had *already* educated their children about the horrors of slavery, and abstained from sugar consumption. The subsequent discussion about travelling to Africa was also seemingly a tense exchange in which Equiano solicited an independent response directly from Panton (then eight years old) and Josepha (six or seven years old), who in reply – perhaps uncertain of what he wanted to hear – attested to their own deference to their father's authority. In a sense, Equiano had challenged them to exceed the agreed limits of their independence by signing up to an imagined trip to Africa without their father's assent. They chose instead to stand firm to their established boundaries; an act that nonetheless required an active decision about which adult's

---

[93] SA 1066/9 (1792), f. 10.
[94] Vincent Carretta, *Equiano, the African: Biography of a Self-Made Man* (2005), 355.
[95] SA 1066/17 (1793), ff. 5–7.

expectations to frustrate.[96] This once again emphasises that, at least for the Plymley children, adherence to parental authority on the question of different forms of antislavery activity represented a *negotiated* form of juvenile agency.

## IV

In 2002, political scientists Michael McDevitt and Steven Chaffee formulated a revisionist model of 'trickle-up influence' perceiving children as acting agents, whose views and actions were capable of affecting the outlook of their parents. Family interactions and the responses to ongoing political events could lead to the re-evaluation of political positions. As they explain, 'the intrinsic forces of family adaptation ... can make the home a powerful incubator of citizenship'.[97] The history of children's involvement in the antislavery cause exemplifies how the intergenerational transmission of political and moral judgements could be dialogic as well as straightforwardly pedagogic. Affective relationships and dynamics of authority inflected juvenile anti-saccharism in complex ways, and post hoc claims of uninfluenced juvenile leadership tended towards idealising constructions in service to personal or family identity narratives. While the notion of antislavery activism as an unmediated form of juvenile political expression may be compelling, agency manifested most often as a result of recursive negotiation with adults' expectations and demands. Put another way, emotional pressures and family dynamics were crucial influences on children's agency, but they did not in any simple sense override it.

The evidence of the Plymley archive demonstrates how children's activities in the cause of antislavery positively affirmed adult positions. In her study of American girls' diaries from this period, Martha Blauvelt has drawn attention to the 'emotional labour' required of her young subjects.[98] Such an observation appears apposite to the Plymley children. They had significant expectations placed upon them to demonstrate particular emotional responses, especially to the suffering of enslaved people, in ways that would validate the adults' sense of their individual and family identities. Nevertheless, just as Blauvelt observes that 'emotion work' could function as a 'vehicle through which women

---

[96] For socialisation as a dialogical process in this period see Mary Hilton and Jill Shefrin, 'Introduction', in, *Educating the Child in Enlightenment Britain: Beliefs, Cultures, Practices*, ed. Mary Hilton and Jill Shefrin (Farnham, 2009), 6–8.

[97] Michael McDevitt and Steven Chaffee, 'From Top-Down to Trickle-Up Influence: Revisiting Assumptions about the Family in Political Socialization', *Political Communication*, 19 (2002), 281–301.

[98] Martha Blauvelt, *The Work of the Heart: Young Women and Emotion, 1780–1830* (Charlottesville, 2007).

create a negotiated self', so too could this be a means through which the Plymley siblings defined themselves.[99]

Historical discussion of the sugar boycotts has tended to present them as female-led, and as giving particular expression to female sensibilities.[100] The Plymley archive indicates that family interactions were more complex, and that greater attention needs to be paid to intergenerational dynamics. Mona Gleason has challenged historians to comprehend 'children's compliance with adult dictates from their own perspectives'.[101] This article suggests some of the ways in which this might be attempted, even in the absence of child-authored sources. However, we argue this needs to be within a framework which identifies contemporary attitudes towards, and facilitation of, juvenile initiative. Extant family papers such as the Plymley diaries elucidate how children's activism could be solicited within the home by indicating family practices designed to facilitate particular forms of juvenile response. They are suggestive of why children's agency might have been especially valorised in certain fora, nuancing our picture of the role played by young people in the antislavery movements. Above all, they provide insights into how children responded independently – often in ways that were neither anticipated nor explicitly sanctioned, but nonetheless approved of. As such they illustrate the complex interactions between children and adults – and the highly intricate dynamics within which juvenile political agency needs to be situated.

---

[99] *Ibid.*, 198.
[100] See above, footnotes 7 and 8.
[101] Gleason, 'Avoiding the Agency Trap', 457.

*Transactions of the RHS* 30 (2020), pp. 119–140 © The Author(s), 2020. Published by Cambridge University Press on behalf of the Royal Historical Society
doi:10.1017/S0080440120000067

# UNFINISHED BUSINESS: REMEMBERING THE GREAT WAR BETWEEN TRUTH AND REENACTMENT

## By Jay Winter

READ 17 MAY 2019 AT THE OPEN UNIVERSITY

ABSTRACT. This paper analyses the phenomenon of historical reenactment of Great War battles as an effort to create what is termed 'living history'. Thousands of people all over the world have participated in such reenactments, and their number increased significantly during the period surrounding the centenary of the outbreak of the Great War. Through a comparison with representations of war in historical writing, in museums and in the performing arts, I examine the claim of reenactors that they can enter into historical experience. I criticise this claim, and show how distant it is from those who do not claim to relive history but (more modestly) to represent it. In their search for 'living history', reenactors make two major errors. They strip war of its political content, and they sanitise and trivialise combat.

There has been a world of activity marking the centennial of the outbreak of the First World War. Much of it has been in the sphere of public commemoration. I want to call attention to a particular kind of commemoration called reenactment, since its substantial growth over recent years presents an important challenge to what we historians do.

Reenactment is less reviewing the past, than reliving it. All over the world, men and women put on uniforms, either of the war period or tailored as closely as possible to its materials, and bear arms, authentic if possible, in imitation training and in combat conditions. Verdun, the Somme, Gallipoli, Caporetto have attracted reenactors, either at the site of the original battle, or in places made to resemble them, whenever possible. Reenactment societies exist all over the world, and come together through the internet. Online merchants service them, and on-site auxiliaries enable them to go through their paces. This is internet history par excellence, a kind of computer game come alive. And it is very lucrative for those who make it possible.

In this essay I want to align reenactment with other kinds of commemorative and historical representations of war, and to try to express my view that it is a dangerous and offensive form of both historical and commemorative activity. It is dangerous because it adds elements of excitement and adventure to contemporary notions of war. It is offensive because it lacks respect for the hardship, the suffering and the anguish of men in battle. It betrays the men who fought by sanitising war and turning combat into what we now call infotainment.

This matters on ethical grounds, but it also matters on professional grounds. Much of the public history of the Great War during the centennial in general, and reenactment in particular, takes virtually no notice of what we do or say. To the public, we are hermetically sealed in our profession, and only talk to each other. To outsiders we are minor swimmers in a stream that others propel forward. We do not control the direction of the stream or even the way it is navigated by the millions of people fascinated by the Great War.

How do we answer this challenge? One way is to say we are trained to turn legends into archivally documented narratives. What we offer, as best we can, is the truth, and nothing but the truth, scrupulously based on the sources we cite in our publications. Truth is not a particularly valuable commodity in today's marketplace. All the more's the need for us to insist on standards of evidence and proof when examining historical narratives of all kinds, both within and beyond the academy.

It is important, though, to recognise the force of the challenge presented by reenactors and reenactment. The centennial of the outbreak of the Great War has been marked by a shift in the balance between collective memory and collective history. Collective memory is the memory of collectives, and most of these collectives are relatively small. Collective memory is almost never the memory of the state. We call state-based narratives about the past 'official memory'. Below that level there are groups of people who form an idea of the past through family records or through participating in relatively small-scale commemorative events. The French Presidential Commission on the Commemoration of the Great War found that the overwhelming majority of projects submitted to it for approval and money were of this kind – the history of our town, or our school or our factory in the Great War. Small is beautiful is their watchword, and as a result, the scale of much of Great War commemoration has been reduced to the life-size, the quotidian, the personal.

This is where we historians – we who create collective history – have to pause and take note. In much of this commemorative activity, as well as in television, film and theatre, the complexity of the war has been reduced to the personal level. Commemoration is public history, the performance in different places of narratives about the war using different media. Many of these narratives are framed by stories people tell around the dinner table about their past, their family and their local past. Jan and Aleida Assmann call these stories 'communicative memory'. When they are repeated in public, and last for generations, they enter into enduring stories they term 'cultural memory'.[1] Commemoration of the Great War at its centenary is cultural memory expressed through rituals, objects and images.

Television and museums present stories about the Great War all over the world. They use visual technology to tell stories about the war. Without photographs or other images, televisual history is impossible. So is the history presented in museums, though in those institutions artefacts, and the narratives embedded in them, have pride of place. But in many forms of public history, the kind of history we get is first-person history.[2] When no authentic voice can be found in memoirs, then visual history searches for its story elsewhere. One point to which we shall return below is that this requirement tends to turn television and museums into places where it is difficult to present some kinds of academic history: structural history, the history of the environment, history on the comparative and transnational level, in particular. There are exceptions, but much of public history tells a story visitors already know. The faces on the screen or in the display are like theirs – mostly white and European, or of European settlers. Africans, Asians, Latin Americans, Caribbean people are extras on this extended film set.

This is hardly surprising, since cultural memory comes out of family stories, and the families who have been telling stories about the Great War are by and large European. What matters more is what is left out of even this restricted story. Most of the time, the war that is presented on television or in museums aims at historical accuracy.

Others who tell stories about the war in public are also interested in accuracy – the precision of detail of uniforms, trenches, weapons. They study their subject, war, and come together to reenact combat. This paper focuses in part on this large group of commemorators. The reason I do so is that what they do profoundly distorts our understanding of war. What they offer is not war, but a caricature of war – simplified, sanitised, banalised. We historians need to respond in public to the blurring of the truth about war or its blatant elimination in the public domain. Reducing war to entertainment is simply wrong.

Reenactment societies are not the only culprit. Any historical reconstruction which uses smoke to simulate gas and light bulbs to simulate an artillery barrage betrays the truth. Visitors to such exhibitions are not getting the truth, but a travesty of the truth. That, alas, mars the

---

[1] Jan Assmann, 'Communicative and Cultural Memory', in *Cultural Memory Studies: An International and Interdisciplinary Handbook*, ed. Astrid Erll and Ansgar Nünning (Berlin, 2010), 109–18.

[2] Jay Winter, 'Producing the Television Series "The Great War and the Shaping of the Twentieth Century"', in *Profession 1999* (1999), 10–22.

new Australian Sir John Monash Information Centre at Villers-Bretonneux, which offers its visitors a son et lumière of combat in 1918. Ambient sound in museums suggests that visitors are in a liminal space – on the way to the past. Most of the time, these special effects are used to make people believe that they themselves are really on or near the battlefield, and that they can take a time machine, just for a moment, into the past. This is complete nonsense.

To support my argument, I will present various instances of reenactment and other forms of historical fantasy. Thereafter, I want to add a second charge to my bill of indictment: it is that the reduction of war to the level of personal experience almost always cuts the politics out of it. And there is politics aplenty in this domain. Their omission of the politics of remembrance raises the great danger that in seeking popular ways to honour and glorify those who fought in war, historical reenactors wind up glorifying war itself.

## I Reenactment as 'living history'

A search for what we may term 'authentic history' has led a large number of people to support and engage in false history. The primary impulse behind this shift is a surge of interest in and search for the corporeal experience of war. What history offers are representations and interpretations of the corporal experience of war. For a very large population, that is not enough. What they want is the thing itself.

And they want both more and less than the truth. They want the emotional charge of reenactment, understood 'as a body-based discourse in which the past is reanimated through physical and psychological experience'. 'Once inhabiting this psychological and physiological space … reenactors describe a condition referred to as "period rush" – a state of complete absorption in the reenacted event – followed by difficulty transitioning out of the past and into the present.'

This conversion experience 'take[s] the form of testimonials: reenactors attest to profound experiences that are markers on the hard road to knowledge. They begin as novices (referred to in the reenactment community as "farbs"), undergo trials, acquire skills and experience, and are finally inducted into a community of dedicated reenactors'. In case we miss the religious flavour of the phenomenon, one acute observer of reenactment tells us:

> The epistemological implications of this conversion-testimonial structure are twofold. First, knowledge is the result of individual experience, and, second, it is perceived to be true. Trauma, privation, emotional disturbance, and transformation leave their marks on the body and psyche, and it is to these wounds and scars that reenactors testify.[3]

---

[3] Vanessa Agnew, 'Introduction: What Is Reenactment?', *Criticism*, 46, Special Issue: Extreme and Sentimental History (2004), 327–39.

Wounds, scars, transformations: we clearly have entered into the language of the Eucharist. For many, though not all, Roman Catholics, the wine and the wafer actually become the blood and the body of Christ. Something similar seems to occur for reenactors: they seek to break through the barrier between past and present, and live in the event itself.

I will come in a moment to the price such people pay for converting the profane material of history into the sacred material of quasi-sacred performance. It is relatively easy to see to what extent those who think they are actually at Verdun during the battle are deluded. They miss the otherness, the strangeness of the past in general, and the radical strangeness of that corner of the past in particular. Yet, many of them insist that their reality is more real than any historical account.

Reenactors do what they do for many reasons. For some, their motivation is clear. They are in search of the sacred, and they find it in the horror and suffering of war. Yes, they find other things, too – evidence of courage, fortitude and endurance – but by and large what they seek are limit experiences, extreme experiences to add a new dimension to their lives. One US Civil War reenactor put it clearly when he said that his quest in uniform was similar to the search for the Holy Grail. He found it not in a cup or other artefact but in the scraps of material which made up his uniform.[4]

Reenactors travel. They can be found on all continents. There are dozens of societies of German reenactors of the American Civil War; not surprisingly, most opt for the losing side. On 11 November 2011, there were French reenactors at the inauguration of the Museum of the Great War at Meaux on the river Marne not far from Paris. Other dedicated French amateurs have restaged the battle of Verdun at Verdun, and at the ceremony marking the centennial of the battle there was a march past of French and German units in period uniforms and gear.[5]

Reenactment has long been a lively enterprise in the United States. At Rockport, Illinois, there was recently a 'living history' reenactment of the battle of Verdun.[6] This town was the site of other reenactments of different episodes in the war, including a gas attack and (not surprisingly) American combat in 1918.[7] Similar reenactments were conducted at Parkville, Pennsylvania,[8] and at the Edward Waldo House in

[4] Tony Horwitz, *Confederate in the Attic: Dispatches from America's Unfinished Civil War* (New York, 1998), 388.

[5] www.youtube.com/watch?v=2Kbrr_NwkJY.

[6] www.youtube.com/watch?v=PGLTHlFHGyw.

[7] www.youtube.com/watch?v=XBRBwaZoCqo.

[8] www.youtube.com/watch?v=EtMzFhIDeiQ.

Scotland, Connecticut. Thousands of members of the Great War Association 'experience a living history of the Great War', says the presenter of the cable television programme *History's Guns*, presented by the website 'Shooting USA', an affiliate of the National Rifle Association.[9] These and other similar events may simply be an echo of the much larger phenomenon of the US Civil War reenactment movement. But they are by no means restricted to the United States.

In 2018 the 10th Essex, the Royal Warwicks and the Rifle Corps were on display in full First World War kit and attire at a reenactment by living history groups participating in the Great War weekend at Batemans, a seventeenth-century mansion and its grounds at Burwash, in Sussex.[10] The same group shows those who want to know what British drill instructions were like in the First World War.[11] Near Chelmsford, the 'Queen's Own' Royal West Kent Regiment Living History Group (50th & 97th) manned trenches to mark the centennial.[12] Former history teacher and Great War specialist Andrew Robertshaw dug a trench system in his back garden in Oxfordshire and dressed up archaeologists and reenactors to help them understand 'the individual experience' of soldiers in the line in the Great War.[13] You can also find on YouTube a reenactor displaying his cooking skills at the front.[14] British First World War gear for the Royal Naval Division can be seen (and purchased), from an American source.[15] North of the border, reenactors presented the trench life of the Canadian Black Watch Regiment in 1918.[16]

More surprising was the Great War reenactment 'family day' in the War Memorial Gardens in Islandbridge, in Dublin, in May 2016.[17] Such an event, sponsored by the Irish Great War Society, would have been inconceivable twenty years ago. Two decades later the onset of peace in Northern Ireland created the social space for a commemoration of Irishmen who died in the British army during the Great War. I can recall visiting this site thirty-odd years ago – it was covered by waist-high grass and served well as a field for grazing horses. Now it is spick and span and suitable for reenactment. Other parts of Dublin served

[9] www.youtube.com/watch?v=xsCBet-OSww. Russian soldiers are represented too, and they are on the side of the good guys!

[10] www.youtube.com/watch?v=JTJNkeyb39A.

[11] www.youtube.com/watch?v=vI7jYRMI9vI.

[12] www.youtube.com/watch?v=kck7Y_zWnAk.

[13] www.youtube.com/watch?v=W9dHIPwgVWA.

[14] www.youtube.com/watch?v=g1CsXrSJNUE.

[15] www.youtube.com/watch?v=CDhSbLZuZqA.

[16] www.youtube.com/watch?v=fhofYrtmAb8.

[17] www.youtube.com/watch?v=OeukmSzvSTY.

as living sets for reenactments of the Easter Monday Rising in Ireland in the same year.[18]

There is a secondary market for younger people, too. Legoland offers a display of soldiers in the battle of the Somme, presumably for younger reenactors.[19] There are six other moments in the war similarly displayed, and video games are on sale as well. Evidently reenactment is a profitable enterprise for those who provide the paraphernalia, both for reenactors and for their families. There is no better example of the phenomenon George Mosse described thirty years ago as the trivialisation of war.[20]

Reenactment straddles the globe. In 2017, Slovenian reenactors 'relived' the battle of Caporetto. Despite a major hailstorm, more than 200 soldiers entertained 4,000 visitors at the scene of the battle.[21] At Beersheva in Israel, Australian reenactors staged their cavalry charge of 1917,[22] and they made sure that their hosts were part of the story – note the Israeli flag flying proudly, thirty years before the State of Israel was founded (Figure 1). In November 2017, British troops recaptured Jerusalem again, just as they had done a century before[23] (Figure 2). In 2018, there was a Kiwi reenactment of the liberation of Le Quesnoy, replete with armoured cars and air power.[24] It was repeated on 4 November 2018, precisely 100 years after the battle. Not surprisingly, Gallipoli was reenacted at Lake Kalapiro, in Cambridge, New Zealand, in 2014.[25] So, too, was the use of tanks on the Somme two years later, at the same site.[26]

This range of effort and expense is a global phenomenon, aided by the internet. Arming and clothing a troop of reenactors is easier than it ever was: all you need is access to the web, and then the door is open to anyone who believes that everyone can know, through acting, what it felt like to fight in the Great War.

One aspect of the phenomenon of reenactment that does deserve our respect is its emphasis on emotion. Those who write about war without emotion are suffering from a delusion. The questions that matter are how to express emotion, how does politics frame the expression of

[18] www.youtube.com/watch?v=vGG-q64XMxw.

[19] www.youtube.com/watch?v=dXq7gVjCGEw.

[20] George Mosse, *Fallen Soldiers: Reshaping the Memory of the World Wars* (New York, 1990).

[21] www.youtube.com/watch?v=iPcQAFzuK2k. They even withstood a hailstorm to see the reenactment.

[22] www.youtube.com/watch?v=zntbs_ebxhQ.

[23] www.haaretz.com/israel-news/.premium.MAGAZINE-the-british-conquer-jerusalem-again-1.5628395.

[24] www.youtube.com/watch?v=ep8NsLR-5s8.

[25] www.youtube.com/watch?v=j-9Dq30Yo9M.

[26] www.youtube.com/watch?v=jAvURZzfUX4.

Figure 1 Battle of Beersheva, reenactment, 2017 (note the Israeli flag in the centre). (Source: The PMO, 31 October 2017.)

emotion, and what part of the emotional universe of the past lies within our reach?

## II Emotion and the framing of the past: reenactment, the performing arts, museums

To answer these questions, we can divide the spectrum of approaches to representing the Great War into four domains. On one end of the spectrum is reenactment, sought by those who value what they take to be 'living history' and transformational experience. At the other end is academic history. In between are the performing arts and museums, which I shall discuss below. My claim is that academic history, like the performing arts and museums, engages with representations of war. Reenactment occupies a different domain, that of reliving war. Therein lies the rub.

### The temptations of reenactment

I start with the question as to why people reenact battle. What do they get out of it? There are two frameworks which seem to fit these people and their search for a palpable past. The first is that of 'postmemory', a term coined by Marianne Hirsch in her adept description of the indelible imprint made by parents' stories about their lives, stories which give

Figure 2 Entry of Allenby to Jerusalem, reenactment, 2017. (Source: i24news, 8 November 2017.)

their children an eerie sense of having been there with them.[27] Thus one generation's memories seem to inhabit their children's imaginative reconstruction of their own past. Postmemory can work in a didactic sense too. Thus men whose fathers or grandfathers served in war transmit stories about war which their sons and grandsons want to adopt as their own. Reenactment enables them to do so.

The second framework to account for such phenomena is Alison Landsberg's notion of prosthetic memory.[28] This refers to a more general phenomenon than Hirsch's notion of 'postmemory', since in Landsberg's interpretation, many individuals can attach to their lives a series of stories that may have no family or other direct connection, but that make them feel richer, fuller or more accomplished people. At the extreme, this can arise from psychosis, such as the well-known case of Benjamin Wilkomerski, who truly believed he was a child of Holocaust victims, because he was deeply moved by having seen a photograph of one such child, which, he believed, was his own portrait; subject and object merged. He was not a fraud, just a victim of a prosthetic memory that had seamlessly merged with his own sense of himself.

---

[27] Marianne Hirsch, 'The Generation of Postmemory', *Poetics Today*, 29 (2008), 103–28.
[28] Alison Landsberg, *Prosthetic Memory: The Transformation of American Remembrance in the Age of Mass Culture* (New York, 2004).

This genre of remembering entails a splicing into an individual's autobiographical knowledge of specific elements from other people's lives. The messages adopted come from film, television and the internet, a process facilitated by the way they present stories about the past as free-floating signifiers that viewers and visitors can adopt as their own.

This can lead to activism in social movements, such as participating in marches today to join in some way the great Civil Rights marches of the past. Rabbi Abraham Heschel wrote that when he marched in Alabama in the 1960s, his feet were praying. Why can't ours do the same? Reenactors treat this question not as our engagement with a metaphor, but as our entry into a moment in history; we really join the stream of history at a point of our own choosing.

Reenactment, after all, is both a social phenomenon and a very profitable part of the tourist and leisure industries. My tentative reading of reenactment is the following. War unfolds stories which are based on myths, or eternal themes, like love, brotherhood, sacrifice, suffering, redemption. Those stories have been framed for centuries in the traditional churches. I sense that many of the people who have become reenactors are some of those who have left their churches by the millions in the last two generations and are seeking the sacred in a new environment. Reenactment, which is both intensely individualistic and a collective activity, provides this environment. Total immersion, obviously a reference, intended or not, to baptism, leads to living history, or the visceral ingestion of the past, as part of both body and mind. It is a conversion experience, intensely emotional and personally transformative. It is also sold by some very able marketers who know what they are doing, though reducing it entirely to hucksterism would be a mistake.

It is important to qualify this argument by admitting that reenactment has its attraction for those for whom organised religion is still an essential part of their lives. Most sociologists argue that in the developed world the proportion of the population still devoted to their churches is in decline, but that is not the case everywhere. Churchgoing is still common in the American South, and fundamentalist sects and evangelical churches flourish in many parts of the world, particularly in migrant communities. An annual meeting of the Christian Open Door Church in Mulhouse, France, was the unintended trigger for the spread of coronavirus in 2020.[29] In Lebanon, the blood of Imam Hussein is still shed by the Shia faithful, in the ceremony of the Ashura, marking the martyrdom of the House of Ali. Secularisation and religious fervour are both

---

[29] Tangi Salaün, 'Special Report: Five days of worship that set a virus time bomb in France', Reuters, 30 March 2020, www.reuters.com/article/us-health-coronavirus-france-church-spec/special-report-five-days-of-worship-that-set-a-virus-time-bomb-in-france-idUSKBN21H0Q2.

evident in many parts of the world, requiring us to qualify any correlation between trends in organised religion and reenactment.

There is another reason why reenactment is popular today. It is a celebration of martial masculinity at a time when, for a host of reasons, both war and masculine violence have got a bad name. It is wonderful propaganda for the National Rifle Association in the United States. What better way for those who are troubled by feminism to flee the conflicts around #MeToo and the like than by joining other middle-aged men in a search for the thrill of combat and the scent of danger? Of course, reenactment has nothing to do with the brutal face of war and violence, since if anyone bleeds or shits in his trousers, it is purely accidental. Reenactment is a retreat to a vanished world, one in which men of a certain age can feel safe enough together to celebrate their fascination, their fixation even, with guns and organised violence. Reenactment is even a better fix than drugs or alcohol, since there is no hangover the following day.

## The performing arts

The second domain of the representation of war which flourished during the centenary is that of performative artists, institutions and events. Museums, films, concerts, 'dark tourism', art installations and other performances are the central media in which history and memory come together in forms which resist the two extremes – total immersion in emotion in reenactments and total refusal to express emotion in some scholarly quarters.

Did the directors of the very successful play based on Michael Morpurgo's book for children, *War Horse*, engage in reenactment? No, because the social convention which binds theatre companies to their audiences is that they are watching a representation of reality, and not reality itself. The South African puppeteers Adrian Kohler and Basil Jones, and their Handspring Puppet Company, created a maquette of a horse whose body was transparent. The two puppeteers creating his uneven cadence and his equine movements stand under, and work in, the maquette. It is so evidently not a horse that, when their artistry brought the horse to life on stage, the result was utterly stunning (Figure 3). When Steven Spielberg put the book to film, his realism was less true to life than was the artifice of the Handspring Puppet company. In their stage production we saw a living, breathing horse on stage precisely because artists of immense talent used suggestion rather than false special effects designed to 'recreate' reality.

The same contrast can be seen in two versions of R. C. Sherriff's 1929 play *Journey's End*. With Laurence Olivier in the lead, the original presentation was set in one dugout on the Western front just before the

Figure 3 Michael Morpurgo's *War Horse*, National Theatre, London. (Source: *Theatre Times*, 16 November 2018.)

launching of the March 1918 German offensive. The claustrophobia of the underground war was captured on the stage, and when everything was blown to pieces at the end of the play, we knew that the offensive had begun. The part stood for the whole. A film version released in 2018 reproduced most of the dramatic action in Sherriff's original play, but it ends oddly with German soldiers poking around the ruins of the British trench they have just captured. Cinematic realism failed to convey the tension and destructive force of war as well as did the indirection of Sherriff's theatrical treatment of the theme.

In Britain many of the most striking imaginative works on war that have been produced during the centennial were not realistic in character or form.[30] One way to understand reenactment is as a form of amateur theatrical work trying to touch war, or to present it as a living reality, while disseminating a hidden agenda that war is honourable and so too is the possession and use of guns and ammunition.

It is possible to argue that reenactment is just a form of open-air theatre, or an open-air version of war films, in which the actors are people like you and me. The difficulty with this argument is that both theatre and film present an imagined alternative reality, one that we know did not happen in the way shown on stage or screen, whereas

---

[30] Jenny Waldman *et al.*, *14–18 Now: Contemporary Art Commissions for the First World War Centenary* (London, 2019).

reenactment presents an experienced alternative reality, one which enables participants to leap over the proscenium arch directly into the past. When staged performances become in the eyes of those staging them a pathway into the heart and soul of the past, then they go beyond the art of performance and enter the domain of enhanced reality.

One of the most successful ventures in drawing on all the arts in the commemorative period was a British project called 14–18 Now. It was a publicly financed organisation which presented and funded over 100 works of art about the war. Among these works are William Kentridge's play about African porters and soldiers in the First World War, *The Head and the Load*, which premiered at the Tate Modern in London, moved to Germany and then to New York. It is a brilliant representation of Africans at war, using techniques from Brecht's Berliner Ensemble, as well as puppets and *latèrna magica* effects, to bring out the price Africans paid during the war (Figure 4). Another such imaginative project sponsored by 14–18 Now was the pilgrimage to many destinations of one part of Paul Cummins's *Blood Swept Lands and Seas of Red*, the installation of poppies around the Tower of London in 2014. A third was the performance of the music of John Taverner on 4 August 2014.

All three of these projects touch on the sacred themes of suffering, death and sacrifice. But they do so from within a theatrical framework which announces clearly that these are representations of sacred themes, set in different languages of representation. They are clearly within the category of staged performances. Reenactment goes beyond representation, and therefore beyond history.

That is why it is dangerous. Of course we need to reach out to the vast public concerned with, indeed obsessed by, the Great War. But we must never pretend that we offer them 'the war experience' as did the Imperial War Museum (IWM) from 1990 to 2014 in their permanent and vastly popular exhibit 'The Trench Experience'. The IWM has sobered up and moved on, but a great many people have gone the other way.

Reenactment does present real challenges to historians. We operate within the realm of representations and use documents to create narratives about war. We all know that war is a limit experience. It entails observing the pain of others, as Susan Sontag put it.[31] It is not possible, therefore, to treat writing the history of war the way you would treat the history of prices or population movements. Images and objects carry emotion, and thus have a particular role in both the academic and public history of war. Since emotion is an essential element in the waging of war, it must be so in the history of the waging of war. But

[31] Susan Sontag, *Regarding the Pain of Others* (New York, 2003).

Figure 4 William Kentridge's *The Head and the Load*. (Source: 14–18 Now.)

writing about such emotions does not mean going down *Alice in Wonderland*'s rabbit-hole. We are outside the story, and those who claim they are inside it are either deluded or dangerous.

An analogy may be useful here. Many, perhaps one-third of, American Roman Catholics believe in the miracle of the Eucharist, when the wine and the wafer become the blood and the body of Christ.[32] Two-thirds of those who regularly go to Mass believe in the miracle. But aside from these weekly churchgoers, many Catholics are sceptical or take the ritual as a metaphor. Reenactment takes place in the realm of belief; artistic representation, history in museums, and academic history remain in the realm of metaphor.

## Museums

Museums occupy a space between reenactment and metaphor. They share with reenactors the privileging of artefacts which were used in war. They borrow from the metaphors of the imaginative arts the organisation of objects and captions in such a way as to convey a story, which is

[32] Gregory A. Smith, 'Just one-third of US Catholics agree with their church that Eucharist is body, blood of Christ', Pew Charitable Trust, 5 August 2019, www.pewresearch.org/fact-tank/2019/08/05/transubstantiation-eucharist-u-s-catholics/.

set out in space like a story. It is not battle itself but an account of battle, and therefore approaches what academic historians do.

Of course, we need to adapt the organisation of museal space to the culture of the internet and the cell phone. Interactive design can facilitate learning in a host of ways. The technology is not the problem. What is more troubling is how time horizons have shrunken. What is driving forward many of these attempts at creating virtual reality is the overpowering tendency of the internet to make communication (and perception) instantaneous and (whenever possible) spectacularly visual. Museums are inevitably part of the world of entertainment, and therefore compete for attention with many other attractions including reenactment. But they are also part of the world of learning and, implicitly or explicitly, present to the visitor a social contract, a kind of Hippocratic oath, that their exhibition designers will do the truth no harm.

Most of the time, museums of the First World War keep the faith. But we should note the elements of museal representation which move towards reenactment and thereby implicitly make the false claim that what they provide is the *experience* of war.

There are at least three areas in which we can see how museum designers try to attract a population bombarded by, indeed inundated with, electronic reality. The first is sound; the second is landscape; the third is experiential, specifically the effort to identify the visitor with the warrior or with the victim of the warrior, to make him or her – if only for a moment – part of the experience of war. All three aim at bringing visitors inside historical experience, rather than leaving them outside the past. They suggest that visitors can try on a certain element of past reality and see if it fits. They ask us to enter the mood of war, and if we close our eyes, we can begin a voyage into the past.

Regarding all three museum strategies of bringing visitors into an intimate relation with the past – sound, landscape and a vague notion of 'experience' – I admit to being a purist. The reason is simply that compromising on these points leads almost inevitably to the falsification of history and its refashioning as sanitised entertainment. Consider sound, for instance. Before you enter the Musée de la Grande Guerre in Meaux, near Paris, you hear the sound of artillery projected from below ground. Then, to introduce you to the period, you enter an orientation space, where time moves backward and you hear the sights and sounds of yesteryear. Until the war breaks out. Then you are ushered into the narrative structure of the museum, which does indeed have much of interest in it. Sound here is transitional, a way of telling you what is coming, and preparing you for the voyage you are about to take into the past. The sound is false, and so is the sense that we can really hear the artillery of the Great War. No one can.

The designers of the In Flanders Fields Museum in Ypres initially used sound as a kind of audio soundtrack to accompany visitors. But after consultation with visitors, with their own staff and with others in the profession, they turned the sound off. They recognised that there was no need to add a tonal boost to help visitors understand the tragedy of the war.

There is sound in many of the displays in the Ypres museum, heard privately through earphones, or in enclosed spaces. Some of the most effective representations are films of actors reading historical texts, such as the words of Harvey Cushing, the American neurosurgeon. He is one of what the museum terms its 'iconic people'. Here we are right on the boundary between history and entertainment, since there is a false touch to the surgical gown worn by the actor reading his lines. I am prepared to accept that the text is more important than the props or the staging, but I still feel that the story is being fashioned to suit audiences used to BBC costume dramas. Perhaps this is a necessary compromise, since the words of Cushing (visually and dramatically presented) subvert any notion of the war or human suffering as redemptive.

The second arena of negotiation between entertainment and history is in the presentation of landscape. I have noted that some years ago the IWM finally scrapped its old, and highly popular, displays of 'The Trench Experience'. But the new Great War Museum at Meaux gives us a plastic trench painted to look like the real thing. Whenever present-day products are used to imitate historical artefacts, then the game is up. We glide between the false and the true like politicians, and immediately lose any idea that what we see in a museum is real. I admire the presentation in the In Flanders Fields Museum of a tree ring, showing damage to the tree during Great War bombardment (Figure 5). This is not a representation of a tree, but the tree itself, a document on which the war is written in black, indicating when the tree was almost killed at the time. It is like a man who has a shrapnel wound in his back and goes on living with the embodied traces of war. Showing it is history *pur et dure*, and nothing but the truth.

Representations of landscapes in museums are very similar to sets in theatre or opera. They provide ambience, mood and (literally) a setting, not a kind of frozen reality. One comic example from television history made this point in an unforgettable way. In the 1989 BBC series *Blackadder Goes Forth*, there is an exchange where General Melchett surveys a map of the land 'recaptured since yesterday'. He asks his adjutant what is the scale of the map. The answer is 1:1; what the General was looking at *is* the land taken from the Germans: 17½ feet.[33] So much for

---

[33] Richard Curtis and Ben Elton, 'Blackadder Goes Forth: Advanced World War I Tactics with General Melchett', www.youtube.com/watch?reload=9&v=rblfKREj500, at 2:22.

Figure 5 Tree trunk and tree rings displayed in In Flanders Fields Museum, Ypres. (Photo: author.)

any artificial landscape providing a point of entry into the lived experience of the battle of the Somme or any battle like it.

The third area of compromise concerns the representation of what is usually termed the landscape of battle. By that I mean a certain ambience of desolation, shown for example in a large display in the US National World War I Museum in Kansas City. Its purpose is to bring the visitor into an alternative world of massive destruction and danger (Figure 6). The problem is that such artificial installations, being inherently false, cannot convey 'what it was really like' to be at war. No one who visits a war museum can enter into the landscape of war, and any attempt that pretends to make that possible is doomed to fail.

A similar problem confronts visitors to the US Holocaust Museum and Memorial in Washington, DC. Entrants are given a card on which is written the name of someone who was trapped in the Nazi state or in countries they occupied, and who became a victim of its racial policies, leading to genocide. Identification with the victims is understandable; moving into their experience is not. It constitutes precisely the kind of 'prosthetic memory' that reenactors conjure up from their day on the beaches of Normandy or in the forests of Poland.

Figure 6 Trench design, National World War I Museum and Memorial, Kansas City. (Photo: author.)

Museums can represent the experience of war but they cannot bring visitors into it. And that is the key choice that they, and all of us, have to make. In the Historial de la Grande Guerre, the designers of the museum (of whom I was one) decided to stylise the arrangement of objects in the *fosses*, or dugouts, to suggest that we are not in the business of creating a false sense that visitors can enter the domain of warfare by looking at a dozen objects soldiers used in the trenches (Figure 7). False realism is the danger lurking in this field, and the more designers gesture towards realism, the more they come up against the hard truth that much (if not all) of the experience of war lies at or beyond the limits of representation.

### III Conclusion

Reenactment of battlefield history falsifies the truth on a host of levels, no matter how authentic the uniforms or weaponry may be. It is not only naive; it is also dangerous, because sanitising war – by separating it from terror, pain and bloodshed – makes it thinkable, and therefore, doable in the future.

The second major flaw of reenactment is the exclusion of politics from the domain of war experience. Reenactors are in search of a reified

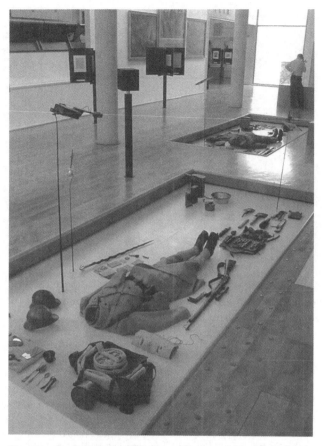

Figure 7 *Fosse*, French soldier's uniform and kit, Historial de
la Grande Guerre, Péronne. (Photo: author.)

experience, almost always masculine. Some New Zealand nurses on a
pilgrimage I led to Gallipoli, though, could not resist the temptation to
put on the uniforms of their sisters who served in the war, as though
the cloth could convey or offer a privileged point of entry to an earlier
reality. Once more the absence of the idea that war is a political act is
palpable. The reality of war, and in particular the reality of the Great
War, was bound up in national sentiment supporting state power
arrayed with tenacity against other state powers just as determined to
see the struggle through to victory. Reenactors bypass this essential
meaning of war, and thereby present a reified image of battle, as an
engagement in violence outside of politics.

Figure 8 Military history enthusiasts dressed as Nazi troops take part in a stage battle 'Summer 1941' near the village of Ivanovskoye, some 60 km outside Moscow, on 22 June 2014. (Source: Dmitry Serebryakov/AFP/Getty Images.)

If the exclusion of the political distorts the Great War, you can imagine what it does when German reenactors put on Wehrmacht uniforms of the Second World War, and recreate the 1941 invasion of the USSR (Figure 8). Here is infotainment at its worst: a mixture of the obscene and the idiotic. Even if reenactors were to try (for an hour or two) to show solidarity with the victims of the German invasion of Poland, the Baltic states, Ukraine, Byelorussia and Russia, by pretending to walk alongside them, they would betray them, since we (and they) cannot know what they went through. Marking such events is important; staging them borders on absurdity. Turning suffering into entertainment is the worst kind of kitsch, and no historian worthy of the name wants to promote that.

It is important, though, to recognise the attraction of reenactment, and the money it generates, in order to understand the difficulties museum directors have in resisting it. Yes, museums have had bumper years of attendance during the centennial, but now (2020) that season is over. Now what? Will declining revenues require a more user-friendly approach to conveying the experience of war? If so, then I urge the museum world to turn to presenting theatre like *War Horse* or installations like Philippe Prost's *Ring of Memory* near Arras, France, or music like Benjamin Britten's *War Requiem*. The imaginative arts do not attempt reenactment. They do much better than that. They provide what Viet Thanh Nguyen terms 'Just Memory'.[34] They tell the truths no reenactment can convey.

In much recent commemorative activity, the complexity of the war has been reduced to the personal level. This in part is a reflection of the increased significance of the visual in our internet-driven culture. Photographs, as Barthes has shown us, are powerful reminders of mortality, including our own, and they serve as indexical documents, perhaps as much as, or at times even more vividly than, do written documents. The personal can be conveyed by letters and objects, to be sure, but when these letters or objects or faces are captured in photography, they take on an additional aura of authenticity.[35]

Museums show artefacts to bring that feeling of authenticity to the visitor, but even better is when they can juxtapose real objects with film or still photographs of the objects in use. This accounts in part for the success of the Historial de la Grande Guerre at Péronne, Somme, where small video screens perched on poles show the objects around them in action. The same use of objects, and of images of objects used by people, dominates television history. Without photographs or other images, televisual history is impossible. Much internet-driven history, like genealogical research, is first-person history, and when no authentic voice can be found in memoirs, then visual history searches for its story elsewhere. To be sure, what we now call the history of material culture has brought the richness of ancient and medieval societies to large populations both in museums and on television. As Ken Burns's path-breaking 1989 American television series on the history of the American Civil War showed, hearing actors reading aloud the letters contemporaries wrote to their loved ones is a powerful way of conveying history to millions. In the age of the witness,[36] the voice of the individual living through war understandably has become an essential part of televisualised history. When the voice matches the face of the man or woman who went through war, then we viewers can be both moved and informed at the same time.

The problem remains, though, that there is much important historical writing which focuses on issues beyond the biographical and the personal. That is why much of the best new historiography we have is not represented to any significant degree in the public domain. While the internet has put online an astonishing array of documents, it still privileges the history of individual men and women, moments of whose

---

[34] Viet Thanh Nguyen, *Nothing Ever Dies: Vietnam and the Memory of War* (Cambridge, MA, 2016).

[35] Jay Winter, *War beyond Words* (Cambridge, 2017), ch. 2.

[36] Annette Wieviorka, *The Era of the Witness* (Ithaca, 2006).

lives are captured vividly in particular in photographs and in letters. And most of these men and women are white. The work of artists in initiatives like 14–18 Now has helped to change the colour of the archive, but it is still true that the voices and faces of white participants in the war are prioritised in public history whereas people of other skin colours are marginalised.

The online archiving of mountains of war records both enriches visual history and virtually closes off other avenues of historical thinking and representations. While the internet has democratised the archive, by adding millions of voices and records to it, it has also pointed scholars in the direction of questions that can be answered by reference to online sources alone.[37] What of the vast majority of archives that cannot afford digitisation, which is the case in much of Africa, Asia and Latin America? Are their holdings so far off the beaten path – the online path – as to be consigned to oblivion?

The better path for us to take is to accept the conditions and limits of public history, while expanding the range and nature of the sources it uses and the questions it poses. Furthermore, we must keep on trying to insert in the discourse of public history the fruits of our archival research in all kinds of archives, both on- and offline. We must continue to insist on the complexity and messiness of history and on the stubborn fact that there are some facets of war that simply cannot be reenacted.

A little bit of humility is no bad thing in the work both we and they do. It can make some people stand back from turning war into the subject of a theme park and history into a light consumer durable good. We all have a moral obligation to do better than that.

[37] See Jay Winter and Antoine Prost, *The Great War in History*, 2nd edn (Cambridge, 2020), ch. 9.

*Transactions of the RHS* 30 (2020), pp. 141–163 © The Author(s), 2020. Published by Cambridge University Press on behalf of the Royal Historical Society
doi:10.1017/S0080440120000079

# THE 'MARTYRDOM OF THINGS': ICONOCLASM AND ITS MEANINGS IN THE SPANISH CIVIL WAR*

## By Mary Vincent ⓘ

READ 10 MAY 2019

ABSTRACT. The anticlerical violence of the Spanish Civil War has received significant scholarly attention in recent years. However, there has been relatively little focus on the iconoclasm, even though the destruction of objects was easily the most common form of anticlerical violence. Nor has the effect of iconoclastic violence on those who treasured or venerated these objects been examined. This article looks at the emotional significance of the material artefacts that came under attack during the Civil War. It argues that, while some objects were treated simply as the material of which they were made, most provoked more complex interactions. In contrast to most earlier episodes of iconoclasm, these also left a visual record, which shows how the memory of the violence was shaped not only by textual accounts but also by photographs that memorialised and aestheticised it.

> … [A]s well as the chalices, ciboria, monstrances, vestments, retables, confessionals, images, Holy Week floats, altars etc. they destroyed roofs, ceilings, doors, windows, grilles, balconies, floors, bells etc. leaving only the walls.[1]

In 1961, Father (later Bishop) Antonio Montero Moreno published the definitive reckoning of the anticlerical violence of the Spanish Civil War. This meticulous delineation of the 'religious persecution' of 1936–9 confirmed the deaths of nearly 7,000 religious personnel, 13 bishops, 4,184 diocesan priests, 2,365 monks and brothers and 283 nuns.[2] The anticlerical onslaught took place largely during the first months of the Civil War, a period of regime collapse when central

---

*The work for this article was funded by a Leverhulme Trust Major Research Fellowship: MRF-2016-109 'Religious Violence in the Spanish Civil War: Iconoclasm and Crusade'. Along with many other historians, I am grateful to the Trust for their generous support.

[1] Letter from parish priest, La Alberca (Murcia), Archivo Histórico Nacional (AHN) Causa General (CG) Legajo 1068 Pieza 10a.

[2] Antonio Montero Moreno, *Historia de la persecución religiosa en España, 1936–9* (Madrid, 1961); see further Vicente Cárcel Ortí, *La persecución en España durante la Segunda República* (Madrid, 1990), 234–43.

authority was disrupted and de facto power lay with spontaneous revolutionary committees of trade unionists and militiamen. Arson attacks on ecclesiastical buildings – 'church-burning' – entailed widespread destruction, while searches of ecclesiastical buildings – either for 'treasure' or for arms – caused great damage and served as invitations for looting. Religious objects were also confiscated during searches of private homes.

In and of itself, this extensive episode of iconoclastic violence has received little historical attention. Studies of the Republican rearguard examine violence in more general terms and tend to concentrate on violence against the person.[3] Similarly, the historiography of anticlericalism in Spain has focused on the protagonists, seeing iconoclasm as one of a range of transgressive actions that cemented bonds between newly formed revolutionary groups.[4] The anticlerical repertoire is well established, and several studies speculate as to motive and intention. But the effects of the iconoclasm, particularly on those who owned, venerated or loved these destroyed or damaged objects, remains unexamined.[5]

The anticlerical violence of 1930s Spain was intertwined with both the wider Civil War – which allowed the violence to rage unchecked – and the preceding Second Republic, which established the Church as a political protagonist. The political historiography has tended to regard anticlericalism as a secondary issue, one factor among several that fuelled the left/right divide. In contrast, clerical commentators tend to disregard the wider political context, seeing instead a history of religious persecution and martyrdom that began with the secularising legislation of the Second Republic. Given the scale of the killings, which clearly fitted the Christian idea of martyrdom, this is perhaps not surprising.[6]

---

[3] José Luis Ledesma, *Los días de llamas de la revolución: violencia y política en la retaguardia republicana durante la Guerra Civil* (Zaragoza, 2003) and 'Qué violencia para qué retaguardia o la República en guerra de 1936', *Ayer*, 76 (2009), 83–114; Julius Ruiz, *The 'Red Terror' and the Spanish Civil War* (Cambridge, 2014); Mary Vincent '"The Keys of the Kingdom": Religious Violence in the Spanish Civil War July–August 1936', in *The Splintering of Spain: Cultural History and the Spanish Civil War, 1936–39*, ed. Chris Ealham and Michael Richards (Cambridge, 2005), 87–8.

[4] The fullest study of the perpetrators is Maria Thomas, *The Faith and the Fury: Popular Anticlerical Violence and Iconoclasm in Spain, 1931–6* (Brighton, 2013); see also her 'Sacred Destruction? Anticlericalism, Iconoclasm and the Sacralization of Politics in Twentieth-Century Spain', *European History Quarterly*, 47 (2017), 490–508; and José Luis Ledesma, 'Enemigos seculars: la violencia anticlerical', in *Izquierda obrera y religión en España, 1900–39*, ed. Feliciano Montero and Julio de la Cueva (Alcalá de Henares, 2012), 219–44.

[5] See further *Feeling Things: Objects and Emotions through History*, ed. Stephanie Downes, Sally Holloway and Sarah Randles (Oxford, 2018).

[6] See Julio de la Cueva, 'Religious Persecution, Anticlerical Tradition and Revolution: On Atrocities against the Clergy during the Spanish Civil War', *Journal of Contemporary History*, 33 (1998), 355–69.

The first beatification causes were opened in the late 1940s and, though they came to completion only after 1986, testimony was collected even before the war had ended. The memory of the violence was thus handed down through the voices of the victims and – as this paper will show – by the objects themselves.

These testimonies acknowledged the huge scale of violence against buildings, monuments, images and objects, as did Father Montero in his final chapter on the 'martyrdom of things', which drew heavily on the first attempt at some kind of overview of material loss, Castro Albarrán's *La gran víctima* (1939). Both authors interpreted iconoclastic violence as a sustained and coordinated attempt to drive religion – that is, Roman Catholicism – out of Spain. Indeed, Canon Castro Albarrán had been prominent in formulating the arguments for 'holy war' that were used to justify the military rising of July 1936 and proved instrumental in baptising the ensuing war effort as a 'crusade'.[7] The iconoclasm was used as evidence – perhaps even as proxy – of the intentions of their adversaries. The 'martyrdom of things' was defined by the nature of the enemy: barbarous, pitiless, insensate and Satanic.

The rhetorical point was to underline the attack on religion, the prevention of Christian worship and the injury to Catholic culture. Barbarism – denoted by terms such as vandalism, pillage and sacking – converted the anticlericals into a savage horde, intent on wreaking unimaginable destruction. As Gamboni has noted, in the modern period 'ignorance' became 'a key concept in the stigmatization of iconoclasm', and descriptions of the iconoclasm always emphasised its 'vandalism'.[8] References to pillage and sacking underlined the lack of regard for beauty or history. 'Energumens' acting under diabolic instruction targeted the tabernacle, then the altar and then the crucifix, finally setting fire to 'all vestments, images, reredoses and whatever else they might find', destroying art and heritage alongside religion.[9]

It is the fact and the scale of the iconoclasm that is of concern in these descriptions, and which is, in turn, assumed to reveal the truth about the perpetrators. Unlike human beings, 'things' are always 'innocent', Montero argued. Their sacred nature in and of itself demonstrated their assailants' intent to extirpate Christianity. As he pointed out, there can be no military motive for 'destroying an image of the Virgin,

[7] Aniceto Castro Albarrán, *Guerra santa: el sentido católico del movimiento nacional española* (Burgos, 1938).

[8] Dario Gamboni, *The Destruction of Art: Iconoclasm and Vandalism since the French Revolution* (1997), 13–20, at 13.

[9] Joan Estelrich, *La persecución religiosa en España* (Buenos Aires, 1937), 52–9, at 57; Luis Carreras, *The Glory of Martyred Spain* (1939; first published in Spanish, Toulouse, 1938), 76–85, esp. 78.

burning a reredos, or trampling on corpses'.[10] Again, 'martyrdom' lay in the intention and purpose of the assailants, as well as their choice of targets. The assumption was that these were sacred objects: images, tabernacles and Eucharistic paraphernalia. In Catholic tradition, there is a liminality to these objects, notably those that represent the body.[11] Not only are human beings made in the image of God, but God also took human form. Images are thus both material and immaterial, just as is, in another example, the consecrated Host.[12] The tabernacle had its own place within the church and was treated with a veneration that had been significantly enhanced by modern eucharistic practices such as 'watching' and, under Pius X, frequent communion.[13] Reverence towards these objects was not necessarily the preserve of believers. Militiamen searching the Claretian church in Barbastro, ostensibly for arms, stopped before the tabernacle when one said 'Careful! Only a priest can open this; I know something about these things.' And, indeed, they asked a priest to open it.[14]

This particular class of 'holy' object – and, indeed, this kind of magical thinking – was surely what Fr Montero had in mind when he wrote that 'their obliteration highlights the hatred of what lay behind them, [that is] of God, which they represent'.[15] But these were not the only targets of the anticlericals nor did they represent the limits of the iconoclasm. As the destruction was usually undiscriminating, it encompassed sacred objects (images, relics, tabernacles, chalices, ciboria, vestments), secular items (paintings, pews, retables, glass- and metalwork) – both of which could include valuable, and even priceless, works of art – and everyday objects of little intrinsic value (candles, food, cutlery, linen etc.). Similarly, while contemporary accounts focus on 'church-burning', it only accounts for part of the material destruction. Searches of ecclesiastical buildings and private homes led to the confiscation of personal and domestic religious objects which, like those from destroyed churches, could be treated in various ways. Many items were burnt, destroyed or deliberately defaced; others were stolen, looted or lost; some were

[10] Montero Moreno, *Historia*, 627.

[11] David Morgan, *The Embodied Eye: Religious Visual Culture and the Social Life of Feeling* (Berkeley and Los Angeles, 2012).

[12] W. J. T. Mitchell, *What Do Pictures Want? The Lives and Loves of Images* (Chicago, 2005), 97.

[13] For the Spanish context see Mary Vincent, *Catholicism in the Second Spanish Republic: Religion and Politics in Salamanca, 1930–6* (Oxford, 1996), 82–108.

[14] Jesús Quibus, *Misioneros Mártires: Hijos del Corazón de María de la Provincia de Cataluña sacrificados en la persecución marxista* (Barcelona, 1941), 45.

[15] Montero Moreno, *Historia*, 627; the questionnaire circulated by Madrid diocese's Vicaría de Reorganización only asked about 'cosas sagradas' and did not include any request for inventories or exact numbers, though parish priests were asked about monetary value. *Boletín Oficial del Obispado de Madrid-Alcalá*, 15 June 1939, 137–8.

reused, requisitioned or stored. But whatever their fate, it depended on an interaction with human beings, and one that was governed as much by the materiality of the object as by the intention of the person.

There is little hint of this complexity in Montero Moreno's 'martyrdom of things', nor of the materiality of the things he is discussing. They are martyred, not by their own choice or agency, but by their sacred nature, that is their liminality, and the evil intentions of their assailants. There is no precision to his – or anyone else's – statistics, no typology of the different types of damage, no differentiation of the material destruction. In an entirely specious table, categories such as 'liturgical objects destroyed' and 'churches partly destroyed, profaned and sacked' are recorded as 'almost all', 'all of those affected' and, for 'churches destroyed', 'several'.[16] Similarly, according to Castro Albarrán, in Seville, in one afternoon, seven churches were 'reduced to ashes', another six 'sacked by the mob' while 'other churches that we won't go through now as it would never end' lost 'for ever a countless number of paintings, sculptures, garments, sacred vessels, objects in ceramic and metal, embroideries, tapestries, grilles, jewellery, reliquaries … the list would be interminable'.[17]

There is no doubt that, apart from buildings, the damage was hard – and is now impossible – to catalogue. This was due in part to the scale and complexity of the iconoclasm, in part to the length of the war and in part to a lack of inventories.[18] Numbers became another way to represent the criminal barbarity of indiscriminate destruction, though the attention paid to monetary value acted as a reminder that these items were also property. The attempts at accounting may have served as a coping mechanism, surveying and quantifying the damage in a way that made it seem manageable, even as it served as a claim to restitution.[19] But, even so, there is a vagueness around material damage that not only permeates contemporary commentary but also came to structure the historical record. Paradoxically, this persists even through the lists that punctuate every account of the violence. As with the accounting measures, these lists purport to catalogue but, as none of the terms are

---

[16] Montero Moreno, *Historia*, 629–30, cf. Aniceto Castro Albarrán, *La gran víctima: La iglesia española mártir de la revolución roja* (Salamanca, 1940), 130–1.

[17] Castro Albarrán, *La gran víctima*, 90–1.

[18] The Republican Ley de Tesoro Artístico (1933) was intended to protect and catalogue national heritage, including that in ecclesiastical hands; it remained in force until 1985. Rebeca Saavedra Arias, *Destruir y proteger: el patrimonio histórico-artístico durante la Guerra Civil* (Santander, 2016), 158–9; Miguel Cabañas Bravo, 'La Dirección General de Bellas Artes republicana y su reiterada gestión por Ricardo de Orueta, 1931–1936', *Archivo Español de Arte*, 82 (2009), 169–93.

[19] David de Boer, 'Picking up the Pieces: Catholic Material Culture and Iconoclasm in the Low Countries', *BMGN – Low Countries Historical Review* 131 (2016), 59–80, esp. 73–8.

defined, fail to provide even a taxonomy of lost objects. The list simply becomes another device to emphasise the scale of the losses and the vandalism of the attackers.

The sharp contrast between the generalities with which the iconoclasm is treated and the forensic data-gathering around those who had died is unmistakable and characterises all the accounts and memoirs – collectively known as 'martyrologies' – that we have. As Montero relied on these accounts, it is not surprising that, in contradistinction to his 'figures' on material damage, he provided detailed lists of names of the religious personnel who were killed, their dates, place of death, place of origin and, where possible, the manner of their execution.

There thus appears to be a significant difference in the confidence with which religious authorities approached violence against human beings as against that directed at material objects. Priests and religious knew how to recognise, define and, crucially, how to write about martyrs, hence the steady production of martyrologies and, later, of beatification causes. The Francoist state also collected information on the anticlerical violence – most notoriously in the extraordinary archive known as the Causa General, essentially a prosecution of the Second Republic for crimes against Spain – but it relied on the Church for information on anticlerical violence. The stereotypes and vague reckonings are thus repeated in the official record, which is far fuller and more precise in its documentation of violence against the person than of material damage, of which, however, we can find tantalising traces.

So, what then are we to make of the 'martyrdom of things'? Why this strange formulation for an episode that most clerical commentators actually seem to avoid in some way? One answer may lie in the political instrumentalisation of the anticlerical violence and the sacralisation of Franco's war effort, that is, the construction of the Crusade.[20] Alternatively, Montero's own argument may suggest a more metaphorical reading, whereby the sacrifice of blameless objects underlined the innocence of the clerical victims, in contrast to the war dead, who died bearing arms.[21] Each has some validity, but neither engages with the actual nature of iconoclasm, that is, the materiality of material destruction. Given that the sources largely do not engage with this either, this is probably not surprising. But a close and sometimes cross-grained reading

---

[20] This is the only area that has received substantive historiographical attention; see e.g. Julián Casanova, *La iglesia de Franco* (Madrid, 2001); Peter Anderson, 'In the Name of the Martyrs: Memory and Retribution in Francoist Southern Spain, 1936–45', *Cultural and Social History*, 8 (2011), 355–70; Miguel Ángel del Arco Blanco, 'Before the Altar of the Fatherland: Catholicism, the Politics of Modernization, and Nationalization during the Spanish Civil War', *European History Quarterly*, 48 (2018), 232–55.

[21] Mary Vincent, 'The Martyrs and the Saints: Masculinity and the Construction of the Francoist Crusade', *History Workshop Journal*, 47 (1999), 69–98.

of them reveals much about the 'martyrdom of things' and not simply in terms of the attentions of their assailants.

Martyrdom is a voluntary act. It entails the willing acceptance of death for a higher cause or purpose, an act of resignation that renders that death sacrificial. If martyrdom is a sacrificing of the self then, clearly, there can be no 'martyrdom of things' as 'things' have no subjectivity. They do, however, have a materiality that makes certain demands of those who interact with them. And interaction with material objects – images, 'holy' pictures, rosaries, medals, scapulars, prayer cards and, above all, crucifixes – was definitional in the everyday practice of Catholicism.[22] The 'agency of the object' structures human actions when engaged with that object, both in ordinary circumstances and at the moment of their destruction. The different and varied ways in which religious items were treated during the 'martyrdom of things' tells us much not only about the iconoclasm, but also about the nature of Spanish Catholicism.

## I Burning and breaking: the forms of destruction

In its strictest sense, iconoclasm means image-breaking.[23] There is clear evidence that this very particular kind of object – an icon/idol – was sought out by those intent on attacking the physical presence of the Church in 1936. In the large towns and cities, left-wing activists, usually mobilised through trade unions and now forming spontaneous revolutionary committees, used arson to signal the end of the old social order.[24] As militia groups formed, armed columns then took the incendiarism out to the pueblos, where they found no shortage of collaborators to help strip the churches, and, often, torch the buildings. As the contents were emptied, however, a distinction emerged in the way different objects were treated, with some apparently being seen for what they were and others as what they were made of.

There is no clear categorisation here. The same kinds of objects were treated in different ways on different occasions. But there were some patterns. Invariably, the assailants piled furnishings, altars, statues and whatever else they could find into a large pyre, either in the church or on the street outside. One parish priest in Madrid, for example,

---

[22] *Feeling Things*, ed. Downes *et al.*, 27–96; Abigail Brundin, Deborah Howard and Mary Laven, *The Sacred Home in Renaissance Italy* (Oxford, 2018), 113–48.

[23] On the history and nature of iconoclasm, see Mitchell *What Do Pictures Want?*, 28–56, 125–44, 158–66; Gamboni, *The Destruction of Art*; Alain Besançon, *The Forbidden Image: An Intellectual History of Iconoclasm* (Chicago, 2000); and Andrew Spicer, 'Iconoclasm', *Renaissance Quarterly*, 70 (2017), 1007–22.

[24] See further Thomas *The Faith and the Fury*, 74–99; and Ledesma, *Los días de llamas de la revolución*, 244–69.

specified the burning of 'some twenty-five prie-dieux', while in Olot (Girona) a bonfire was made in the Carmelite church of 'the usual combustibles … retables, images, confessionals, benches, doors'.[25] The religious images found inside Spanish churches were predominantly made of polychromed wood and so were easy to burn. Indeed, 'the burning and destruction of images' was the 'most common' anticlerical act: crucifixes and statues of the Virgin and saints were invariably the first items to be removed.[26] In Linares de la Sierra (Huelva), local Socialists tried to save the images, removing them from the parish church before the altars, pews and other furniture were burnt inside it. But more militant elements insisted that the images be burnt too; they were only 'branches of orange trees', they told the villagers, before using them to stage a mock bullfight and throwing them on a bonfire.[27]

As this example clearly shows, the actions of the iconoclasts were provocative, usually performative and always transgressive. They were also complex; hence the bullfight with the Virgin's veil as a cape, and a statue as the charging bull, both animated by human action in a spectacle designed as entertainment. Breaking taboos formed a collective bond and hardened a revolutionary identity rooted in socialist and proletarian values. The Church, long allied to the political right, was singled out as the enemy of the people, and ecclesiastical property of all kinds assaulted. The enmity of the 'people' – or at least of the revolutionaries – was clear. However, while the 'power' of the Spanish Church remains the go-to explanation for anticlerical violence, it was an easy target. Despite endless rumours of stockpiled arms and priests firing from bell towers, ecclesiastical buildings were undefended, and the objects inside them, by definition, offered no resistance. (See Figure 1.) Indeed, this may have contributed to Montero's insistence on their 'innocence'.

The result of this powerlessness was enormous destruction. Famously, Spain's only known work by Michelangelo, a statue of the infant John the Baptist, was smashed to pieces, while El Greco's Risen Christ had its arms and feet hacked off.[28] The threat posed to national heritage was

---

[25] Archivo Histórico Diocesano de Madrid (AHDM) Legajo 2585 (Nuestra Señora de Los Angeles), letter dated 17 Dec. 1942; Simón María Besalduch, *Nuestros Mártires: Religiosos Carmelitas asesinados en España, por causa de la fe, durante la guerra contra el comunismo Soviético que empezó con el Glorioso Alzamiento Nacional del 18 de Julio de 1936 y terminó el 1 de abril de 1939* (Barcelona, 1940), 363.

[26] Saavedra Arias, *Destruir y proteger*, 119, quoting report now held in the Archivo General de la Administración (AGA).

[27] George A. Collier, *Socialists of Rural Andalusia: Unacknowledged Revolutionaries of the Second Republic* (Stanford, 1987), 150–1.

[28] El Greco's only known surviving sculpture. Seventeen fragments of the San Juanito survived, a mere 40 per cent of the original. http://es.fundacionmedinaceli.org/actividades/ficharestauracion.aspx?id=14.

Figure 1 Convent of Mother of God, Ronda (Málaga), after a search for arms. (Reproduced with kind permission of Biblioteca Nacional de España.)

immediately recognised by the Republican government, which established an official body to protect 'artistic heritage' on 1 August 1936, five months before equivalent measures were taken by the Francoist side.[29] There was widespread horror at the destruction – particularly

---

[29] Saavedra Arias, *Destruir y proteger*, 53–109; see further *Arte protegido: memoria de la Junta del Tesoro Artístico durante la Guerra Civil*, ed. Isabel Argerich and Judith Ara (Madrid, 2009); and *Arte en tiempos de guerra*, ed. Miguel Cabañas Bravo, Amelia López-Yarto Elizalde and Wifredo Rincón García (Madrid, 2009).

from those with a background in art or heritage work – which was blamed on 'incontrollables'.[30] Indeed, the effective steps the Republican government took to protect artistic heritage may well reflect the profound discomfort caused by having to take such measures against those on their own side.

As the war progressed, a more stable Republican government requisitioned religious objects to protect and catalogue them.[31] Significant works were recoded as art, that is, as museum objects rather than active subjects – and agents – of devotion. 'Great' religious art and architecture was preserved, but as heritage; faith and worship were, in effect, consigned to the past. As this substantial official initiative was, however, a *response* to the destruction, it has been argued that the anticlerical violence was, in fact, the continuation or completion of the Second Republic's secularising project 'from below' and by non-legislative means.[32] The same argument emphasises the materialism of the proletariat, which, rejecting the 'opium' of religion, and deeply critical of the wealth of the Church, took measures to alleviate their own poverty after years of resentment towards Christian charity and religious communities who demanded prayers and gratitude from those who came to them in need.[33]

Many objects were taken from ecclesiastical buildings, a process depicted by clerical commentators as 'pillage' and by some historians as a redistribution or *reparto* but which most closely resembles looting. Though we have almost no information about some of the most common – and most useful – church objects, in general looted objects have to be both portable and desirable, either because they are valuable or because they serve a practical purpose. In Alberca de Záncara (Cuenca), the militiamen took 'the bells, wax and vestments that were left' after the church was stripped. Similarly, all the alms-boxes went from Nuestra Señora de los Angeles parish church in Madrid; metal objects, including a gold reliquary, disappeared along with 'useful items' from the Capuchin monastery in Santander; chalices, patens

---

[30] Joan Cid i Mulet, *La guerra civil i la revolució a Tortosa (1936–9)* (Barcelona, 2001), 42–116; *Tres escritos de Josep María Gudiol i Ricart*, ed. Arturo Ramón and Manuel Barbié (Barcelona, 1987), 89–109; *Un testimonio oficial de la destrucción del arte en la zona roja: el libro de actas de la Junta Republicana del Tesoro Artístico de Castellón* (Bilbao, 1938?), 11–90.

[31] The Libros Inventarios de Cuadros list 22,670 canvasses while the Libros Inventarios de Objetos have 16,279 entries, though 48 of these are blank, Archivo de Guerra, Instituto de Patrimonio Cultural, Madrid.

[32] Thomas, *The Faith and the Fury*, 45–73, 131–44; Juan Manuel Barrios Rozúa, *Iconoclastia 1930–6: La Ciudad de Dios frente a la modernidad* (Granada, 2007), 345–405.

[33] The classic exposition is Joan Connelly Ullman, *The Tragic Week: A Study of Anticlericalism in Spain* (Cambridge, MA, 1968); see also Joaquín Romero Maura, *La rosa de fuego: el obrerismo barcelonés de 1899 a 1909* (Barcelona, 2012), pp. 525, 532–4; the argument has recently been revived by Thomas, *The Faith and the Fury*, 20–44.

and ciboria were taken from the sacristy of the Daughters of Charity in Almería.[34] The subsequent fate of these objects is usually obscure; some will have been sold while others moved into domestic space. We know, for example, of items repurposed as drinking vessels and cooking pots – one Cantabrian militiaman apparently made a point of drinking red wine from a chalice – while candles and other small items could simply be used as they were.[35]

However, metal objects in particular seem to have been viewed primarily in terms of their material. Altar railings and grilles were removed and bells taken down, with profound effects on local soundscapes: the writer Concha Espina remarked that now only cowbells were heard in her Cantabrian valley.[36] Studies of the north-eastern dioceses of Cuenca and Barcelona show that bells were taken systematically, quite often simply by dropping them from the belfry.[37] The lack of heed paid to damage to the bells – let along the fabric of the church – underscores the point that the assailants wanted the material, and not the artefacts themselves. Metal has a clear intrinsic value, it is very useful in wartime and, crucially, it is not combustible. The effort required to remove railings and, especially, bells was amply rewarded by the valuable raw material that they yielded.

Melting down and recasting metal is hardly a domestic enterprise. Cloth, on the other hand, can be reworked at home. Again, textiles were often burnt – as at Malvarrosa (Valencia) where the Hospitallers' vestments, habits and church linens blazed in a great pyre – but there are also many cases of cloth being saved from the flames.[38] In the province of Almería, vestments and altar cloths were taken from the city church of San Sebastián and the parish church in Leitor, while the Sisters of Mary Immaculate lost both church and household cloths.[39] At the Dominican house in Calanda (Aragón), after a general looting

---

[34] Sebastián Cirac Estopañán, *Martirologio de Cuenca* (Barcelona, 1947), 28 (NB: this is the only reference I have found to wax); AHDM Legajo 2585, letter dated 17 December 1942; Buenaventura Carrocera, *Mártires capuchinos de la provincia del Sagrado Corazón de Jesús de Castilla en la revolución de 1936* (Madrid, 1944), 235–6; AHN, CG, Legajo 1164-1; Saavedra Arias, *Destruir y proteger*, points specifically to the ambivalent status of 'collectable coins and ecclesiastical gold and silverwork', 66–8.

[35] Concha Espina, *Esclavitud y libertad: diario de una prisionera* (Valladolid, 1938), 77.

[36] *Ibid.*, 114; church bells became a point of contention in many areas after 1931; see my *Catholicism in the Second Spanish Republic*, 186–7, 215–16; Fernando del Rey, *Paisanos en lucha: exclusión política y violencia en la Segunda República español* (Madrid, 2008), 167–70.

[37] As at the church of Sant Vicenç de Sarrià, Josep M. Martí Bonet, *El martiri dels temples a la diòcesi de Barcelona, 1936–9* (Barcelona, 2008), 152–3 and *passim*; Cirac Estopañán, *Martirologio de Cuenca*.

[38] Orden Hospitalaria de S Juan de Dios, *Violencias, profanaciones y asesinatos cometidos por los marxistas en los establecimientos de S Juan de Dios* (Palencia, 1939), 27.

[39] AHN, CG, Legajo 1164-1; Legajo 1015-2 Ramo 44.

in which 'some took clothes, others food from the dispensary, the animals and poultry; others clocks and typewriters … they broke the images, burnt the altars, and the sacristy cloths and vestments were shared between the women'.[40] In this mixture of looting, iconoclasm and *reparto*, the women's role is distinctive. It does not seem to have been unusual for women to take the lead in seizing church textiles, presumably because they were the ones who would remake or reuse them. There is clear evidence of recycling, with women making cushions and curtains from 'chalice cloths' and vestments, 'espadrilles, trousers and shirts' from other church fabrics, and underwear – presumably heavy woollen petticoats – from 'white religious habits'.[41]

Though it seems clear that these fabrics moved into domestic space, and were repurposed for practical use, we know little of how they were used, or even what kind of cloths were taken. Church textiles range from fine lawn through cotton and linen to heavily embroidered silks, while habits and cassocks were made of heavier stuff, such as wool. As the historical record runs out at the point at which they were taken, we do not know how these garments were viewed, if they held any memory of their own history, or were passed down with stories as to their origin. The ornate embroideries commonly used as chasubles and outer vestments would have been distinctive in both quality and pattern and, as they were fragile, may not have survived for long. But, again, we do not know the effect these repurposed garments had on others or if they were genuinely only seen as practical pieces of cloth. Certainly, religious images treated as fuel did not simply become wood. When the Hospitallers' church in Malvarrosa (Valencia) was dismantled – a process that began on 15 August 1936 – the shattered images were taken to the kitchen 'where Brother José Miguel had to go through the pain, which made him collapse, of burning the remnants of those objects that had inspired such devotion in him in the days of his religious life'.[42]

Garments, too, are objects with meaning. They have an intimate relationship with humans – perhaps the closest of any objects – and are invested with emotional meaning through family association, gift-giving and personal memory.[43] For ordained priests and professed religious, clothing also has a ritual purpose and significance and is an integral part of the ceremonies that mark their entry into community

---

[40] Literally 'sacristy clothes', Manuel García Miralles OP, *Los dominicos de la provincia de Aragón en la persecución religiosa* (Valencia, 1962), 17.

[41] Thomas, *The Faith and the Fury*, 114–16; Alexandra Walsham, 'Recycling the Sacred: Material Culture and Cultural Memory after the English Reformation', *Church History*, 86 (2017), 112–54, discusses similar examples in a different historical context.

[42] *Violencias, profanaciones y asesinatos cometidos por los marxistas*, 27.

[43] Daniel Miller, *The Comfort of Things* (Cambridge, 2008), 32–45.

or the clerical life. Church embroideries were frequently bequeathed or presented to religious communities, often to commemorate these clothing or profession ceremonies. Similarly, vestments were commonly given as ordination presents, often by close relatives.

When the young Jesuit priest José María Lamamié de Clairac – who died at the front as a military chaplain – celebrated his first Masses in September 1935, he wore a chasuble embroidered by his mother, which had first been worn at her own wedding, and the alb his grandmother and great-aunt had made for his uncle's ordination.[44] As with many church items, these had a family history as well as a religious one. But the soutane was a highly personal item. Priests and religious often regarded their distinctive dress with great affection, and were reluctant to abandon it, even in the face of death. One jailed Capuchin, RP Domitilo de Ayóo, refused to remove his habit, or his beard, saying he would rather die than 'take off the habit I've worn since I was ten'. Indeed, one attempt to change failed when he appeared briefly in lay dress, highly agitated, to tell his companions, 'I feel very bad like this.'[45]

Few cases were as extreme as this, but other monks delayed removing their habits or did so only with 'the sadness you might imagine'.[46] As with the images, these objects are not simply the material of which they are made, and it is inconceivable that the iconoclasts did not recognise this, not least through the effect they had on others. Indeed, it is hard not to see Brother José Miguel's 'collapse' as the result of deliberate intention. Religious statues – even bad ones – had the animation so commonly attributed to art objects through terms such as 'vivid' or 'lifelike'. Many are dressed, including Jesus the Nazarene, which – unlike clothed images of the Virgin, which are usually simply a frame – has a full polychromed body which is intended to be stripped as part of the Passion story. Even in a liturgical context, then, clothes are designed to be put on and taken off. That is, to echo W. J. T. Mitchell, what they want. So, during the Civil War, clothed images were often stripped – as were clergy – and others dressed up. Headgear, that long-standing staple of caricature, was the most common choice for these parodic re-dressings of religious statues, with militia caps a frequent addition. The Sacred Heart in one Madrid convent spent the first months of the war 'with a militia cap, a red rag, and a rifle in its hand'.[47]

[44] Antonio Pérez de Olaguer, *"Piedras vivas": Biografía del capellán Requeté José María Lamamié de Clairac* (San Sebastián, 1939), 68–9, 72–3.

[45] Carrocera, *Mártires capuchinos*, 213–14; for other examples, Vincent '"The Keys of the Kingdom"', 87–8.

[46] Carlos Vicuña, *Mártires agustinos de El Escorial* (El Escorial, 1943), 57.

[47] María Luisa Fernández and María Leturia, *Catorce meses de aventuras bajo el domino rojo* (Rome, 1939), 312; the statue was then demolished.

Human bodies too were dressed up as vestments became a staple of carnivalesque performances. This is hardly surprising. Vestments 'want' to be put on; they are, at one level, a specialised theatrical prop and so were well suited to parodies of religious ceremonies or processions, which were sometimes, apparently, carried out just for fun. One militiaman in Alboloduy (Almería) created a costume from 'the tunic from an image' and various vestments, while parades or mock processions round pueblos 'in ecclesiastical dress' with 'the intention of mocking and ridiculing religion and the ministers of the Lord' were common.[48] As with other transgressive behaviours, this burlesque of religious rite was a breaking of taboos, a clear signal of disrespect or contempt, and a demonstration of the powerlessness of sacred objects. The performativity has received less attention, but it is quite possible that this quality of liturgical objects as props or costumes is reflected in the theatricality of the iconoclasm, which is quite unmistakable.[49]

## II 'They dragged the saints through the streets'

The same performative quality was seen, repeatedly, in the ritualistic ways images were treated by the iconoclasts themselves. In Montoro (Córdoba), for example, 'they dragged the saints through the streets' as the Holy Week figure of Jesus the Nazarene was taken to the river with other images from the church. Similarly, the figure of Christ from the chapel of the Augustinian nuns in Madrid was 'mutilated and pulled through the streets with a rope around its neck'.[50] Many images were 'drowned' by being thrown in rivers – often after burning – while the bonfires themselves were often located at some kind of threshold, the church door, the boundaries of the pueblo, a riverbank.[51] The same process of dragging or parading was enacted on priests' bodies – both dead and living – in a clear demonstration of the interchangeability of person and object, priest and image. Religious statues – that is, simulacra of the human body – were thus treated in very similar ways to the living bodies of priests. As the post-war summary of the destruction from the diocese of Córdoba succinctly put it:

---

[48] AHN CG Legajos 1038 (Almería), 1044-1 and 1044-2 (Córdoba); for another example, this time by a woman, Miguel Batllorí SJ, *Los Jesuítas en el Levante Rojo: Cataluña y Valencia 1936-1939* (Barcelona, 1941?), 116. Press photographs clearly show the theatricality, not least in the fact that they are posed.

[49] For a local example, Lucía Prieto Borrego, 'La violencia anticlerical en las comarcas de Marbella y Ronda durante la Guerra Civil', *Baetica*, 25 (2003), 751–72.

[50] Vicuña, *Mártires agustinos*, 40; Besalduch, *Nuestros Mártires*, 321.

[51] AHN CG Legajo 1038 Almería: Alboloduy (burnt on riverbank with clothes); Legajo 1044-1 Córdoba: Montoro and Palma del Río (thrown in river); Legajo 1041-2 Huelva: Almonaster la Real (burnt at boundary).

All the IMAGES were profaned as well. As to how, the profanation varied: they were battered, their hands and feet were cut off, their eyes were gouged out, their heads were split, they were shot with all manner of equipment, the place where the heart would be was perforated, as were hands and feet, and other similar methods were used, that could only have been dictated by an infernal hatred.[52]

Catholic Spain has, of course, a long history of hierophanic images, their apparent physicality accentuated by the plasticity of polychrome sculpture. Statues of Jesus, the Virgin Mary and various saints were credited with human qualities – moving, weeping, sweating or bleeding – as well as with intercessionary powers.[53] But ideas of 'living' images went very deep. In Santander, for example, militiamen spoke of burning images 'alive'.[54] This interchangeability between people and images was seen repeatedly, as when the Madrid Augustinians encountered two Dominican fathers 'bleeding like an Ecce Homo', or the archdiocese of Seville listed 'consecrated persons' alongside churches, 'sacred images' and 'the Holy Eucharist' in a register of what had been defiled.[55]

Such a strong sense of animation would seem to go beyond a simple notion of magical objects whose charm could be broken by the straightforward fact of treating them as blocks of wood. There is evidence of magical thinking on all sides, not least in the blinding of statues that could not see and the torture of images that could not feel. We do not know if any of the objects looted from churches were kept for use as talismans and good luck charms but it must be highly likely.[56] Similarly, claims that food tasted better if cooked over wood from images and church fittings may have been simple bravado, but may also have been – or been understood as – referring to some innate quality, or magic, that 'holy' wood possessed.[57] In other cases, of course, objects were taken for profit, with gold- and silverwork an obvious target. (See Figure 2.) In Barcelona, anarchists immediately took such objects in order to buy arms. Some were sold and melted down into ingots, others stored until they could be sold abroad, including on an individual

---

[52] Obispado de Córdoba, Contestación al cuestionario 22 Nov. 1940, AHN, CG Legajo 1044-2. For attacks on heads and hands, see further Pamela Graves, 'From an Archaeology of Iconoclasm to an Anthropology of the Body', *Current Anthropology*, 49 (2008), 35–57.

[53] William A. Christian Jr, *Moving Crucifixes in Modern Spain* (Princeton, 1992), and *Divine Presence in Spain and Western Europe, 1500–1960* (Budapest and New York, 2012), 45–96.

[54] Espina, *Esclavitud y libertad*, 104, 158; she reports '"quemarla viva" – según frase miliciana', 112.

[55] Vicuña, *Mártires agustinos*, 47; *Boletín Oficial Eclesiástico del Arzobispado de Sevilla*, 8 Sept. 1936, 187.

[56] On the talismanic use of religious objects, see *La religiosidad popular*, ed. Carlos Álvarez Santaló, María Jesús Buxó i Rey and Salvador Rodríguez Becerra (Barcelona, 1989).

[57] For such claims, Thomas, *The Faith and the Fury*, 114.

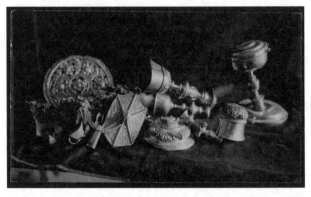

Figure 2 Broken chalices and eucharistic objects (Morón de la Frontera, Seville). (Reproduced with kind permission of Biblioteca Nacional de España.)

initiative.[58] But even this, entirely secular, illegal export of artworks was depicted as 'a simple flight into Egypt' as virgins and saints crossed the border from Spain.[59]

The veneration of images has been crucial historically in establishing Catholic identities, that is, a sense of who is Catholic and who is not.[60] Those who do not respect or venerate religious images are placed outside the Catholic fold, whether Jews, heretics, Protestants or anticlericals. But the same principle worked in reverse, as was shown by an order given by the local defence committee in Sabadell (Cataluña) on 8 September 1936 confiscating all personal religious objects. If any remained in private homes after a certain date, their owners would be seen as 'seditious'.[61] Such orders were followed up by searches. Domestic space was to be denuded of devotional objects, and personal religious faith was to have no outward expression. Religious objects are here being taken emblematically, as a badge of identity, and some private devotional items had, of course, long been used in just this

[58] 'Diario de José S', in *Diario de un pistolero anarquista*, ed. Miquel Mir (Barcelona, 2006), 175–7, 181–2, 190–2; for anarchist involvement in the black market in artworks, Saavedra Arias, *Destruir y proteger*, 157–90.

[59] Castro Albarrán, *La gran víctima*, 122.

[60] The Reformation and Counter-Reformation are the most obvious historical examples, but Marcelino Menéndez Pelayo's account of the 1868 revolution includes destroying churches and convents, shooting images and burning artworks and altarpieces. *Historia de los heterdoxos españoles* (Madrid, 1992), II, 1337–8, 1353–5.

[61] Bonet, *El martiri dels temples*, 17.

emblematic way. Door plaques, particularly to the Sacred Heart of Jesus, had long been encouraged as both a pious practice and – from the nine-teenth-century 'culture wars' – a political identity.[62]

Under conditions of war, these emblems were both reassuring and dangerous. Crucifixes, rosaries and religious pictures were common domestic items, part of the material culture of everyday Spanish life. One Jesuit priest interrogated in Valencia insisted his rosary was 'a memento of my mother' while, in Madrid, a woman refused the anarchist militias' orders to take down a crucifix and picture of the Virgin, on the grounds that 'as well as an emblem of our faith' they were 'a reminder of our parents'.[63] Many religious items were miniature, and commonly carried: crosses, scapulars and medals were all relatively easy to conceal, including by Republicans. A militiaman in Toledo showed the discalced Carmelites in hiding in the city 'with some complacency the holy scapular and medals he wore hanging at his breast'. These may have been carried as charms but, presumably, he revealed them as a sign of his trustworthiness; certainly he did not betray the friars, though nor would he help them escape to Madrid.[64]

Carrying religious objects in the first months of war was undoubtedly dangerous. Their emblematic nature meant they could reveal someone's true identity if discovered, which was a particular danger for priests in hiding. At least two Jesuits in Barcelona disappeared after being betrayed by their breviaries while, in Valencia, a Dominican found with a rosary in his pocket was driven off to be shot, the rosary around his neck.[65] Together with crucifixes, rosaries and prayer books were the items most commonly kept by priests and monks, with breviaries used to struc-ture the day, say the daily office and follow the liturgical year.

*Pensions* sheltering priests in plain clothes, groups of nuns living clan-destinely in flats and Catholic homes were subject to repeated searches. The Handmaids of the Sacred Heart had their rosaries and profession crosses taken – ostensibly to be melted down to make bullets – while the small image of the Virgin 'which had heard our private prayers and dispensed so many graces in those distressing situations' was thrown from the balcony to crash on the street.[66] Some people resisted

---

[62] Raymond Jonas, *France and the Cult of the Sacred Heart: An Epic Tale for Modern Times* (Berkeley, 2000); Luis Cano, *"Reinaré en España": la mentalidad católica a la llegada de la Segunda República* (Madrid, 2009), 29–136; Christopher Clark and Wolfram Kaiser, *Culture Wars: Secular–Catholic Conflict in Nineteenth-Century Europe* (Cambridge, 2003).

[63] Fernández and Leturia, *Catorce meses de aventuras*, 60–1.

[64] Evaristo de la Virgen del Carmen, *Martirologio de los Carmelitas Descalzos de la Provincia de Nuestro Padre S Elías de Castilla en la revolución marxista de 1936* (Avila, 1942), 59.

[65] Batllori, *Los Jesuítas en el Levante Rojo*, 10–12; García Miralles, *Los dominicos de la provincia de Aragón*, 65.

[66] Fernández and Leturia, *Catorce meses de aventuras*, 208–9.

or dissembled, but most hid or disguised the objects. On 12 October 1936, after hearing of a search, Concha Espina buried in the garden a silver rosary, religious pendants, her granddaughters' *medallitas*, and two crucifixes, one of ivory and the other her late father's. A picture of the Virgin she had had since childhood was concealed behind a Velázquez reproduction.[67] These were the items they saved. Others were presumably left in place so as not to arouse suspicion.

The list gives a sense of the texture of domestic devotional life and its dependence on material objects. Less affluent households also risked saving at least some religious items. Two women in Cuatro Caminos (Madrid), for example, made frequent reference in their correspondence with the bishop to their small altar to Mary, Help of Christians, the rosaries they said every Saturday, and the miracles the image had worked during the war, when the altar must have been hidden.[68] It was not simply the preservation of these objects but the pious practices and devotional routines associated with them that were important. This was particularly true of the rosary, the domestic devotion par excellence: in Concha Espina's house it was said daily, before an improvised bedroom altar made with a prayer card.[69] Even in jail, where many priests and male religious were detained, along with numerous Catholic laypeople, all deprived of religious paraphernalia, they made rosaries from string, with knots or olive stones for the beads, as well as carving crosses, medals and crucifixes with knives, and making rings with threads from matting.[70]

It is this personal quality – the emotional life of objects – that comes through most clearly when looking at these domestic items. People risked much to retain or replace them; they had a resonance which was not confined to religious virtuosi but which priests and religious clearly demonstrated. Many of those in hiding had taken small, personal, religious objects with them, usually rosaries, scapulars or crucifixes. These items carried considerable emotional weight: those detained or under threat of execution kept them close wherever they were and for as long as they could. Often, this meant until the moment of death. One Capuchin father, arrested in a boarding house in Madrid, slipped a crucifix into his sleeve while collecting his hat and later died holding it.[71] A Jesuit from Manresa (Barcelona) left with only his Vow Crucifix,

[67] Espina, *Esclavitud y libertad*, 107, 214; they also hid their best clothes and household linen.
[68] Correspondence, AHDM Legajo 2585, letters dated 27 July, 25 Nov. 1948.
[69] Espina, *Esclavitud y libertad*, 43, 244; on the domestic rosary, Brundin *et al.*, *The Sacred Home*, 97–100.
[70] Rafael María Saucedo Cabanillas, *¡Hasta el cielo!: Biografía y martirio de 54 Hermanos Hospitalarios de San Juan de Dios* (Madrid, 1952), 161; Vicuña, *Mártires agustinos*, 102, 116; Batllorí, *Los Jesuítas en el Levante Rojo*, 176, 213.
[71] Carrocera, *Mártires capuchinos*, 33–5.

kissing it before hiding it in his jacket pocket and fleeing across open country, through which he was tracked and killed.[72]

Many bodies were found with – or identified by – religious possessions: a scapular, a small image of the Virgin, a crucifix, a medal, a prayer card.[73] Sometimes these were bloodstained. The crucifix taken from the pocket of one of the Talavera Hospitallers by a militiaman was thrown away, but retrieved by 'a pious woman' and returned to the community, where it was received as a relic.[74] Similarly, when the bodies of three old order Carmelite monks were exhumed in Hinojosa del Duque (Córdoba) in January 1940, the author of the community martyrology identified one of the bodies. 'With my own hands', he wrote, he took his 'handkerchief, his rosary, a scapular and a crucifix that I wear round my neck with the same veneration with which St Pancras carried the blood of his martyred father'.[75]

The relationship between people and objects thus continued to the moment of death and beyond. These were not, in themselves, 'martyred' objects. They had accompanied the 'martyrs', but not been attacked themselves. Rather, these small pious objects acted both as testimony – they had, after all, witnessed the events – and as conveyors of memory. On occasion, these relics were selected – even curated – by the martyrs themselves. One Dominican who managed to keep his rosary with him in jail in Valencia when 'they took medals, rosaries, scapulars from everyone and broke them and shot them' wrote of it as 'a sacred memory. It has been in my hands in the most difficult moments; it has been my best friend. I have put it to my lips in very bitter times; it has slept next to me and been the language I have for the Virgin.'[76] He survived the war and gave the rosary to his mother, presumably as testimony not only to his suffering but also to his providential survival. The Barbastro Claretians were not so fortunate but they too managed to keep their breviaries while in prison, as well as the rosaries, and crucifixes they took with them to their deaths. One, Esteban Casadevall, who made his final profession in prison, was given the founder's crucifix to kiss on the eve of his execution, as he no longer had his own. They also left writings, including a farewell letter on a handkerchief and a chocolate wrapper they had inscribed with their names and phrases such as 'Long Live Christ the King!', 'Grace and Glory to

[72] Batllorí, *Los Jesuítas en el Levante Rojo*, 72; for a similar case in Valencia, 107; Jesuits are presented with a crucifix when they make their first vows.

[73] E.g. Antonio Torres Sánchez, *Martirologio de la Hermandad de Sacerdotes Operarios* (Salamanca, 1946), 125; Carrocera, *Mártires capuchinos*, 259.

[74] Cabanillas, *¡Hasta el cielo!* (Madrid, 1952), 37.

[75] Besalduch, *Nuestros Mártires*, 279.

[76] García Miralles, *Los dominicos de la provincia de Aragón*, 73.

God', 'Long live the martyrs', 'Long live Catholic Barbastro' and 'Forgive my enemies'.[77]

Objects thus became relics, vessels of memory of those killed. In Barbastro, as elsewhere, they are now displayed in a small museum dedicated to the 'martyrs', who are also now beatified by the Catholic Church.[78] However, objects also had the potential to create their own relics, by, for example, being snatched – or 'rescued' – from the flames. This was the case with the hand of Christ of Piera (Cataluña), and a smoke-blackened figure of Christ from a crucifix in Calera de Leon (see Figure 3).[79] More commonly, fragments and broken images were brought together as photographic assemblages. Headless, faceless or armless statues were grouped together; decapitated heads of statues were pictured in close-up, portrait-style or brought together in a series, the counterpart to the maimed and mutilated images seen in other photographs. In every case, the image of the debris accentuated that of the lost (whole) original.

Many of these images are by anonymous photographers selling to the press or documenting the damage for those charged with assessing it. In either case, they come to us through the Francoist press and propaganda agency. But named photographers also worked in this field, notably Pelayo Mas Castañeda, who specialised in art history. His highly aestheticised prints presented assemblages of mutilated crucifixes, in various ways, with standing crosses as a Calvary, or fragments on the ground as at Golgotha. (See Figure 4.) There was thus a double mimesis: the very familiarity of the form of the broken image – particularly in the case of the crucifix – made it easy for the viewer to reconstruct it imaginatively. Whole and part, the original image and its damaged relic, came together in a new aesthetic of religious destruction. The beauty of the original image was preserved in the fragments that remained.

Pelayo Mas Castañeda's photographs also echoed the theology of suffering that is fundamental to Christian thought. Man was made in the image of God; religious images were vehicles for a divine presence. Breaking an image was thus an assault on the divine. The broken images echoed Christ's broken body on the cross, the suffering of the images, his Passion. But, of course, scripture tells us that Christ's body was *not* broken. The Church's teaching on 'wholeness' prohibited the veneration of 'mutilated' images, with a few specific exceptions. The

---

[77] Quibus, *Misioneros Mártires*, 95, 118–19, 121–5; Francisco Javier Román Solans, '"They went to their death as if to a party": Martyrdom, Agency and Performativity in the Spanish Civil War', *Politics, Religion and Ideology*, 17 (2016), 210–26,

[78] www.martiresdebarbastro.org/en/museo.html?jjj=1554919115649.

[79] Manuel Delgado, 'Culte i profanació del Sant Crist de Piera', *Miscellanea Aqualatensia*, 7 (1995), 87–114.

Figure 3 Carbonised figure of Christ pulled from the ashes, parish church of Santiago Apóstol, Calera de Leon (Badajoz). (Reproduced with kind permission of Biblioteca Nacional de España.)

broken image must be restored or destroyed; they do not survive, although the major images were then replaced – including the Christ of Piera, which incorporates the original nails in the new crucifix. But, just as an infirm or disabled priest was unable to say Mass in public,

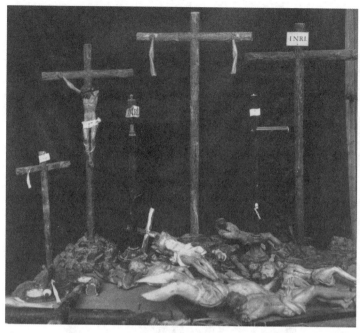

Figure 4 Pelayo Más Castañeda, Assemblage of Broken Crucifixes. (Reproduced with kind permission of Postulación para las Causas de los Mártires, Archdiocese of Toledo.)

broken images were not displayed. Some of the thousands of items retrieved after the Civil War were returned to their owners, others were stored, while those beyond repair were destroyed, including by burning.

So, even as 'the rubble was cleared away after the fact to make place for new altars', the memory of the breaking remained.[80] It survived in a remarkable body of photographic images that memorialised the breaking, aestheticising the broken icon and recuperating it from the defacing intent of the iconoclasts. This was done through familiar techniques of devotional representation. Decapitated, mutilated and eyeless images were photographed as single objects against a plain background. Indeed, eyeless images feature particularly heavily in the photographic

---

[80] Koenraad Jonckheere, 'The Power of Iconic Memory: Iconoclasm as a Mental Marker', *BMGN – Low Countries Historical Review*, 131 (2016), 141–54, at 142.

record, particularly 'blinded' virgins.[81] The framing encouraged the watcher to engage directly with the image, to concentrate upon it as an encouragement to prayer, just as with a crucifix by Velázquez or Pacheco or an Ecce Homo by Gregorio Fernández.[82] In this way, the photograph transformed the image itself, creating a memory that would overlay the original 'icon' even as it confirmed its reliquary power.[83]

These remnants, the 'piles of debris' left by the iconoclasm, were thus transformed into what de Boer refers to in the sixteenth-century Netherlands as 'ruined beauty and things sacralized in the course of the storm'.[84] The broken objects are no longer sacred; they are revealed as material objects, just as the iconoclasts intended. They are no longer to be venerated; they are, still, expelled from churches. But the photographic record has allowed them to become totemic. The intimate relationship between people and objects – a shared martyrdom – established during the violence meant that they now represented an experience and not just an event. The power, the 'charm', of the object continued, even when that object no longer existed.

[81] Eyeless virgins were used as the cover images for Castro Albarrán's *La gran víctima* and *L'Illustration*, January 1938, 'Le martyre des Oeuvres d'Art'.

[82] Alfonso Rodríguez G. de Ceballo, 'The Art of Devotion', in *The Sacred Made Real: Spanish Painting and Sculpture 1600–1700* (2009), 45–57.

[83] Jonckhere, 'The Power of Iconic Memory', 147–9.

[84] de Boer, 'Picking Up the Pieces', 79.